Th...
Devo...
Village Book

For

Mum & Dad

Welcome To Devon

All our Love

Simon & Sabha.

THE VILLAGES OF BRITAIN SERIES

Other counties in this series include:

Bedfordshire *

Berkshire *

Buckinghamshire *

Cheshire *

Cleveland *

Cornwall *

Cumbria *

Derbyshire *

Dorset

Durham *

Essex *

Glamorgan *

Gloucestershire *

Gwent *

Hampshire *

Herefordshire *

Hertfordshire *

Kent

Lancashire *

Leicestershire & Rutland *

Lincolnshire *

Norfolk *

Northamptonshire *

Northumberland *

Nottinghamshire *

Oxfordshire *

Powys Montgomeryshire *

Shropshire *

Somerset *

Staffordshire *

Suffolk *

Surrey

East Sussex

West Sussex *

Warwickshire *

West Midlands *

Wiltshire *

Worcestershire *

East Yorkshire *

North Yorkshire *

South & West Yorkshire *

* Published in conjunction with County Federations of
Women's Institutes

The Devon Village Book

Compiled by the Devon
Federation of Women's Institutes from notes
and illustrations sent by Institutes in the County

Published jointly by
Countryside Books, Newbury
and the D.F.W.I., Exeter

Countryside Books
3 Catherine Road
Newbury, Berkshire

ISBN 1 85306 078 X

Cover Photograph of Otterton
taken by Jane Primmer

Produced through MRM Associates Ltd.,Reading
Typeset by Acorn Bookwork, Salisbury, Wilts
Printed in England by J. W. Arrowsmith Ltd., Bristol

Foreword

With a coastline both north and south, and Dartmoor and the southern fringe of Exmoor within its boundaries, this large county attracts a vast number of visitors. Yet there is much more to Devon than seaside and moorland. Visitors often miss the delights of villages and hamlets approached by the deep, narrow lanes which are such a feature of this county.

The places written about in this book, by members who know them, will surely inspire the reader to search them out and will add to the pleasure of visitor and resident alike.

I am delighted to have this opportunity to thank our Co-ordinator, Pat Macdonald, who has worked on the project with enthusiasm. Here we have a book which gives us an overall picture of the county so many think of as Glorious Devon.

Betty Aust
County Chairman

Acknowledgements

The task of co-ordinating the work for this book has been an enormous personal pleasure and privilege and I have had many a nice exchange of greetings with fellow-members from the four corners of our large county as a result. Thank you all for the tremendous effort you put into supplying the material which has gone into this fine publication of which we can all be proud.

Pat Macdonald
Project Co-ordinator

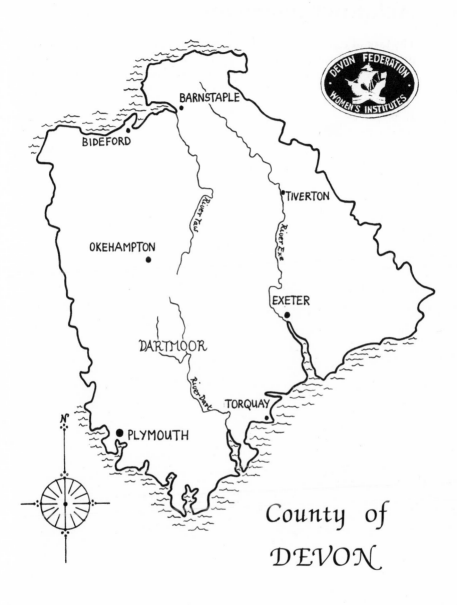

County of
DEVON

Judy Barber.

Abbotsham 🌿

Abbotsham is a delightful village, situated in a gentle fold of the hills some two miles west of Bideford and about one mile from the rocky cliffs bordering Clovelly bay. There were two 'streets', roughly parallel, but recently the intervening space has been filled by pleasant housing, mainly inhabited by retired and by professional people, many of whom commute to Bideford or Barnstaple.

The row of cottages on the old Bideford to Clovelly road is still a pleasure to behold, leading down to the tree-encircled church of St Helens, much of which dates from the 13th century. Probably the most fascinating feature of this lovely church is the carved bench ends. Close by stands the school, formerly the poor house.

Nowadays the original school building is quite inadequate for the number of pupils, especially since the neighbouring village of Alwington's school was closed, and the children transferred to Abbotsham. A new school is projected, behind the pleasant recreation field provided largely by voluntary effort. Since 1924 a parish hall has completed the central group of buildings and this is well used by local organisations.

One great and historic event is thought to have occurred in the parish of Abbotsham, long ago in AD 878. This was the battle of Cynuit fought against the Danes, led by their fearsome leader Hubba. The Anglo-Saxons had taken refuge in their rough fortifications on a small hill, now to be found between Bideford and Abbotsham. All traces of military occupation have been obliterated by agriculture, trees and footpaths.

Commanded by Odda, the Earlorman, the local men took the Danes by surprise and routed them, killing 1,200 men including Hubba their leader. Odun, with his own hand, captured the Raven Standard, embroidered by Hubba's sister and credited with magical powers. This victory allowed King Alfred to emerge from hiding and, subsequently, to drive the Danes temporarily from England. Folk memories survive and within living memory a mischievous boy has been called a 'Woe's Bird' ie a raven.

The site of the encounter now overlooks an elegant flyover, part of the new Bideford bypass. Nearby stands a castellated house (now a hotel) called Kenwith Castle, in the grounds of which there is a small lake.

The lordship of the manor of Hame was granted in AD 981 to the Abbot of Tavistock, and the abbey continued to hold the parish of 'Abbot's Hame' until the Dissolution of the Monasteries in 1539. The oldest house in the parish is Coombe, built circa 1616 by a Daniel Berryman, whose plaster label of 1632 can be seen in one of the rooms.

Unlike many small villages, Abbotsham can still boast a pub and a shop-cum-post office, as well as a school, a church and a Baptist chapel.

Abbotskerswell 🦋

This beautiful village, dating back to before Tudor times, nestles in a valley near Newton Abbot. Amongst many interesting features are the lovely old church of St Mary The Virgin, still bearing some scars of the ransacking by Henry VIII's men, and the lychgate which is almost the oldest in the country, at least one Devon longhouse, and many interesting thatched houses and cottages. Church House, one of the oldest buildings, was built for the use of people coming to church who wished to rest between services, men in one part, women in another.

There are several wells which provided water before the mains supply came to the village. The water in Ladywell is supposed to be beneficial for bad eyes. There are two pubs, one of which formerly housed the blacksmith. The other has a Quaker room over the front door, and a Quaker burial ground nearby.

From the village there is a footpath used by pilgrims in their travels to Torre Abbey, a long walk, even from Abbotskerswell.

The Parish Council room, which is very small, was once the public bath house, and before that a pound house. A cider factory existed close to the main road, but this was closed, and no more scrumpy was made in Abbotskerswell. It was said that the scrumpy was the most potent in Devon! In the centre of the village there was once a chestnut tree and commemorative lamp-post in the middle of the road. These were removed many years ago, and quite recently a mini-roundabout has been sited there.

Overlooking the village on one side is St Augustine's Priory, now converted into luxury retirement apartments. Not officially in Abbotskerswell, it is understood that when 'beating the bounds' took place, two men only were allowed through the priory, others had to go round on the road. According to the map only the graveyard is in Abbotskerswell.

On the other side is Court Grange, once owned by Mrs Marcus Hare and then by the Rev and Mrs Deuce, who gave it to the Royal National Institute for the Deaf. The boys are taught social and vocational skills and have the only field gun-crew manned by deaf or partially deaf boys.

New housing has been built over the years which has expanded the village considerably. Many of the older residents, and indeed some of the newer ones, can remember when there were a lot more fields. There were of course several farms in the village, but sadly, only one farm remains.

All Saints & Smallridge

Until Queen Victoria's reign no-one had heard of All Saints; even today the Ordnance Survey map has not noticed it.

But then they built a chapel in a corner of Chardstock, and under an Act to divide populous parishes, All Saints was created. All Saints had only a few old farms, with their clusters of cottages, with names like Wagg's Plot and Churchill, possibly the original home of that great family.

Towards its west side the parish is cleft by a deep valley and a nameless stream. It is the ancient boundary between Devon and Dorset. To make All Saints, a small area with the village of Smallridge was taken, not only from Axminster, but worse, from the county of Devon itself. Indeed, but for another stroke of the pen which restored the whole area to Devon in 1896, All Saints would have no place in this book.

Smallridge has the history which All Saints lacks. A manor before the Conquest, it was Smarige in the Domesday Book. The family of Walter Raleigh owned it for ten generations, but not the great Sir Walter himself, as his grandfather had been heavily fined for 'misprision of treason' and had to sell Smallridge to raise the cash. The historian, Prince, called it 'a sweet and pretty place'.

The manor was broken up in 1771 and the farms sold separately. The manorial rights went to a Mr Pitt for £10, and he sold them to a relation for a hogshead of cider.

The break-up of the manor probably started the decline of the rural community, while the enclosures of 1854/6 were as traumatic for the cottager and small farmer as they were profitable for the landlords and the bigger farmers. Smallridge Moor in the centre of the village was enclosed, and now, over a century later, is threatened with building development. The vast open acres of All Saints disappeared behind a network of hedges.

By the end of the century no more brides and grooms had to sign the register with their 'mark'. The dame schools had done their work, augmented in 1849 by a parochial school – later demolished because the Bishop, by an unfortunate accident, had consecrated its site as holy ground! A larger school was built nearby and is still in use today.

All Saints has not only the school, but a church and chapel, pub, post office, shop, village hall, and cricket ground. In these days, what more can a village ask?

Alphington

Alphington is on the Alphin brook, on the edge of Exeter. The village probably originated as a Saxon settlement between two ancient British trackways.

The modern day Marsh Barton trading estate, between Exeter and Alphington, used to be marshland and there has been regular flooding of the village over the centuries. For example in July 1760, the brook overflowed and destroyed twelve houses, barns and fields of corn. Again in 1960, the brook flooded and many people had to be rescued by boat. The church paid for the cost of coal for drying out the houses.

During the first half of the 19th century Alphington was noted for its cattle and horse fairs. The horse fair was established in 1632 at Michaelmas. There were 23 public or 'bush' houses opened in the village for the sale of beer and cider and the Admiral Vernon Inn cooked as many as 60 geese during the fair. The Admiral Vernon is one of only two pubs now in the village, but is not the original, which was burned down in 1875 and stood on the site of the old village school. Many gypsies bought and sold horses at these fairs while their wives told fortunes. The fair ceased in 1870.

The house known as the Gables at the far end of the village is one of the old Alphington manor houses of about 1730, with over 20 rooms. At one time it was used as a prison and has a tunnel through which prisoners were taken for hanging. In 1839 Charles Dickens took Mile End Cottage, still standing, for his parents to live in, and it is said that Dickens wrote some of *Nicholas Nickleby* there.

The most prominent building is the 15th century church, dedicated to St Michael and All Angels. It is built on the site of an earlier Norman church, of which little remains except the font. Said to be the finest of its type in the country, it is carved with scrolled roundels, St Michael attacking the dragon with a lance and other mythical animals. Major repairs and decorations had to be undertaken in 1986 after a disastrous fire destroyed much of the roof, vestry and organ. A peal of eight bells hung in 1749 are still regularly rung. A notice in the porch asks worshippers to remove their pattens, so the noise would not disturb the congregation. Pattens were worn to lift shoes out of the muddy lanes, which must have been very necessary in this marshy area.

Church of St Michael and All Angels, Alphington

There are three 13th century granite crosses in the parish; the present war memorial cross was found in the garden of Fairfax House and the shaft at the corner of Mill Lane.

In the 1930s the population was 1,280, mostly employed in market gardening, farming and quarrying, and there were many orchards, particularly where the comprehensive school now stands. The famous firm of Messrs Veitches Nurseries moved to the village in 1931.

Until the 1930s there were a number of local charities. When a baby was due, two pairs of sheets and 'Widdlin' bands were loaned, and another charity was for the provision of bread for the villagers every Thursday during Lent from the village hall.

The Teign Valley Railway, opened in 1903, joined Exeter with the villages of Alphington, Ide, Longdown, Dunsford and Christow, via 24 bridges and two long tunnels. The railway did not go to the seaside, so for many years Farmer Loram took waggon loads of children to St Thomas' railway station for a trip to the sands at Dawlish Warren. The line and bridge in Alphington is now removed, but the embankment conveniently screens new housing estates from the main roads in and out of the City of Exeter.

Although Alphington has expanded rapidly in recent years with a series of small housing estates, it has retained a scale and character in keeping with the old village street and red sandstone church at the centre.

Appledore 🦐

Steeped in a history of seafaring, shipbuilding, rope-making and smuggling, the village lies at the end of a promontory and is at the meeting point of the Taw and Torridge estuaries. The streets are narrow, with some Elizabethan and Georgian houses. There was a village here in 1069 called Tawmutha, but the name Appledore first occurs in the 14th century, spelt Apildore.

St Mary's church was built in 1838 and has some fine stained glass windows. In September 1988 the Bishop of Exeter commemorated the 150th anniversary year of the church and also consecrated the newly structured St Anne's Lady Chapel.

Salmon fishing in the estuary has been carried on since Saxon times. In past years the season would give employment to up to 100 men, but the present reduction in licences, in order to conserve fish, reduces employment and the catch.

Shipbuilding has been the main industry of Appledore through the centuries and in the late 1960s the Appledore Shipbuilders Ltd were involved in the building of a new shipyard in the Bidna Marsh which was to become the largest covered shipyard in all Europe at that time. Much larger ships were built than ever before in Appledore. The shipyard was nationalised in 1974, the first in Britain. Another boatyard was famed for the knowledge of ancient skills and tools with which they built replicas of the *Golden Hind*, the *Nonsuch* and the *Valkyra*, a Viking longboat.

Sadly the decline in shipbuilding in Britain generally is now reflected in Appledore and the associated manpower has been reduced. This workforce now find employment in local towns. There is still a busy trade in the export of sand and gravel. In the summer there is a tourist trade supplying accommodation and restaurants, and there are several adventure schools for the young holidaymaker.

In 1588, in recognition of the service of Appledore's seamen and ships against the Spanish Armada, Queen Elizabeth I granted Appledore a free port for all shipping – this still applies in that no charges are made on shipping entering, berthing or mooring in the harbour.

Older inhabitants remember a self-sufficient community. Three dockyards provided employment and trade. There was a Customs House and office, police station, doctor, dentist and chemist. The owner of a small cinema installed the first public lighting (two electric lights on the quay),

Salmon Fishing, Appledore

15

powered from a generator under the cinema. Gas works were run by a private family. There were three bus services, milk and vegetable deliveries by roundsmen with horse and cart, a tailor, drapers, chandlers, bakehouses and made-to-order oilskins.

Irsha Street, with its fascinating courts and the slipways to the river, was once a separate hamlet. Parallel with the quay runs Market Street. In the past a weekly pannier market was held here. Now several small stores and a studio are part of the picturesque houses, some with bow windows.

On the hilltop are housing estates built in the 1960s and 1970s. A fine house built circa 1856 for a shipyard owner stands proudly. 'The Holt', as it became known, now comprises self-contained flats and the grounds form part of the new estates.

Docton House, the oldest building, is thought to have been built by Cistercian monks in the 14th century and occupied by them until the Dissolution of the Monasteries. Owned by the Docton family in the 16th century, little is left to denote its former glory. The family coat of arms is visible.

Appledore's modern high-speed lifeboat is at its estuary mooring and an in-shore lifeboat at the slipway. Both are kept very busy in these hazardous waters. Trinity Pilots board the ships crossing the Bar to and from Appledore and Bideford.

There are many organisations here – church and secular, including a splendid Silver Band and several choirs. Annually held are the Regatta, Carnival and the Torch-light procession. For a seemingly tranquil village, it is very active.

Ashburton 🐚

Ashburton is situated within the National Park on the southern slopes of Dartmoor, nestling in a valley with the river Ashburn winding its way through historic buildings.

There are four ancient bridges in this small friendly town, but King's Bridge was the only crossing into the town centre. In days past children used to believe that an evil water sprite, named Cutty Dyer, lived under the bridge. Although this frightening being is generally forgotten now, older residents still remember his story.

It is believed that Ashburton was inhabited as early as 500 BC during the Iron Age. Earthworks can be explored in three different locations in the parish – Boro Wood, Ashburton Down and Tower Hill. It is believed the reason for settling in this area was tin.

In 1305 Ashburton was designated as a Stannary town. Tin mining, and later the wool industry, brought prosperity to this little town although neither remains today. Until the end of the 1960s the famous Ashburton marble was still being produced, and it was in world-wide demand. It is predominantly black with delicate traces of coral pink running through it.

With prosperity many large houses were built. One of the most famous is the 17th century Card House in North Street. It was a gambling house, so named because of the clubs, diamonds, hearts and spades forming the pattern on its slate-hung facade. On the corner of North Street was the famous Mermaid Inn (now the local ironmonger's) where General Fairfax – the Roundhead leader in the Civil War–had his headquarters for a few days after defeating the Royalists nearby. Here there is a unique example of a granite archway.

Near the base of St Andrew's tower is the grave of a French officer prisoner of war who died just 28 days after the battle of Waterloo, a reminder that French prisoners were billeted here on parole during the Napoleonic Wars.

The town's Saxon heritage still exists with the office of a portreeve. The name comes from 'port' meaning market town, and 'gerefa' meaning an official. Today he is, along with his portrevene, the social head of the town. His most famous duty is that of joining with the Leet Jury of the Ale Tasters and Bread Weighers and one evening knocking on the door of each public house to enjoy a sample of their beer. Not an easy task when we consider there are ten public houses in Ashburton! The bread weighers weigh the bread from the baker's shop, and if the bread is found to be up to standard a certificate and a piece of evergreen strip is given. These days the bread is then auctioned at the local recreation ground whilst a ram roast is in progress.

Ashburton's present outdoor market opened in 1910. Before this animals were sold in the streets. There are nine sales a year – one for lambs, one for the famous Dartmoor ponies, usually in October, the rest for store cattle.

In 1791 a private undertaking brought water to those wealthy enough to live in East Street, known as the East Street Conduit. It has been restored and if one looks around Ashburton streets there are many small alcoves let into the walls. In many there are traces of where taps were fixed. It was not until the beginning of this century that there was a public water system. Electricity came to the town in 1930, while gas had been installed since 1840.

Ashprington ✣

This peaceful village is a pleasant three mile drive from Totnes. If you should feel energetic you might like to try the river walk to Ashprington, which starts at the edge of Totnes and for most of the way follows the course of the river Dart.

When you reach Ashprington you will find a picture postcard village of little stone cottages, with lattice windows and roofed doors. It may remind you of days gone by for you won't find any yellow lines on the roads, any lamp posts or ugly signs here. Its lanes quickly become bridle paths which lead down to the banks of the river.

The 18th century refurbished Durant Arms was named after Richard Durant, who became lord of the manor of Sharpham House in 1841. In the pub you can still see the window from which the estate workers used to be paid their wages. Next door there is an interesting black and white timber and plaster coach house.

The church is dedicated to St David, unusual outside Wales, and built on an ancient site. Outside you can both admire the view over the village to the surrounding hills and also the tall 14th century tower. The church has been newly decorated, the parishioners having raised the necessary funds. The white walls make a fine backcloth for the large Norman font, which contrasts with the ornately carved modern pulpit.

Ashprington is a sunny village picturesquely arranged on the side of a hill. Near the old hump-back Bow Bridge, where the river Harbourne runs into Bow creek, is the pretty stone Waterman's Arms. The road leads on beside the creek to the village of Tuckenhay, with its old paper mill buildings and the riverside Maltsters Arms.

Not only are the residents of Ashprington spoilt for choice when it comes to attractive pubs within easy walking distance but the village still boasts a small post office cum village store where you can be sure of a friendly welcome. There is a warm community spirit in this village and good use is made of the quaint village hall. Here twice yearly get-togethers are held when as many as can be fitted in enjoy lunch together. The first Saturday in August sees the annual village fete.

Visitors to Ashprington can see over Bowden House with its photographic museum and can stroll around the beautiful gardens which are open to the public at Avenue Cottage. But if you should want to catch sight of Sharpham House, a Palladian mansion set beside the river Dart, then you ought to take one of the boat trips from Totnes to Dartmouth and you will have it pointed out to you as you round Ashprington Point.

Ashreigney 🖋

Ashreigney is a hilltop village approximately 550 ft above sea level. Included in the parish are the hamlets of Riddlecombe and Cottwood. The village is situated twelve miles south-east from Great Torrington.

The parish is surrounded by beautiful countryside, with large wooded valleys, part of the original Eggesford Forest. To the north are views of Exmoor and south is Dartmoor.

Ashreigney is basically a farming community, but not so dependent upon it as in the past. Many of the working age residents now travel further afield to South Molton, Barnstaple and Exeter for employment. In the parish there is now only one general store and a part time post office, although in the past there was a much larger variety of shops and trade, including wheelwrights, tailors and rope makers.

Down through the centuries Ashreigney has also been known as Rings Ash, which was possibly an informal name used by common people, while the gentry used Ashreigney. Evidence of Rings Ash still remains today, as the public house takes this name, along with Zion Methodist church, which belongs to the Rings Ash Circuit. On a stone in the parish church, which dates back to 1701, the words appear in this order, 'Ashreney also Ringsash'.

A Roman road runs through the village from Pensford to Tittywater. During the Civil War, Sir Thomas Fairfax, Chief of the Army under Cromwell, is reputed to have spent the night at Ashreigney, prior to his attack on Great Torrington in 1646.

St James's church takes up the central position in the village, approached by a path dividing the village green. There is some controversy as to the age of the church, and some authorities think that it is no earlier than the 15th century, but it is thought that there must have been an earlier church on the same site, as the font is 13th century. The church is built in stone in the Gothic style, with an unusual north sited tower. Ashreigney also had its own rectory and rector, but in common with other parishes these days, now shares its vicar, who lives in Winkleigh.

During the summer months the village is a hive of activity, with the Annual Garden Show & Sports Day, Clay Pigeon Shoot, and Country Fayre. The Country Fayre is a big day for the village, attracting visitors from all corners of the South West.

Atherington

Atherington is stated by a 16th century authority, to have got its name from King Athelstan, who drove away the Danish invaders and made Umberleigh his royal seat, including land at Atherington and High Bickington. The history of St Mary's church is inseparably interwoven with that of Umberleigh, as some of the furnishings came from the old Umberleigh Manor.

The Baptist chapel was built in 1839. In the 1900s there were two schools, one run by the church and one by the chapel, with about 60 pupils in each. An Attendance Officer from Chittlehampton used to call at the schools every week in his pony and trap to make sure that no children were absent.

The occupations of the villagers used to be all connected with agriculture, market gardening and soft fruit. There were many of the famous 'mazzard' cherry orchards, which originated from France. There was a blacksmith, thatcher, cobbler, carpenter, mason, undertaker and a chimney sweep, who used to go around the neighbouring villages with a donkey and cart. Today the village has a post office, tearoom and gift shop, a general stores and hairdressing salon and a thatcher. The majority of the people who live in the village today are not connected with agriculture but commute to Barnstaple and other towns.

In the early 1900s there used to be two clubs, the Rational Club run by the chapel and the National Club run by the church. The highlight of the year was a Club Day held in June in a field near the village when there would be various entertainments like a fair, races, stalls etc and a public tea.

Legend has it that many years ago a man who lived at Dobbs Cottage committed a murder and he was told that if he could empty the river Taw of sand by picking up a grain of sand a day he would be saved. Of course, that being impossible, he was hanged. There is a deep fishing pool in the river Taw known as Dobbs Pool. It is said that a strange black dog sometimes seen at night and called the Black Dog of Torrington is the ghost of Dobbs.

There were once three pubs in the village – now there are none! In 1900 the rector, Rev W. W. Arthur, took over the White Hart Inn, the last remaining licensed house, and ran it so that profits went to the Church National School. The White Hart is now a private house.

Aveton Gifford

Aveton Gifford, pronounced 'Awton Jifford', is at the head of the estuary of the river Aune or Avon, which is tidal as far as the weir. At the beginning of this century the river was used for communication and trade, the local inhabitants transporting coal, stone and lime.

The bridge was built in about 1420, and has been widened once. Today it is part of the A379 Plymouth to Kingsbridge road and will continue to be so even when the long promised bypass is built.

The rector defended this bridge during the Civil War, trying to prevent Cromwell's army crossing. He manned a cannon on Pittans Hill, but the attempt failed, he escaped and was hidden in one of his former parish churches.

The original church of Aveton Gifford was built in the 13th century, situated on a hill a short distance from the village. The beautiful church which had stood for centuries was destroyed in minutes on 25th January 1943 at 4 pm, when bombs rained down on the church and village. Ten houses and the rectory were almost totally destroyed, 17 people were hurt and a little girl killed. The church remained a ruin until 1951. The rebuilding was completed in 1957 but soon afterwards the tower was found to leak badly. The people of Aveton Gifford raised money and rebuilt the tower but it was twelve feet shorter with no bells and was only re-dedicated in 1970.

The name of Aveton Gifford comes partly from the river Aune or Avon. Walter Giffard was William the Conqueror's Standard Bearer and was given the manor in 1100. The site of the old manor near the church is probably Court Barton.

It has always been a village of builders and masons. Robert Macey, who built numerous churches and theatres in London, including the Adelphi and the Haymarket, was born the son of a mason in Aveton Gifford in 1790.

The school was built in 1857 on the site of the old poor house and has been up-dated and is now well equipped although the structure remains unaltered.

The Taverners and the Ebb Tide are the only remaining inns. Around 1840 there were five and more before that. There is a village green which is part of the old manor lands, known as the town common or dump. There is a children's play area and recently a tennis court has been added.

The village is a thriving community with many farm buildings now turned into living accommodation.

Axmouth 🦡

The village has the character and calm of a very ancient place. The earliest evidence of human activity is a large hand axe of about 25,000 years ago, found on the south-west shoulder of Hawkesdown, the steep hill with its Iron Age hill fort overlooking the Axe valley. Coins of the Durotriges (the Celtic tribe here before the Romans) have been found. A gold coin of Nero was found 40 years ago and, recently, five pieces of Roman lead sling shot.

The first written record of Axmouth is in the will of Alfred the Great. He died in AD 901 and left the manor of Axanmouth with other west country properties to his younger son Ethelward. The manor remained part of the royal demesne until well after the Norman Conquest in 1066.

The Fosse Way, which runs across country to Lincoln, probably had its southern end at the mouth of the Axe – later extended to Exeter. The Axe estuary was an important haven on a difficult coast, but the pebble bank which formed between 1350–1450 partially closed the entrance and slowed the river which silted up, creating the marshes. Great efforts and large sums of money were expended with little effect on widening the entrance. Nevertheless, coastal trading, as far as London and sometimes up the east coast, continued until the arrival of the railway in 1868. Two of the old warehouses remain as interesting homes.

St Michael's church is a delightful small church. One version of the Anglo-Saxon Chronicles mentions it as the burial place of an earl in the early 10th century. The structure contains work of almost every period from Norman to Victorian. There are some very early wall paintings and the effigy of a 14th century priest. There is an undated mass burial under the south wall of the churchyard, which is a mystery. Battle or plague? The number of victims is very large.

A very early ford crosses the river just near the church and heads for the deserted medieval village of Fleote on the west bank. A ferry also crossed the river on the seaward side of the bridge to Seaton. This coast, with its sheltered combes and small population was ideal for smugglers and, no doubt, the local folk were involved.

This has always been farming country but huge machines have replaced men and women. Few now work on farms but are mainly employed outside the village.

Two good inns, one very old, the other a replacement for one burned down, add to the scene. The village hall was the school until about 25 years ago. Outside is a quern of great age, used for grinding corn.

If Axmouth had an early manor house it has not been identified. Stedcombe House had that position when, in about 1550, the house and manor were granted to Walter Erle. The house was burned down during the Civil War and the present house was built in 1695 and is currently being refurbished.

Bampton 🐚

Bampton, lying on the river Batherm in north-east Devon, had its origins as a small Celtic settlement. Saxon farm names suggest this area was the meeting place of penetration from the west and the north. All the tracks still lead in to the centre called Newton Square, meaning the New Town.

About a mile to the south is Ha'penny Bridge, so named after the tax that was collected, whereas to the east is Holwell Farm, the reputed haunt of the ghost of an 18th century maiden who drowned herself in a lake. To the north, Bampton once had a castle, besieged by King Stephen in 1135, but only some out-works now remain.

A visit to the church, mainly 14th and 15th century, should not be made without noticing the tablet on the west wall –

'In memory of the Clerk's son
Bless my little iiiii's
Here he lies
In a sad pickle
Kill'd by an icicle
In the year 1776'

There is also a sundial, bearing the date 1586, on the exterior south wall and the old stocks are by the church tower, still remarkably well-preserved.

In the Middle Ages, life was dominated by the noble families, especially the Bourchiers – The Earls of Bath. By the 16th century their mansion was below the castle on the site of the present Castle Grove, which is Georgian. The vast majority of the town houses are of local quarry stone and show attractive 18th century features. At this time, Brook Street was an open stream called Duckpaddle with railed walks on either side. The age of the turnpike brought the toll house at the top of Briton Street, alongside Packhorse Way, which was part of a very important packhorse route passing through Bampton at that time, sections of which are still preserved to the south-east and north-west of the village.

Nowadays, most of the working population have to travel elsewhere to find employment although there is some local light industry. During the last century and the earlier part of this, the local quarrying industry provided work for many inhabitants with the building of houses, railways etc. It is interesting to note from a directory of the 1930s that the residents included innkeepers (there were more than eleven inns including the Cyclist's Rest and the Druggist's Arms), a town crier, a coachman, two butlers, three chauffeurs, a blacksmith, a charwoman, various labourers and platelayers and, last but not least, the lord of the manor.

Bampton Fair is still renowned throughout the West Country. Originally a three-day fair, its charter being dated 1258, it is now a one-day event, taking place on the last Thursday in October. At first, it was a sheep fair, emphasising what has always been the main occupation of the area but in the 19th century the sale of ponies was included. The wholesale seasonal movement of animals by rail was a feature of the Exe Valley Railway for many years until its closure in 1965. About a fortnight before the fair the pick-up goods train from Exeter carried a few empty cattle wagons up to Bampton. By the day of the fair there would be some 50 wagons waiting to load the ponies and convey them to Tiverton. Sadly, it is no longer a cattle fair, but efforts are being made to revive old crafts.

Bampton church

Beaford ✒

Beaford is situated on the B3220, south-east of Great Torrington.

There was a church in Beaford long before the present mainly late 15th century building, since the font is Norman, dated between 1086 and 1106. All Saints' tower was rebuilt in 1802 and again replaced in 1909. One of the bells is dated 1432, cast by an Exeter bellfounder named Robert Norton.

Extracts from a gazetteer of 1851 indicate that Beaford was quite a bustling village with a population of 666 and an acreage of 3,203. There were masons, carpenters, glaziers, shoemakers, tailors, grocers, drapers, higglers (egg collectors), a blacksmith, a gunsmith, and other trades and services within the village. Robert Heard was landlord of the Gunsmith's Arms and several other Heards ran local businesses.

In 1927 Beatrix F. Cresswell read a paper before the Women's Institute which described how Beaford in former years seems to have envied the privileges of its larger neighbour Torrington as a borough town. Failing to reach this dignity the village annually elected a Mayor, took him round the parish in a wheelbarrow, and finally threw him out on the green. Borough towns of dignity frequently complain of the trouble it is to find individuals willing to serve as Mayors; one has an idea it must have been most difficult to persuade any parishioner to accept the doubtful honour of being, even for a brief time, Mayor of Beaford.

Present day Beaford has one shop cum post office. The school is now an Area School and takes pupils in from nearby St Giles and Roborough, at present numbering 100. The Globe Inn is now the only public house, but a mile down the road is the Beaford House Hotel. The inhabitants now travel to Torrington, Bideford and Barnstaple to work, but farming is still a way of life here.

The Beaford Centre, formerly 'Green Warren House', was bought by the Dartington Trust in 1966 and is used as an Arts Centre. Many events and exhibitions take place here and it is also open for schools from all over the country for educational visits. This was also where the (now Barnstaple-based) Orchard Theatre started life.

The population at present is 350. Beaford, however, has several holiday cottages and, with the hotel, there is quite an annual influx of people to the village. New housing in the village has had a very gradual progress in the past 20 years, but with eight new bungalows built in 1988 and 29 houses due, Beaford is now a growing village.

Beer 🌿

The valley in which the village of Beer lies, has known habitation since prehistoric times. There are (or were) flint beds on Beer Head and these were worked and traded with other inhabitants of Devon.

The Romans worked the stone in the Old Quarry at the head of the valley and Beer stone is to be found in the Roman walls of Exeter. The Romans moved the stone by sea and they first drove a road from the quarry to the sea, which is now the line of the village street.

After the Norman Conquest the village became part of the lands of the Abbot of Sherborne and supplied the abbey with fish and wine, the grapes for which were grown on south facing hillsides. Within living memory the village allotments were known as 'The Vineyards'. The Normans continued exploiting the quarries and there is Beer stone in every church in East Devon, in Exeter Cathedral, and in many churches in South Devon in places accessible from the sea. Beer's own church was built only in 1877, on the site of an earlier chapel.

In the late 1500s Flemish immigrants brought lace-making to East Devon, and Beer became an important village. At the height of the industry there were 400 registered lacemakers in the village and in the 1840s part of Queen Victoria's wedding dress was made there. The Lace Shop still stands where the agent collected the lace for transport by cart to Honiton, then by stagecoach to London. The trade died out, replaced by machine-made lace, and the last old lady who tried to earn a living with her 'lace pillow' died in 1942.

Fishing was important from Tudor times and continued to be so until the 1950s. Before the Second World War Beer was the third port in Devon in weight and value of fish landed. One December morning in 1936, 600,000 herrings were sold off Beer beach. After the war it was found that the herring had changed its migration course and the loss was catastrophic.

The fishing industry had been sustained by the evolution of the Beer lugger. This was a 30 ft open boat with three sails. It gave the boat great speed and was ideal for smuggling, since it could outsail the slower Revenue cutters. From the late 1600s most of the fishermen were engaged in 'the game' to supplement their meagre income. The principal pick-up port was Alderney, and the inward cargoes were usually spirits and tobacco. The best known smuggler in East Devon was Jack Rattenbury – a Beer man. He published his memoirs in 1837, after gout had forced him to 'retire' from his profession. There are people alive who know their families were still engaged in the trade in 1870–80.

On the seafaring side, Beer men were active from Queen Elizabeth I's reign – it is known from Tudor documents that a Beer fisherman was sailing master for Sir Walter Raleigh, and Beer men lost their lives in Raleigh's early attempts at settlement on the east coast of America. From the 1600s on, village men who could not find work in the local boats, joined the 'cod schooners' which fished the Newfoundland banks and sold their catch, dried and salted, in Spain, racing home loaded with oranges which they hoped they could unload before they went rotten. This trade lasted until about 1870 when the schooners were put out of business by tramp steamers. There are men still alive who knew the 'cod' men.

There was a great influx of men into the Merchant Service and from 1890 into the Royal Navy (regular service). Right up to 1945 there were seven Beer men with Master's tickets and scores of others at sea.

The fishermen worked on the 'share' basis and were truly self employed – 'no fish, no money!' It was a hazardous life with little financial reward but it bred a certain bloody-minded independence – 'we don't work for a boss and there is no squire'.

Until recent times the village was fairly isolated and the inhabitants were inbred and closely related. This close relationship meant there were no social classes and this emphasised the 'bloody mindedness'. People from surrounding villages agreed Beer people were different and their term of abuse was 'Spaniards'. This springs from the legend that after a visitation of the plague in 1646, which decimated the male population particularly, a Spanish merchant ship was wrecked in the bay and the men were absorbed into the village. There is no written evidence of this but the folklore is so persistent that it may well be founded on fact.

A few of the present villagers earn their living by fishing, the main catch being crabs, with mackerel fishing in the tourist season. The main occupation now is the tourist industry, catering for summer visitors.

Bere Ferrers 🪶

The village is designated an area of outstanding natural beauty and lies on a peninsula bordered by the rivers Tavy and Tamar, 15 miles from Plymouth. The name comes from the Celtic 'bere' meaning narrow strip of land, and Ferrers after the lords of the manor.

Unquestionably the jewel in the village's crown is St Andrew's church, perched on the bank of the river Tavy. It was built by Sir William de Ferrers by 1258 and rebuilt 70 years later by his grandson William, who established a collegiate church with five priests to pray for himself and his wife in perpetuity. He installed rare stained glass obtainable only from France, and the east window, showing himself and his wife Matilda offering his church to the Lord, remains, together with some examples in Exeter Cathedral, the oldest glass in Devon.

In 1979 St Andrew's was declared beyond repair, but the village community of 250 folk decided against redundancy and to restore the church. Nine years later, after hundreds of fundraising activities (and with help from English Heritage) they had raised £80,000 and the major restoration was complete. The Friends of St Andrew's has been formed to mastermind future fundraising.

In the reign of Edward I Bere Ferrers was renowned for its silver and lead mines. The area was for 200 years the most highly specialised mining community in Southern England. Bere silver had its own stamp and in the 14th century mines were reserved for the King's exclusive use. The rivers were the main artery of the community, used for the import of timber, lime and coal, and the export of minerals, fruit and flowers, until the advent of the railway.

Apart from the heyday of the mining era in the 13th and its revival in the early 19th centuries, the Tamar valley was engaged in horticulture. The mild climate and south-facing slopes were ideal for the early production of fruit and flowers. The opening of the London and South Western Railway in 1890 brought great changes, markets opened up throughout the country and the valley's black cherries, pears, plums and strawberries, already famous, brought prosperity.

There are now only three farms, specialising in narcissi bulbs and market gardening, but Hensbury, the pick your own farm, is popular with visitors.

Today the railway line to Waterloo is non-existent but there are regular trains along the Plymouth to Gunnislake line, presently being promoted as a tourist attraction. There are also bus services to Tavistock.

The village is still a farming community though there has been an influx of people who commute to Plymouth and Tavistock. The indispensable church hall was formerly the village school, which closed in 1933. People shop in the post office-cum-general store, and bread, fish, fruit and vegetables are delivered. A doctor's surgery is held weekly.

There was a vineyard of repute on the south-east slope of Vinegar Hill in 1585. Today there is still a vineyard – Birlanda, which concentrates on the white wines, Schonburger and Riesling.

Orchard Pottery fires traditional stoneware and porcelain, employing local outworkers and exporting virtually worldwide. There is an inn, The

Plough, and the social club has new premises where billiards, darts and euchre are enjoyed. The Lanterna is a small family hotel, and there is a Methodist church. Naturally water sports are popular but salmon fishing has declined.

In 1986 the ten acre Marsh Field, an important wildlife habitat, was bought by two local businessmen, to prevent its being developed for housing.

Berrynarbor ✤

Berrynarbor is a delightful village and parish nestling between Ilfracombe and Combe Martin on the North Devon coast.

In the 13th century, there were two influential families, the Berrys and the Nerberts. When they intermarried in the 14th century, the village was called Berry Nerbert, changing to Berry Narbor in the late 17th century.

The centrepiece of the village is the church of St Peter, an ancient structure, some parts dating back to the 12th century. Once inside, besides finding peace and sanctity, there are monuments to the Berry and Nerbert families, and an engraved portrait of John Jewel, an illustrious theologian born in the parish at Bowden Farm in 1522.

In the early 19th century, the Basset family were the principal land-owners. They had a stone, castellated mansion built. When the last hereditary owner, Mrs Penn Curzon, died, this, together with the estate was sold, and is now Watermouth Castle, a very important tourist attraction.

Near the church is all that remains of the former manor house, and the hall is now used for village activitites. The well-attended primary school was built in 1847.

Over the years Berrynarbor has changed from a completely rural area, to one incorporating farming with tourism. Many new residences have been built, blending in with the older properties. A butcher's, and two village shops, one the post office, cater for all needs.

In the 18th and 19th centuries, entertainment centred around the church, and the first Sunday in July was celebrated as the Berry Revels, when an early morning service was followed by a day of festivities and tests of skills. Unfortunately the custom died out, until in the 1970s it was revived, only this time taking place in August, so that the many visitors could appreciate the village atmosphere.

Being a competitive village, Berrynarbor has gained several certificates

29

of High Merit for Britain in Bloom. It also gained the Best Kept Village award in 1985 and 1988, both occasions being sponsored by a very active Youth Club.

For the energetic, there are lots of interesting walks and colourful gardens to visit. The stream gurgling through Berrynarbor on its way to the sea attracts ducks, and herons prospecting for the odd trout.

Bickington (North Devon) 🐚

The 'village' of Bickington, a large and ever-growing area which is fast becoming a part of neighbouring Barnstaple is, in reality, a hamlet of Fremington. This parent village of Fremintone, as it appears in the Domesday Book, takes up most space in the history books, leaving Bickington with fewer records.

In the reign of Edward the Confessor, Bickington belonged to the parish of Tawstock. Many of the streets, roads, fields and rights of way are named after Saxon warriors and gods, and some fields still carry their original Saxon names.

Fremington Quay, situated between Bickington and Fremington, gave employment to many Bickington men. Coal was imported and clay from local clay-pits was exported. A narrow gauge tramway (horse-drawn) was opened in August 1848 and ran to Barnstaple from the quay. It was superseded by a steam-hauled broad gauge line which ran through to Bideford, in 1855.

The clay-pits contained many erratics, large rocks which had been brought down by glaciers in the distant past and which were eagerly sought by geologists. Some large granite examples can be seen acting as gate-posts in the Combrew area.

The first St Andrew's mission church was built in 1911 next to the school on land provided by Mr W. Pitts Tucker. Its match-boarding interior and corrugated iron exterior caused a few irreverent villagers to refer to it as the 'cast-iron cathedral'. It was burned down on Thursday 5th January 1956 and a new St Andrew's was built in its place.

White's History and Gazetteer says that a 'School Church' was erected of brick with stone dressings in 1870 at a cost of £600, and that divine service was held in the room on Sunday afternoons. This must be what is today the church hall and what was until the late 1950s the village school.

The date over the door of the chapel at the top of Bickington Hill is 1835 but the Congregational and United Reformed records show the date as 1839. Nonconformist services were held in people's homes earlier than this.

The general store and the combined post office, newsagent and store have taken the place of the bakery, bootmaker and old-fashioned shop smelling slightly of paraffin, barley meal and cheese.

In the more recent past the aerial view of Bickington must have been like a herring bone because it consisted of a long main road with lanes leading off. Now it is growing and will in time become a large built-up area.

There are two pubs. The more recently opened one is in what was a former private house, believed to have, at one time, been a coaching inn.

Bickington (South Devon) 🦢

The ancient village of Bickington (formerly Bickentone or Buketon) lies three miles north-east of Ashburton and four miles north-west of Newton Abbot. Its modern name means 'the town on the brook'. The brook is the Lemon, which rises near Haytor. In former years it supplied water to a flock mill and a bone mill in the village. These are now private houses but the water-wheel at Bone Mill, now Chipley Mill, has been restored and is in full working order. The Lemon, which has caused disastrous flash floods in Newton Abbot within living memory, has undergone a flood protection scheme just below Chipley Mill.

Bickington and the hamlet of South Knighton one and a half miles to the east have both lost many village amenities over the last 50 years. South Knighton within living memory had a slaughterhouse cum butcher's, a bakery, a dairy, a shop, a market garden and a pub called the Ship Inn. None of these remain. Bickington had two grocery shops, a blacksmith's, a bakery, a wheelwright's and a post office. Today only the post office remains though not on its original site. Later developments now include a small factory making jockey silks, a racing stable, a garage and a caravan site. In both villages agriculture continues as ever.

The 15th century church of St Mary, Bickington is well documented. It has an ancient lychgate with a room on top. The graveyard tells the story of village families, such as the Bickfords, on its headstones. In 1885 the church was restored. A vicarage was built to replace the curate's house, and in the same year the Wesleyans built a chapel. Today both the chapel and vicarage are private houses.

Chipley and (Bickington) Barton Quarries are not worked any longer, although Barton is particularly famous for its rare species of bat. Indeed during the 1980s the Devon County Council built a tower over their cave entrance to protect them. The quarry is now used as a timber yard.

The cottages close to the church are interesting. Church Cottage was once used as a house for 'fallen women', then it became a post office. When the fireplace at Dove Cottage next door was renovated a large oven, full of clay pipes, was discovered. This is thought to be a relic of the days when both cottages were used by the monks who built St Mary's. Recent other finds in the village include an authenticated Stone Age flint and some flat iron shoes used on oxen when ploughing.

The mains water supply was connected to Bickington in 1962 and the occasion is commemorated by a plaque on the church lychgate.

South Knighton and Chipley have few, very narrow lanes which take local traffic. Bickington on the other hand, being on the main route from Exeter to Plymouth, has had three major roads over the last 300 years. All three can be seen just below Barton Quarry. The original road, past the quarry, the church and down Old Hill into Lemonford, encounters a very narrow dangerous bridge over the Lemon.

The second, known as the 'Old A38', was originally a turnpike road. The turnpike trustees were required in 1755 to improve the communications from Chudleigh to South Brent, through Bickington. The toll house is still to be seen at Goodstone Cross very close to the village. The final road is the dual carriageway linking the M5 to Cornwall.

Bigbury

Bigbury is a large parish, bounded by the English Channel and the Devon Avon to the south and east and by rolling farmland. It is approximately 17 miles from Plymouth.

The original village is relatively unchanged with thatched cottages, a small but pretty village green, a post office and village shop and the Royal Oak public house. The parish church of St Lawrence dates from the 12th century and has two fine brasses, an interesting lectern and a peal of six bells.

Bigbury-on-Sea also forms part of the parish and is some two miles from Bigbury village, while St Ann's Chapel and Easton lie about half a mile and one mile away respectively. Both Bigbury-on-Sea and St Ann's Chapel have their own small stores, while Easton is purely residential but was the home of the old village school and original rectory.

Bigbury-on-Sea, known for its golden sand, is popular for family holidays and for days out for people from Plymouth, Ivybridge, etc. It was hoped in the 1920s and 1930s to make it a garden village by the sea and some development took place on this basis. Other homes, mainly retirement housing or holiday homes, have been developed since the Second World War on a very restricted basis.

Burgh Island lies off the coast at Bigbury-on-Sea and is accessible by foot across the sand at low tide and by sea tractor from the car park at high tide. It is from the hotel on the island that Agatha Christie wrote some of her books and many famous people, such as Noel Coward, frequented the hotel in the 1930s.

St Ann's Chapel, the first of the Bigbury hamlets to be reached on the road into Bigbury, has its own pub The Pickwick Inn, and the Memorial Hall (the village hall) built to the memory of those of the parish who gave their lives in the two World Wars.

Bishopsnympton 🪶

Bishopsnympton is a village in a scattered rural parish with 760 inhabitants, on the southern edge of Exmoor.

The village is shaped like a pole on a base, with the main street as the pole, and the base comprising the church (a large one because the area was part of the estate belonging to the bishop of Exeter), a triangular green, primary school and Hall. St Mary's church is mostly 15th or early 16th century, restored in the 19th century.

Some of the cottages are thatched, there are council houses and old people's bungalows, a chapel, a shop-cum-post office, a pub, a pottery and a small leather-working manufacturer. There are several thriving organisations – WI, gardening club, MU, drama group, playgroup, football and Over 60s club. But best of all, is its kindly and contented people: newcomers are welcomed and readily accepted, and in no time at all feel at home in Bishopsnympton, a village rich in community life, traditions, folk tales, good neighbourliness, and all that is best in Devon life.

Bishops Tawton 🪶

Bishops Tawton, 'the stockaded farm beside the Taw', is thought to have once been the seat of the bishops of Devon. The bishop's palace, now Court Farm, was used on episcopal journeys around the see until at least 1440, and remained in Church hands until the Reformation.

Adjoining Court Farm stands the 14th century church of St John the Baptist. The sanctuary ring, set in the heavy oak door, is a reminder of troubled times and desperate fugitives.

The church contains many memorials to members of the Chichester family, whose family seat known as 'Hall', lies a couple of miles from the village. The present 'Squire' Chichester is a cousin of Sir Francis Chichester of seafaring fame. The family coat of arms, with the motto 'Ferme en Foy', can be seen over the doorway of the picturesque 15th century thatched inn which bears their name.

The new road between Barnstaple and Exeter cuts a swathe through the village, isolating the church and Court Farm from the oldest part of the village with its old cottages and its two inns. The old road threads its way past The Three Pigeons, a 15th century building which has been an inn since 1623. It still bears traces of its time as a coaching inn and is haunted, some say, by a restless monk.

The local hunt meets annually in December in front of The Chichester Arms to take a stirrup cup before moving off up the valley.

The old road continues past the site of the old cattle pound, and coaches then turned to go down a steep hill, across an old stone bridge which spans the South Yeo, and climb steeply again to Stage Cross. At the foot of the hill lies a 14th century Devon longhouse which bears traces of its past as both a meeting house and an inn.

The South Yeo is a tributary of the Taw, and once boasted a quay where barges unloaded limestone for firing in the four kilns on the quayside. The lime-kilns, together with the quarries on Codden Hill and a lace factory, provided work for the villagers in days gone by. Then, as now, however, the main industry was agriculture, especially dairy farming and sheep rearing. Few villagers can boast of being born and bred in the village. The majority have moved in as the village expanded along the Taw valley, and their occupations have become many and varied as commuting to Barnstaple and beyond has been made easier.

Some aspects of village life, however, never change. Elvers are still trapped in the Taw, and anglers still fish the banks for mullet and, hopefully, salmon and sea trout. Cattle still graze the marshes and summer still sees a rash of strange craft struggling to navigate the river, when the Raft Race is run towards Barnstaple from beyond Newbridge. The village Revels were allowed to lapse some years ago, but attempts are now being made to revive some of the old community spirit with an annual fair. Codden Hill still broods over the village, a large part of it still open to the public, thanks to the annual ritual of 'firing the hill'. In October, when the bracken turns Codden into a great brown bear, the village children set off daily for a week to set fire to the bracken, and thus claim the right of public access for another year.

The beacon lit to commemorate the Armada was the latest in a long line of beacons stretching back to pagan times. Each year, by the light of the beacon, farmers fashioned an effigy of a bull from straw and mud, which was set up on Codden as a fertility symbol. Each man carried home a small image of the bull to nail on the lintel of the farmhouse door. This ritual was carried on until at least the middle of the 19th century, but perhaps the magic lingers on to ensure fertility now and in the future. Certainly Codden will remain to protect Bishops Tawton no matter what changes the future will bring.

Bishopsteignton 🐚

The village of Bishopsteignton is situated by the side of the river Teign, two miles from Teignmouh and four miles from Newton Abbot . In early Saxon times there was a settlement here, but there are signs of an even earlier habitation.

It was in AD 927 that Leofric established a Benedictine monastery at Radway, on the site now known as 'Old Walls'. After the departure of the monks in the next century the building became a palace for the bishops of Exeter.

Fore Street, Radway Street, West Street and Ash Hill are the main old streets in the village and go back to Elizabethan times and before. The house next to the Ring of Bells (Cloche Merle) was said to be a plague house, and there was a space set aside in the churchyard for the victims.

The parish church is probably the oldest building still standing in the village, built about 1130 by the Normans. The only parts that can now be definitely identified as Norman are the beautiful arch of the main west doorway, the font, and the tympanum on the outside of the south wall where there was formerly a doorway and porch. This is a fine example of Norman work. There are only a few of these in Devon, and this is said to be the earliest carving in the country depicting the Adoration of the Magi.

Behind the church, to the east, the sanctuary chapel of St John the Baptist was erected in the 13th century – a dedication later transferred to the parish church itself. In this sanctuary chapel fugitives from justice could take refuge. There are sufficient remains to show the outline of the original building, which is believed to have been demolished at the

Reformation, when the land on which it stood passed out of the hands of the Church. Today it is laid out as a garden of rest.

In the 1700s a great deal of the development of the central part of the village as we know it today took place. Residences, said to have been built by 'Gentlemen Merchant Adventurers of the highest calibre', were erected – Cross House, Kittoes, Teign Lawn, Lendrick and Huntley. All the grounds of these properties adjoined and all had access to one another's gardens. In those days owners planned for the future by planting rare trees within the grounds which were brought from all corners of the world, and once Bishopsteignton was said to vie with Badminton in having the greatest variety of trees in the country. Alas, with modern development and tree felling that honour is no longer ours.

The village school originated in 1719 for the education of 20 poor children of the village. In 1729 a schoolhouse was built with a residence for the schoolmaster. In 1949 the school was finally taken over as a County primary school, and in 1972 moved to a new location in Cockhaven Close. The old buildings now form the community centre, and play a large part in the social life of the village.

It is often said that the triangle formed by Clanage Street, West Street and Fore Street was formerly the village green. There were some buildings on the land, variously described in old documents as Church houses, poor houses or almshouses.

Street lighting was taken over by the Parish Council in 1897, the lighting then being by oil lamps. These were not lit four days before and four days after the full moon.

The centuries have seen many changes in the life of the village and the rate of change has accelerated in recent years. While the growth of population and the building of many new houses must inevitably change the appearance of Bishopsteignton, it is hoped that future developments will not change the beauty of this ancient village.

Blackawton

Blackawton is situated in the picturesque South Hams district of South Devon. Although it is four miles from the sea by road, the sea is visible from most parts of the village, and the rays from Start Point lighthouse sweep the surrounding countryside. Most of the year the hedgerows are ablaze with flowers.

Blackawton is one of the earliest Saxon settlements in this area. There has been a church in Blackawton since at least Norman times, as the font dates from that period, but the present church of St Michael was consecrated in 1333. In this church is a splendid rood screen. On the lower panels are the initials of Henry VIII and Katherine of Aragon, while on the panels above is portrayed a pomegranate, Katherine's personal emblem. A claim to fame for Blackawton church is that Sir Walter Raleigh is said to have married Elizabeth Throckmorton here. This cannot be authenticated however and other churches make similar claims.

Blackawton is a mixture of old cottages and new houses. On the outskirts of the village are the ruins of the old manor house of Oldstone, which sadly was destroyed by fire in the 1890s. The house originally belonged to the Cholwich family and was sold to the Dimes family in 1837, in whose possession it remained until the fire in 1895. One of the daughters of the house made a secret marriage and was found drowned in a pond in the woods. Her bridegroom was charged with her murder, but he was finally proved innocent. There are many tales of ghostly sightings in connection with the house.

There is very little employment in the village, the majority of the inhabitants having to commute to Dartmouth, Totnes or beyond. There are farms but they are worked by the families owning them. There are two shops, one a bakery/general store and the other a post office/general store. In the past there was a wheelwright, carpenter, blacksmith, shoe repairer, three working mills, and in the last century even a bellfounder. There is still evidence of his work in the village, a bell in the church and a pump at the back of some old cottages. There are two inns in the village, reputedly built in the 14th and 15th centuries.

Vineyards are being developed, and there is also a small brewery, which used to be in the centre of the village but is now situated on the outskirts.

Blackawton was one of the villages evacuated in the Second World War to clear the area so the American Forces could practise for the D-Day landings. A meeting was held in Blackawton church to inform all the inhabitants of the villages concerned to evacuate the area by 20th December 1943 – six weeks notice to clear the area of people and livestock. The aforementioned rood screen had to be dismantled and removed for safe keeping. Sheplegh Court, another large house, was the headquarters of General Eisenhower during this period. Since that time Sheplegh Court has been a naturist hotel, but has now been turned into apartments.

An eccentric inventor once lived in the village, who ingeniously made car fuel out of chicken manure!

There is a charity in connection with the church which dates back to 1699, whereby bread is distributed each Sunday morning after morning service in perpetuity to the poor of the parish. These days it is given to the children, who clamour for it and apparently enjoy eating dry bread!

Bovey Tracey 🌿

Bovey Tracey, the traditional 'Gateway to the Moor', has for the past few years been a very rapidly expanding community, due, in the most part, to the county's expansion programme.

A settled community at Bovey has been known to exist since before the Norman Conquest, when the manor was held by Edric, a Saxon thane. It was a rich holding by 11th century standards and like many Devon manors had freeholds attached to it, which in the main still exist today as farms or hamlets within the Bovey boundaries.

The 12th century saw the originating of the first of the Bovey legends, the long-surviving tradition that one of the four murderers of Thomas a Becket built Bovey church as penance for his part in the conspiracy. This is not proven and open to much dispute, but it is a very commonly held view – and who can dispute the fact that Bovey church is dedicated to St Thomas of Canterbury and the living is still a gift of the Crown.

Bovey's next notable event occurred during the Civil War of the 17th century. Here again fact and legend are intertwined. It appears that Royalist troops stationed in Bovey were playing cards in the establishment now known as Front House when they were surprised by Roundheads, whereupon the Royalists threw their stake money away and while the poorer Roundheads scrabbled for it on the ground, the Royalists made their escape. There does seem to be little doubt that an important battle was fought upon Bovey Heathfield, and it is said that ghostly soldiers have been heard upon the adjacent Chudleigh Knighton Heath.

Agriculture apart, Bovey has seen some industrial development. In the late 18th and early 19th centuries the unique Granite Tramway carried stone from the Haytor quarries bound for the Teignmouth docks. It ran through what is now part of the Stover Country Park and the newly instituted Templar Way follows this industrial trail for most of its length.

Because of the special qualities of the clay found in the Bovey basin it is in demand for many industries, but especially in the production of fine pottery, and the Bovey Potteries were an essential part of the town from the 19th century until the recent past. Craft pottery in Bovey is also represented by the internationally renowned Leach family concerns.

Lignite, a fossil fuel half-way between peat and coal, was mined in Bovey as part of the economy measures of the Second World War, and its quarry pits now form nature reserves.

In the last few years Bovey's traditional landmark, 'The Wheel' has become the centre for the Devon Guild of Craftsmen. It is reputedly the best craft centre west of Southampton. Bovey's other traditional craft industry is a flourishing handloom weaver's, which can claim Royal patronage and links Bovey to its distant past as an integral part of the West Country woollen trade.

Bow ✒

Bow lies midway between Crediton and Okehampton and consists of Bow, or Bow Town, where a double row of houses line the main road (which was at one time one of the main thoroughfares from Exeter to Cornwall) and Nymet Tracey where the church, the old rectory and a few houses are situated. A century ago Nymet Tracey contained over 80 houses, which were destroyed by a disastrous fire.

Bow is very conveniently situated in the 'dead centre' of Devon and although the railway line was closed for public use some years ago, there is a good bus service between Okehampton and Exeter on weekdays. There are two garages, three general stores, a post office, and another shop which sells clothing, toys, gifts, wool etc.

The oldest house in the village is known as the Old Brewhouse or Malt House and is now a grocery store which has been in the same family for a hundred years. The King's Arms Inn next door probably took that name in the 17th century, when the licence was transferred from the Old Brewhouse. By the numbers of houses listed in old deeds, Bow must have been quite a busy and prosperous place at that time when the wool trade was still a major industry.

In 1643 the Parliamentary and Royalist forces clashed at Bow Bridge and it is believed the mounds on either side of the road mark the burial grounds of those who fell in battle and are not the earlier type of burial mounds or 'barrows'.

The church is dedicated to St Bartholomew. It was originally dedicated to St Martin and changed in the late 19th century but the exact date and reason are not known. According to local tradition it was built by Sir William de Tracey as an act of penance for his part in the murder of St Thomas a Becket in 1170, and the carved stone head of a Norman knight, now to be seen above the south door, is believed to be his likeness, placed outside because of his crime. Tracey Castle stood nearby but there are now no remains of it left.

In 1694 John Gould (yeoman), whose house in the main street is still lived in, left 'a house and close for the use as a school and almshouse.' This is still standing and lived in and was used as the school until the building of the present one in the 19th century. Part of the original garden, with the produce of which the schoolmaster was supposed to support himself, has now been incorporated in the playground of the primary school.

A number of new houses have been built in the village and the population of Bow is now approximately 1,000. While many old names survive and there is still a strong farming and agricultural connection and allied small businesses, Bow partly owes its recent growth to its popularity as a commuting area for Crediton and Exeter.

Bradninch 🌿

Bradninch is situated about ten miles from Exeter and 20 from Taunton. The population is between 1,900 to 2,000. The main industry here is paper-making.

Most of the farms belong to the Duchy of Cornwall. The farmers pay their rent to the Duchy Steward. The Prince of Wales, later the Duke of Windsor, came in 1921 to open the recreation ground and several members of the Royal family have visited since, including the Queen, when she was Princess Elizabeth, as well as Prince Charles.

Years ago it was said that the mayor of Bradninch took precedence over the mayor of Exeter. One day the mayor of Exeter came to visit the mayor of Bradninch with a letter. The mayor of Bradninch, who was a thatcher by trade, was on a ladder at a house at the time; he wouldn't come down to the mayor of Exeter so the mayor had to climb the ladder to him. It is also said that the Bradninch mayor was not much of a scholar and he read the message upside down. It was said that he would shout from the top of the ladder when working 'Reeds, spars and cider and what I ask for last bring me first'.

The church is almost entirely 15th and 16th century, restored in 1845. It is a beautiful church with a remarkable rood screen, said to be early 16th century, depicting scenes from bible stories. The church comes under the patronage of the House of Windsor.

At one time there were four brothers in business in Bradninch; these being Butcher Webber, Baker Webber, Farmer Webber and Harness-maker Webber. The latter kept a shop on the top of Martins Hill and sold leather goods, dog collars, saddles, nails, etc. He lived alone and when he wanted to step out for a drink he would write on the door 'Back in ten minutes'. The trouble was no one knew when the ten minutes started or would be likely to end! Another well known person was Mrs Bessie Beed, who was still the licensee of Ye Old White Lion public house when she was 100 years old.

Bradworthy 🌿

The village is very old, being originally mentioned in the Domesday Book as the manor of 'Braurdina', and probably founded shortly after AD 700. The name means roughly, 'broad enclosure' or 'broad space' and in the lower part of the village is the village green, known from time immemorial as the Broadhill. At the centre of the village is the Square, the largest village square in the West Country.

People born and bred in Bradworthy are known as 'Horniwinks', the local name for a species of plover, the pee-wit, which used to be found in large numbers on Bradworthy Moors, the common pasture of the old manor. The Domesday Book states one detail unique for this part of Devon. The Norman lord of the manor had, in addition to the usual amount of livestock, '30 unbroken horses', and to this day a road to the east of the village is known as Horse Hill. Bradworthy parish is high, standing 732 ft above sea level at its highest point.

It has seen very great expansion and improvements during latter years, and now has a population of about 1,000, with four new and pleasant housing estates. There is a dispensing doctor's surgery, two veterinary surgeries, a cafe, post office and hairdressing salon, a drapery store and newsagent, grocer, butcher, printer, clockmaker and garage. Of the two large furnishing stores, one also sells hardware, shoes and almost anything needed in a rural area. There are two hotels, one of which is the Bradworthy Inn.

There is a strong village community spirit, shown in the many activities enjoyed here. Pride is taken in the appearance of the village, which has won the 'Best Kept Village Competition'. The church and Methodist chapel play a most active part in village life, and there is a modern school with an energetic PTA.

There is an annual carnival and tug of war across the river, when braver spirits take their annual ducking. The festival of Harvest is celebrated at the churches and at Christmas villagers gather to carol round the Christmas tree in the Square and consume quantities of hot mince pies afterwards. In days gone by there were two fairs, one in June and one in September, and the older people still say of the latter 'After Bradry Fair, comes winter air.' There is still a monthly cattle auction here.

Charles Garvice the writer, whose novels became very popular, was practically unknown when he came to Bradworthy and rented a small cottage. With success came bigger houses, and he built Moorlands and Little Silworthy. At the latter place he took up farming, described in his only non-fiction book, *A Farm in Creamland*.

The most important building is the old and beautiful parish church of St John the Baptist. The village pump was put in the Square on the occasion of Queen Victoria's Jubilee. A water diviner was paid ten shillings to find the right place, and 40 ft well was sunk, which still served the village not so long ago during a water shortage. There is also the holy well of St Peter near the south-east corner of the churchyard.

It has to be said in conclusion, that Bradworthy has an annual average rainfall of 55 inches.

Bratton Clovelly

The village is the centre of the very scattered parish of Bratton Clovelly, which takes its name from the Clavilles, who held the manor in the 13th century.

It is rightly proud of its late 14th century church, and the bells which were cast in 1767. It is one of the few remaining churches possessing wall paintings dating back to the 17th century, now in the process of being lovingly restored. The tower was built with its own separate entrance, so that armed men could go up to keep guard, without desecrating the church.

Many names of families still living in the parish occur as far back as the 16th or 17th centuries, with two or three families still farming the same land. Of a unique position amongst these old families is the Palmer family. The post office has been in the family since at least 1863, when Mrs Betsy Palmer was recorded as postmistress. Her descendant Mrs Mary Jordan, born Palmer, carries on the family tradition as the present postmistress.

The population today is 331, but in 1850 the population was 870, and the village boasted two blacksmiths, three carpenters (now only one), a shoemaker, a mason, a tailor and two inns. The only remaining inn is the Clovelly Arms, renamed from the Packhorse.

The village is justly proud of its new parish hall, which was built on the site of the old war-time building, opened in 1954, and built with voluntary labour. The new hall was opened in 1985 and is the centre of village life. Each June the annual fete week takes place in the hall and its adjoining playing field, when each organisation works hard to raise money for their various funds.

A feature of the community spirit, and taking pride of place in the hall, is a patchwork collage depicting the vital areas of village life.

The village enjoys many visits by confused tourists, looking for the Clovelly of steep hill and donkey fame, but then remaining to enjoy Bratton Clovelly, having discovered, as many before them, that it has great charm of its own!

Braunton 🌿

Braunton used to be called the largest village in England, possibly a dubious description now. Although its population is around 8,000 Braunton is still referred to as 'the village' by its indigenous inhabitants.

It was already an established settlement in the 6th century when St Brannoc blazed the trail for other Celtic saints as he sailed up the Taw estuary towards the unknown. He founded the first church here 'at a place where he should find a sow and her litter', a legend recorded for posterity in one of the roof bosses. St Brannoc is buried, possibly under the high altar, in the present mainly 13th century church, which has a fine collection of bench ends.

The Domesday Book called the village Brantona (Brannoc's town). Old maps consistently spelled it Branton until the first Ordnance Survey map of 1809 slipped in a 'u' and it has remained Braunton ever since. Always a large village, Henry VIII could muster 20 horsemen, twelve archers and 30 harquebusiers here in the 16th century. In Victorian times agriculture and seafaring were the staple occupations – Braunton ketches brought in coal from South Wales, limestone from Caldy Island, and sailed out of the estuary with clay and gravel for pottery and building. Names of master mariners like Chugg, Chichester, Butler and Incledon were as well known as their ships. It was John Chugg who, in October 1891, safely brought home his famous *Two Sisters* from Kinsale with his jib boom, mizzen and all gear washed away in a violent storm.

The village, like most of its size, was self-sufficient a hundred years ago. It could boast three blacksmiths, five boot and shoe makers, four tailors, carpenters, a saddler, a host of small shops and businesses and several pubs, many of which were run by women. There was also a lady chemist, Louisa Tyte, surely a very early example of a woman breaking into the male world of the apothecary. Braunton's museum in Church Street shows the maritime and agricultural history of the area.

The railway opened up this magnificent coast to visitors and the first really local guide appeared at the end of the 19th century – aimed at a select clientele ('Not for giddy trippers' the guide proclaims). And so today Braunton is the gateway to the seven miles of golden surfing beaches at Woolacombe, Putsborough, Croyde and Saunton. For those not lured to the Atlantic breakers the great nature reserve of Braunton Burrows beckons.

Between Braunton and the estuary lies the Great Field, one of only three surviving examples of medieval strip cultivation in the country. At the turn of the century it was divided among some six dozen smallholders but is now worked by only a handful of farmers. The rich grazing land beside the Great Field, home of the famous red North Devon cattle, was enclosed under an Act of 1811 and added to in 1857, when the great estuary bank at Horsey Island was raised to keep out the tide.

The present village of Braunton is a mixture of old and new. Ancient cottages form the nucleus of the village – East, South, Heanton and Church Streets – with the elevated sites on the outskirts occupied by large Victorian, Edwardian and between-the-wars houses. Modern bungalow and housing estates have greatly enlarged the village in the last 20 years, but its attractive openness has been preserved.

Brentor

Brentor is a village of some 300 inhabitants on the edge of Dartmoor, about five miles from the thriving market town of Tavistock. Its greatest claim to fame is perhaps the church of St Michael de Rupe (St Michael of the Rock) which, at 1,100 ft above sea level, stands sentinel over the countryside for miles around. Legend has it that during a violent storm at sea a wealthy merchant vowed that if he survived he would build a church on the first land he saw, which happened to be Brentor. Another legend claims that while the church was being built at the foot of the hill, each night the stones which had been laid were moved by the Devil to the top of the hill – perhaps in the hope that the hard climb would deter the worshippers. The Devil almost had his way – some 700 years later a chapel of ease was built in the village itself!

Having so far escaped the clutches of the developer, Brentor remains a very 'rural' village (it has no street lights or pavements) and this is one of its greatest charms. There is still a very strong farming tradition in Brentor, one farm having been in the same family for over 400 years. Nowadays, of course, a number of the villagers commute to Tavistock, Plymouth and farther afield where they are employed in many different professions.

At one time Brentor had a school, mainline railway station, post office, bakery, butcher's and grocer's shops, now all, alas, defunct. The one remaining business in the village centre is the smithy, producing wrought iron and other metal work as well as undertaking more mundane repair jobs.

All this may give the impression of a village in decline but this is far from the case. There is a tremendous community spirit in Brentor, which has not one hall, but three; the village hall, church hall and Methodist hall. In the 1970s, when the last remaining village shop closed, a community centre was formed and a weekly 'shop' held in the church hall. An army of volunteers would regularly visit the local cash-and-carry to stock the shop and on several occasions the shop was featured on local radio and TV news. Although the 'shop' in its original form has now ceased, there is still a fortnightly coffee morning with local produce on sale and the opportunity for people to collect their books from the mobile library. A monthly newsletter, 'The Brentor News', is also still going strong.

On the outskirts of the village new enterprises have superseded the traditional village shops. There is a flourishing herb nursery, a water garden supplying exotic aquatic plants and a nursery producing bedding plants and shrubs. Within the village itself there are people making beautiful quilts and cushions, and ceramic model houses; there are photographers and leatherworkers.

Bridestowe 🌿

The peaceful unspoiled village of Bridestowe (pronounced 'Briddystow') lies at the junction of two streams, bypassed by the main road, on the western edge of Dartmoor, the only modern development consisting of a small number of country-style houses off the main thoroughfare. Descending into Bridestowe one is often greeted by the scent of wood-smoke from the stone and slate cottages. It is fortunate in still possessing its village school and busy post office/stores together with the 15th century parish church, Methodist chapel, village hall and two inns.

Once the home of tin and copper miners, quarrymen, farm, railway and peat workers as well as those who worked on the big estates, the village today has a well-balanced community. Although still largely an agricultural area there are now craftsmen, artists and professional people among its inhabitants. Until the Second World War people did not move away from the village but today the population sees frequent changes.

Burley Wood Camp, one of the strongest forts on the western moor, consists of a large castle mound, bailey and outworks, constructed in the 12th century, possibly by the Pomeroy family.

The present church, the third on the site, was built c1450 and dedicated to St Bridget by the tin miners, some of whom were Irish. The archway which frames the main entrance to the churchyard was removed from a former church which had become the poor house.

Charles I visited on 30th July 1644 and reputedly stayed at Great Bidlake, an Elizabethan house, said to be haunted by a previous lady of the manor. After the battle of Torrington, Squire Bidlake escaped, pursued by Roundheads and reached home just ahead of them. Changing into a cowman's smock he walked down the drive to meet them and when asked if he had seen the squire, told them he had taken a fresh horse and gone to France.

The old cider press at Bidlake, once used by all the local farmers, is still in working order.

The village has two inns, several centuries old, the White Hart and the Royal Oak, a coaching inn which has a 1714 sundial.

A third, the Fox and Hounds, two miles away on the Tavistock Road, is approached through a magnificent avenue of beech trees, nicknamed 'Bridestowe Cathedral'.

The disused Bridestowe railway station is nearby, now converted to a house. This was almost the highest point on the LSW railway. When warrening was a considerable industry on Dartmoor a statistician worked out that Bridestowe sent away annually more rabbits than passengers. Used by various Dartmoor mining industries and also the Rattlebrook Peatworks, which terminated in 1921, the station, an ordnance depot during the Second World War, was closed down in 1968.

Bridestowe was a very self-contained village during the early part of the century, having its own baker, Co-op store, butcher, village policeman, district nurse and post office, as well as a sawmill which generated its own electricity. Cattle fairs, the Fur and Feather show and the Carnival were highlights of the year.

Every seven years the Bridestowe and Sourton Commoners hold the Beating of the Bounds ceremony, a walk of some seven miles on Dartmoor. Local young people are taken to each boundary stone which is then beaten with a stick by the Commoners, thus ensuring that the tradition is passed on to the next generation.

Bridford 🌿

Bridford, a Teign valley village of the Middle Ages, has a population of some 400 residents within its boundary. The village is a small cluster of buildings clinging to a south-facing ledge in the foothills of Dartmoor, which rises from sea level to over 1,000 ft on a plateau to the west of the river Teign.

It is a working and living village now, as it was over 400 years ago. Not a place of particularly fine architecture, there are two or three worthy houses in the locality; Laployd Barton, Bridford Barton and the Old Rectory. Especially fine is the elaborately carved wooden screen to be found at the church of St Thomas a Becket. The church enjoys a lively congregation with its members taking care of its fabric with love and devotion.

During the Napoleonic Wars, families from Exeter, some nine miles eastward, sought to take refuge from the French militia within the village and the surrounding parishes. They believed that the 'remote' hilly settlement would prove to be out of reach of possible invaders.

This very remoteness and the narrow steep lanes add much to the charm of a place which offers the visitor a breathtaking panorama at every turn. From Heltor Rock, a mile to the west of the village, views of the vast Dartmoor wilderness can be seen, while on a clear day the reddened cliffs of east Devon can be made out to the south-east.

A gazeteer of Devon in 1850 by William White shows that Bridford had 560 'souls' and 4,090 acres of land. The difference in population then and now can be accounted for to some extent by the rise and fall in mining activity in the Teign valley and Bridford itself.

Early in the 19th century mining became a major productive source in the area. Lead, iron ore, zinc, manganese, barytes and silver – though not prolific – were all found and economically worked for at least 50 years. Bridford's barytes mining continued into the 20th century and there are still residents in the village who were once miners or associated with the mining company.

Most of today's inhabitants work in the surrounding towns and in Exeter, although there are still many small farmers in the area for the parish acreage is widely dispersed outside the village confines. If you need a builder, plumber, carpenter or jobbing gardener, these are all local men. The village post office and general food stores is thriving, partly due to the home cooked produce and locally baked bread and cakes.

Bridford is particularly fortunate to have a number of local organisations to cater for all tastes. In July each year Bridford holds its village fete, usually in the grounds of the Old Rectory by courtesy of the owners.

Brixham 🏵

Well, Brixham began as a village, a fishing village. Over the years it has grown somewhat, but still retains its village character.

The original fishing boats were brown-sailed. It must have been a wonderful sight to see them heading out to sea, the wind billowing in their sails. They had their superstitions and were quite serious about them. If they saw rabbits gambolling about on Berry Head, back they would come: most unlucky! It was the same if they saw the local vicar, back into port they would come.

The harbour area was very rough, with ten pubs around it; no 'nice' girl ever ventured there. The local fishwives were a tough breed and would literally haul their husbands out of the pubs. The trawler boys would get into mischief when the boats could not put to sea in bad weather, and threw Brixham's first policeman into the harbour. There was, of course, no refrigeration, so the fishwives took the fish out in carts around the countryside to sell. Some of the fish was dried, strung up on wire in lines on the hill above the village. An old name for the fish drying grounds was 'Rea'. Reabarn Road and Great Rea Road exist today as busy roads.

Brixham was at one time two villages – Higher Brixham, known as Cowtown, and Lower Brixham as Fish Town. They were rivals, and not at all friendly with each other. There was many a fight between them on a Saturday afternoon.

Brixham has a ghost – a monk who is said to walk through the Black House in Higher Brixham. Several people admit to having seen him.

Francis Brett Young, who wrote *The Deep Sea* and many other books, lived in the village in the early 1900s. He was a local doctor at that time. Francis Henry Lite, who wrote *Abide With Me*, was at one time vicar of Brixham.

Until a few years ago there was a busy shipyard, both boat building and repairs. Today Brixham still has a fishing fleet and the fishing industry is a large part of its life. The Torbay lifeboat is based here and covers a wide area, the crew being very dedicated and answering calls in all winds and weathers.

Buckfastleigh

Buckfastleigh is a small rural community of hills and narrow streets set between the river Dart and its feeder streams, the Mardle, Holy Brook and the Dean Burn flowing from nearby Dartmoor.

Small cottages and terraced mill houses with pretty, hidden, flower-decked courtyards line the busy streets. Some newer estates have also been developed. With Buckfast, part of its parish area, it has long been involved in the woollen trade. There are still many flocks of sheep on the hill farms, some having rights of pasturage on the moor itself, known as venville rights.

Once there were five woollen mills in the area giving work and housing to many. Now only a spinning mill at Buckfast remains, but in Buckfastleigh there is still a fellmongery and the grading and packing of wool is carried on. The soft water from the moor is essential to the dyeing industry. Some of the processing of the wool was carried out in the mill cottages in Chapel Street, where the long wooden lofts remain, indicating the drying of the wool on tenter hooks. These cottages are still lived in.

The area also had a history of quarrying, now only one working quarry remains. The limestone quarries had been in use for nearly 1,000 years, King Canute taking stone from them to build the first abbey at Buckfast. The caves associated with the quarries are of world-wide significance and the remains of many prehistoric animals have been found there. Local people have been instrumental in discovering and revealing the nature of the caves system, and have given their names to the caves, Joint Mitnor, Reed, Baker and others. Now a cave research centre has been established – The William Pengelly Trust.

There has always been a country atmosphere here. Though there is a Market Street, there is no market. Produce is still brought in from around and many people shop locally. Children from 'out over' come to the local schools.

The National Hunt race course was well known; established in 1884 and closed in 1960, it is now part of a farm. Race meetings were great festive days – horses coming by train to the local station were stabled behind the inns and in the meadows around the town. There is still a link with the racing scene as a local jockey, Jimmy Frost, won the Grand National in 1989.

Small industries and craft works have taken the place of the larger mills and quarries. The tourist trade is important to the economy of the area. Many visitors come to the Benedictine abbey at Buckfast, where Brother Adam works with his famous strain of bees.

For music there is the John Loosemoore Centre, and there are many concerts held at the nearby abbey.

The parish church of Holy Trinity stands on a hill above the town, a 13th century building with a 15th century nave. There are 195 steps to it, but there is also a road!

Buckland Brewer

Buckland Brewer is a village and parish situated in the beautiful country-side of North Devon, set on a hilltop.

Galsworthy Manor, which is said to be the original home of the family of John Galsworthy, the novelist, and Hela Manor were both mentioned in the Domesday Book. Between 1086 and 1312 the spelling of the village's name changed at least six times, from Bochelanda to Bruweres-bocland.

The ancient church of St Mary and St Benedict has some Norman work, but the tower had to be rebuilt in 1399 after it had been struck by lightning. Some restoration took place in 1879.

Buckland Brewer had a famous postman in the early 1800s. Edward Capern was born in 1819. He became a postman in Bideford, walking to Buckland Brewer every day, six miles each way for the princely sum of ten shillings and sixpence for 17 years. During his three hour rest in the village before returning to Bideford, he composed most of his poetry and ballads, of which three volumes have been published. He always carried a paper and pencil on his rounds and would stop to jot down ideas when they came to him. He retired to Wrafton, after being awarded a pension of £50 a year by Lord Palmerston, the Prime Minister of the day.

Budleigh Salterton

Budleigh Salterton is very well known now as one of the last of the unspoilt places in Devon.

The brook that runs along the shopping thoroughfare is very often full of lady's mantle and pretty water foliage. Running down from Squabmoor, a beautiful part adjoining Woodbury Common, the brook is known to have once contained trout. It has little footbridges over it for access to the cottage homes and for the friends who attend the Methodist church.

Clean streets with friendly little shops, pretty awnings and decorated shopfronts invite shoppers to indulge in purchasing an assortment of items from antiques and lace to Devonshire clotted cream and cider.

The Pebble Ridge beach has a backdrop of red cliffs at the west end and a point of cliffs hang over the mouth of the river Otter and Winkle Rocks, where children love to dip their fishing nets into the water pools left at low tide.

Sir J R Millais painted *The Boyhood of Raleigh* from the 'Octagon', a house overlooking the famous rock wall (now under the threat of demolition) where he portrayed two young boys holding a conversation with a fisherman. One boy in the painting is thought to be an antecedent of a local family, whose descendants are still resident in the area.

Adjacent to the 'Octagon' is Fairlynch Museum, a character building of unique design, with its thatched roof and 'lookout' tower. It is thought to have been of assistance to smugglers, who were able to off-load their 'bounty' by means of tunnels running from the water's edge and under the cottages near Fairlynch. Hurricane lamps would have been lit and hung in the 'lookout' tower of Fairlynch, giving the all clear.

The former owner of 'Watch Hill' was a famed architect who designed many houses in the area of great distinction and some of his drawings and designs are on display at Fairlynch Museum.

Budleigh Salterton is still fortunate to have its own cottage hospital. Generous donations, together with a lot of local charity work and functions, raise the necessary funds in order to maintain this service for the care of families and loved ones in their time of need.

Burrington

Burrington is a small community set between South Molton, Barnstaple and Torrington, on high ground with panoramic views of Exmoor, Dartmoor and the scenic Taw valley. In earlier times coaching routes favoured these high lands well above the valley mud and there is still the Barnstaple Inn (a pleasant village pub with skittle alley and good food) and on the other side of the road London House (nowadays the village store). The post office completes the local services.

Being somewhat isolated the village has retained, and is proud of, its strong sense of community, with several local farms run by the same families over many years. The parish hall, a product of this community spirit, is modern, spacious and well-run and used by all the local organisations, of which there are many! Prominent among the organisations is the men's club with its own skittle alley, darts, table tennis, pool and billiards room. The village school has about 38 pupils and has been fiercely defended by local people when cut-backs were mooted.

The church is well worth a visit; Arthur Mee's *Devon* recorded the 'magnificent screen, one of the finest examples Devonshire has of 15th century craftsmanship. Its cornice is like lace for delicacy; the vaulting of the canopy is exquisite in its intricate carving, and is painted in red and blue and gold. To match this work there is a noble roof over the aisle, with grand beams and 38 little angels.'

There is also a Methodist chapel (1829) and a Brethren chapel. In the Square stands the aged village oak.

The church is dedicated to the Trinity and, at the patronal festival, Burrington Fair is held. Nowadays this takes the form of a cattle sale in Pickard's (agricultural merchants) Yard, lunch and church fundraising. Other events including children's sports are held to celebrate Burrington's week.

Burrington is essentially a work-a-day place, strongly dependent on agriculture, and has retained a population of about 500 for the last 50 years. Though not beautiful, it is a place in which its residents take pride.

Calverleigh ༺༄

Anyone travelling along the B3221 from Tiverton to South Molton will see on their way farms on hillsides, clusters of cottages and houses in valleys, but no real villages. Like so many other parts of Devon these small communities are hamlets. In this most beautiful part of Mid Devon, one such hamlet is Calverleigh, just three miles from Tiverton.

Calodelia, as Calverleigh was called in the Domesday Book, still has its luxuriant woods, arable and pasture lands as described in 1086. In about 1166 the manor and the parish became the property of Sir Patrick Calewood. The old manor house was built at this time and soon after, the manorial chapel was built alongside the manor, which later became the church of St Mary. The manor house was probably built on or near to an old Saxon house.

In 1929 Calverleigh Court and its estates were dispersed to pay death duties. Properties, apart from the Court, that were sold included Calverleigh Mill by the river Swine, which divides Calverleigh from Lurley, and the New Inn, which had originally been a coaching inn and was now a farm. Both are believed to be about 500 years old. Blue-Bottle Cottage, once a cider house, became the tailor's house, and then the post office. The school which was built around 1879, was also sold.

The church of St Mary, in a lovely and sequestered spot, is still in use today. The south aisle was added to the original nave by the Southcotts and houses a monument to three generations of that family. Obviously the church has been lovingly restored over the years, but because of this, much has been lost. For example, the clock on the tower has disappeared and so too has the gallery which was across the western end of the nave, which housed the choristers.

There were three bells in the tower until 1897, one dated 1672, one made in 1790 and one older. Three new bells were added in 1897, making a total of six today. In 1938 the vicar, Rev Fitzwilliam Carter, formed a band of schoolgirl bellringers, the first in England and possibly the world. They were pupils of Ingleside school, housed at Calverleigh Court.

In the churchyard are the tombs of all the Chichester-Nagle family who lived at Calverleigh Court from the 18th century, although the majority of them followed the Catholic faith. Over many years people have been so impressed by the peaceful seclusion of the churchyard that they have expressed a wish to be buried there, hence there are many tombstones with names not connected with the local community. Several of these are now 'listed buildings', not because of the tombstones themselves but the engraving on them. There is, for instance, the tombstone of the tramp who died on his way through Calverleigh, probably tramping his way from the workhouse in Tiverton to the workhouse in South Molton.

'A wayfaring man, name unknown lies here – who died March 6th 1880. I was a stranger and ye took me in ...'

At the bottom of the churchyard is a pond, which has been restored. At one time there were four ponds in this vicinity but all had become overgrown – given time perhaps the other three will be cleared again!

Calverleigh is surrounded by the hamlets of Lurley (Lower Lea), Palmershayes and Frogwell. When in the 1940s it was decided to build a village hall in Calverleigh on the site of the stables of the original manor, residents in the surrounding hamlets were invited to use the hall as their own.

Chagford 🎐

Chagford, originally meaning 'gorse-ford', is perched above the river Teign and boasts some spectacular walks along it, notably from Dogmarsh Bridge past Castle Drogo to Fingle Bridge. Above it are the twin hills of Nattadon and Meldon, both giving wonderful views over Dartmoor and as far north as Exmoor.

This large village was one of the four ancient stannary towns for the assaying of tin, and was prosperous throughout the Middle Ages; many of the old mines can still be seen. Later Chagford thrived as a market town. Today it is a tourist centre for Dartmoor and a farming community, and a favourite place for retirement, with a flourishing Adult Community College branch at the excellent Church of England primary school.

Chagford has a claim to the Lorna Doone legend, though it is more popularly ascribed to the parish of Oare in Somerset. In the chancel of the church is an inscription to Mary Whiddon, shot by a jealous former lover as she left the church after her wedding in 1641:

> 'Reader wouldst know who here is laid,
> Behold a matron yet a maid.
> A modest look, a pious heart,
> A Mary for the better part.
> But dry thine eyes, why wilt thou weep –
> Such maidens do not die but sleep.'

Tradition has it that any girl being married from Whiddon House (now the Three Crowns) will meet the ghost of Mary Whiddon.

Chagford also claims to have been the first place west of London to make use of electricity for street lighting, using water power from the mills at Yeo Farm and Holy Street. In 1891 an electricity company was formed.

The Market House, known affectionately as 'the Pepper-Pot', is perhaps the most distinctive building in Chagford, but the church with its lovely carvings should not be missed. Nor should the Three Crowns, where it is said that the poet Sidney Godolphin was shot during the Civil War, and the ancient hall house next to it – nor the Bishop's House in Lower Street with its medieval porch! New Street has a beautiful curve of granite cottages and at the far end on the right can be found what must be the tiniest public garden in England. It was formerly a pound, and has superb views of the moors, and the sunsets, over Kestor.

Many events are staged throughout the year. The Two Hills Race takes place in the spring, (now a national occasion), and Chagford Show in August. The pony fair comes in October, and the opening meet of the Mid-Devon fox-hounds in November – they also meet in the Square on Boxing Day, and hold a cross-country race at the end of the season. There is a colourful Flea Market held in the Jubilee Hall each Friday.

Charleton 🦢

According to old editions of Kelly's Trade Directory: 'Charleton is a parish and straggling village divided into two parts, East and West Charleton'. The years may have added new housing estates and various barn conversions, all of varying degrees of architectural merit, but Charleton is still a straggling village with two distinct halves about a quarter of a mile apart on the Kingsbridge to Dartmouth road.

The name, Charleton, characterises this village's beginnings as a settlement of 'churls' or countrymen in contrast to today's populace, many of whom are retired town-dwellers. Time brings changes, however, and in recent years there has been an influx of younger people, working in Kingsbridge or further afield. Although the 1981 census put the population at 450, it seems likely that numbers will rise to challenge the 1875 total of 540 – although today's villagers occupy a good deal more than the 125 houses recorded then.

Charleton has kept its link with agriculture and still has three farms (one of which, Croft Farm, was the scene of the horrific and still unsolved Maye Murders of 1936), a pick-your-own establishment and a nursery. Fewer people work on the farms these days and Charletonians have branched out into other occupations. At least four men run successful decorating businesses, East Charleton has its own thatcher and a garage which re-opened recently after several years' closure. West Charleton has a thriving post office and stores which is very much the focal point of the village. 'Anna at the shop' is the repository of all sorts of messages, requests and general news.

Charleton prides itself on being a friendly village with plenty of scope for newcomers to establish themselves and meet the locals. The village hall is well-run and houses various organisations. The local pub, the Ashburton Arms, looks a little modern, but it is an old-established inn, and there is nothing new-fangled about the warm old-fashioned welcome you meet inside.

Charleton church seems to contain few of the features which send architectural historians into transports. Indeed, many of its medieval structures fell prey to a fit of Victorian improvement in 1850. Be that as it may, St Mary's has stood on its present site, watching over the village, since the 13th century. There is a busy Sunday school, a brave band of novice bell-ringers (including half the older children in the village) and a dedicated group of regular churchgoers.

As the church commands the high ground, so Charleton Marsh, partly natural phenomenon, partly the result of forced prisoner of war labour during the Napoleonic Wars, dominates the low ground. Almost every house in West Charleton has a view of the marsh and the estuary beyond and most householders make full use of this amenity.

Cheriton Bishop 🌿

The village of Cheriton Bishop stands 650 ft above sea level some ten miles west of Exeter on the Okehampton road, amid outstandingly beautiful Devon countryside at the very edge of Dartmoor. In fact part of the village is actually in the Dartmoor National Park.

One hundred years ago things were very different in Cheriton Bishop. The only transport to Exeter was by horse-drawn carriage on Tuesdays and Fridays and a 6d toll was paid to the tollhouse keeper at Cheriton Cross. Many villagers preferred to walk the ten miles each way as it was quicker. The smithy at Cheriton Cross was kept very busy, this being a farming community. The roads were very poor. The stones for the main road were brought from the fields and quarries and cut up by old men getting parish relief at 2s 6d per week. The carts cut deep troughs in the mud in winter and in summer the dust was thick.

Every year itinerants would come to the village seeking casual work, summer hay-making and cutting corn and in winter ditching, casting hedges and binding faggots of wood. These people slept rough and on wet days would gather in the smithy to take advantage of the warmth, exchange news and tell a few yarns.

Also at Cheriton Cross there was a washerwoman, a dressmaker (who always worked in her open doorway) and a cobbler. Cheriton Cross was very picturesque with three leafy lanes meeting in a green bower, through which the turnpike road ran. An old inn stood further back and by its side a one-roomed thatched cottage under the tall oak. This was at the corner of the lane leading down to the pretty little parish church of St Mary, which itself is of great historical interest.

The earliest structure is the Norman font carved in the form of a corn sheaf (circa 1075). The chancel dates from the 13th century, the nave and tower are 15th century.

A Church school was established in the village in 1881, supported by subscription and fees. It was originally built where the Spalding Hall now stands. The site of the present school was once the poor house, one room of which was used as an infants classroom. The Methodist chapel stands at Cheriton Cross, there having been more than a century of Methodist worship in the village.

Today Cheriton Bishop retains a character and charm of its own, a friendly village with a great community spirit and a warm welcome for all. The smithy has gone but there are now excellent roads and good public transport. There are two inns, a restaurant, post office, garage and shop. The village school is thriving with an increasing number of pupils.

Cheriton Fitzpaine

Cheriton Fitzpaine is in Mid Devon among the rolling hills and good red earth (nine miles from Exeter and from Tiverton). It was and still is very agricultural with many farms all round, four of which were named in the Domesday Book.

The meaning of Cheriton is 'church town' or 'settlement by the church'. Fitzpaine was added in about 1300 when the family of that name held the manor. The lovely parish church of St Matthew goes back to the 14th century.

At one time there were seven farms adjoining the village, some of which sold milk at the door – but that is all gone! Years ago at the north side of the parish there was a tannery and a butter factory. In the village there were two tailors, two butchers, and two bakers who made their own bread and cakes. One could see the dough machine at work in Locks Lane.

The saddler's shop was a hive of industry and chatter! One could buy so much in that shop, boots, shoes, nails, screws of every description, farm and gardening tools etc. Shoes were mended there and hair was cut! In spite of the changes villagers are grateful to still have a good village store and a post office with its own shop.

The authoress Jean Rhys spent the last years of her life in a little bungalow here and her ashes are buried in the churchyard where her name is recorded. Her best known book, *The Wide Sargasso Sea*, was completed and published while she was here with the help of the then rector, the Rev A. Woodard.

In the time of the Wars of the Roses Cheriton became known throughout the country because of the brutal murder of Nicholas Radford of Upcott Barton, a distinguished lawyer and adherent of the great family of the Bonvilles. Upcott Barton still stands, a fine old house, about a mile out of the village and the lane still leads down to the churchyard where his body was thrown into a grave.

Cheriton Fitzpaine had electric light before there was any in Crediton. It was started in a shed belonging to a Mr George Way, a wheelwright and undertaker, and was financed by local people. The blacksmiths forge was a feature of the village and did not close until 1984 after many years of shoeing horses and mending farm machinery.

The village school is still in good use and goes back to 1876. At one time the present school was an unregulated poor house, then a workhouse. It is a long thatched building – one of the very few thatched schools in the country, with what is probably the longest roof.

The almshouses near the school bear the date 1717 and the name of Andrew Scut. Originally there were two cottages but now they have been made into one dwelling, though still administered by a board of trustees. At the other end of the village were five little almshouses put up in 1594 in thanksgiving for the defeat of the Armada. They have now been modernised inside and converted into three houses, privately owned, but the outside walls still stand to remind us of the history of this old village and the part it has played in the life of England.

The Ring o' Bells public house, Cheriton Fitzpaine

Chillaton 🦐

Chillaton is a small village – population 296 – which lies about seven miles north-west of Tavistock. At one time it was a collection of small grey-stone cottages lying in the valley on the banks of a small stream, itself a tributary of the river Lyd. The centre point was the square, from which roads ran to Lifton, Lewdown and Tavistock. Today these cottages have been joined by a number of modern houses.

Several of the buildings are very old indeed, at least in part. Park and Forda in the centre of the village and Billacombe on the road to Lifton can boast a mention in the Domesday Book.

About a mile from the village centre is Sydenham House, standing on the banks of the river Lyd. It was built in 1603 by Sir Thomas Wise and remained in the family until 1937 when the estate was sold. It then had a chequered career, even at one time becoming a boarding school for girls, but has now reverted to being a family home. It is a most romantic house and it is said to have at least one secret passage leading down to the banks of the river.

Mention must be made of the small hamlet of Quither, closely associated with Chillaton. The name means 'rubbish heap' and it too was recorded in the Domesday Book. Part of East Quither Farm is said to have been the retreat for the monks of Tavistock Abbey.

At one time the people who lived in Chillaton were mostly associated with the land or the mining of manganese, which was carried out on Hogs Tor. The spoil heaps can still be seen in the valley bottom as grassy hummocks. Later quarrying for stone was started to the east of the village.

Naturally such a thriving, busy community had a variety of associated occupations. There was a blacksmith's shop, a carpenter's shop, and a butcher's, a mill at Splatt, a general stores, and at one time Park was a tannery. Later there was a separate post office, a garage selling petrol and two public houses.

Since the Second World War however the picture has changed and many people from the village now work in Tavistock and Plymouth. There is a large proportion of retired people. Some still work on the land and some at the local milk factory and the stone quarry is larger than ever although mechanised and not employing any labour, but the result is that nowadays there is only one public house, a general shop/post office and a thriving motor repair business. The village school too is shut and the children go by bus to Milton Abbot or Tavistock.

Chillaton does not have a church within the village and for many years lay within the parish of Milton Abbot, a village three and a half miles away. Of later years however it has been part of the parish of Marystowe and the church of St Mary the Virgin stands on a small hill overlooking the village.

Chittlehampton 🦋

Chittlehampton is a delightful village, lying to the south of Exmoor. It is unusual in having its own saint called Urith. On 8th July each year a procession walks from the lychgate of the towered church at the top of the square, to the site of her martyrdom. She was killed with scythes, and a spring of water is said to have gushed from the ground where she fell, and flowers to have burst into bloom. The well is blessed, and the procession returns to the church where her special hymn is sung and children lay posies of flowers on her tomb. The legend dates from about the 8th century.

This is a thriving village of all age groups, with pub, school, church, post office, and a village shop that sells all you might need in a hurry. There are two thatchers to keep the roofs sound on the many pretty cottages, builders and electricians and plumbers to take care of every emergency. There is a pottery and the post office sells many crafts, from woodwork to delicious Swiss chocolates made locally. At one time there were seven beerhouses in the village, but these are now only remembered in house names, such as The Barley Mow and Rolle Arms. Other house names recall old businesses, The Bakehouse and The Old Brewery.

Old stories of the village tell of a hoard of silver, meant to have been buried in the Wilderness at Hudscott, a large local house, by the owner and his butler, because of a family feud. It has never been found. And of the days of the horse-drawn fire engine, which because the horse was out on his bakery rounds when a thatch fire broke out, had to be pulled to the fire by the firemen. Another legend concerns a black dog who haunts a crossroads near the village, where his master died. If you see him, beware of standing in his path. The owner was a member of the Rolle family who enjoyed dressing in rough clothes and working with his men.

Chittlehampton lies between South Molton and Barnstaple, both busy market towns and buses go in twice a week, so people without cars do not feel cut off. In the summer, numbers of visitors come to stay and enjoy this unspoilt village.

Christow

Christow means 'a place dedicated to Christ', and lies on the banks of the river Teign, but people were living here long before the Christian message came to England. Among the ancient hut circles just above the village, some chisel-edged prehistoric implements were found, dating back to the Bronze Age.

The Benedictine abbey of Bec, in Normandy, became the main landlord for this area after the Norman Conquest. A church was built and a few isolated farmhouses began to appear. During the time of the Crusades, an inn was established and named The Artichoke. The village began to grow despite the poor soil and the isolation. But Christow was not allowed to be isolated from the outside world for much longer. Disaster struck in the form of the bubonic plague. In 1591 there were so many deaths in the parish, that the recording of them was stopped for six months.

Then silver, lead and zinc were discovered in the area. Miners and their families moved in, many from Cornwall, to work in the mines. The Wheal Frankmill mine employed 150 men, and the Wheal Exmouth, 30 men, twelve women and ten boys. Christow had never seen anything like it before! Two extra pubs were opened, and equally swiftly, two chapels as well. The gaps between the farmhouses were closed one by one, as more cottages were built to accommodate the extra workers.

Although for many years the cattle market had been held five times a year at the Teign House Inn, which had a special all day licence, the railway brought the prospect of better prices at Newton market, provided that you loaded your own cattle onto the train at the station, and drove them yourself through the streets of Newton, at the other end! Then disaster struck, the rich seams of mineral wealth petered out, and one by one the mines closed, leaving the ruined chimneys as the only proof that they had once existed, and played such an important part in the life of the village. However, the railway remained, and Scattor Rock Quarry was opened, just up the hill (never mind that it was the steepest hill in the area). There was still work to be had, and an overhead railway was built to take the rock down to the station in the valley. Also, it was decided to build a series of reservoirs in the hills to serve the expanding area of Torbay, so clay from the village was taken, by horse and cart at 18d a load, to line the reservoirs.

By the time Arthur Marshall, the well known author and broadcaster moved into the village, and began writing about life at 'Myrtle Bank', the railway had closed, the lanes were being widened, a bus service introduced, a sewerage system built to accommodate 1,000 houses, lorries were coming for the sheep and cattle, a village hall had been constructed, and the motor car had opened up village life.

Christow became, once again, an attractive village in which to live. More new houses were built for those new villagers, and although Christow is nowhere near self-sufficient, some of the old skills are making their reappearance; the butcher, the baker, the electrician, the plumber, the painter and decorator and builder, and the farmers, who have always been there.

Chulmleigh ✣

Chulmleigh stands in a prominent position overlooking the tranquil Little Dart valley, with beautiful views of distant Dartmoor. Its origins date back to Saxon times.

A charter was granted to John de Courtney in the year 1253 by Henry III for two annual fairs and a weekly market. One, the Lammas Fair, was to be held at the time of the Church patronal festival. This is the famous Chulmleigh Old Fair which survives to the present day and is celebrated at the end of July.

In 1803 and again in 1878 many thatched houses were destroyed by fire, but there are still traditional Devon cob/thatched cottages to be seen, and other one-time merchant's houses, some dating back to Tudor times. Chulmleigh has a Town Hall, although it appears never to have had a mayor. As recently as the beginning of this century, the Court Leet and Court Baron were held in the Town Hall, the bounds were beaten and the portreeve, bailiff, ale testers, bread weighers, town crier and scavenger were appointed.

Chulmleigh cannot boast of any famous 'sons', although the town has produced many worthy characters. One such was John Flower, a famous wrestler of his day who died in 1830 at the age of 46. He had been a wrestler since the age of 16. A 'man of Herculean strength, but of an extremely mild and peaceable demeanour', he was known for his honesty, never taking a bribe, which was a rare attribute in those days.

Charity Joint, still remembered by the older residents of Chulmleigh, was a carrier who lived in East Street. A carrier was one of the most important people in a rural area, picking up goods from the larger towns and taking market produce and passengers to other venues. Charity was a large, tough woman who collected coal, beer and other commodities from Eggesford station. She would load the barrels onto the cart herself, was reputed to be as strong as any man and could keep up with them in the drinking of beer. Such a formidable sight was Charity that she would certainly deter any would-be thieves. She was given the task each week to take the town's police sergeant and constable to South Molton to collect their wages.

Chulmleigh was a prosperous place up to the late 19th century, with a woollen industry and cattle markets and many employed in agriculture. As the woollen trade died away and farms became mechanised many were put out of work. Women supplemented their husbands' income by making border lace at home. This was collected each week and paid for by the yard. However, in the early 1800s a new turnpike road, and a few years later, a new railway, both from Exeter to Barnstaple were built. This provided work for local men. Rival gangs patronised rival pubs (Chulmleigh boasted of 14 at one time) and much blood was spilt! Today, employment is found in Barnstaple, Exeter or South Molton, while the local businesses, shops and schools provide some work. The local crafts of saddle-making, blacksmithing, tailoring and shoe-making have gone, but there are two young thatchers who live in the town.

Churchstow ✍

Churchstow is a rural community two miles north-west of Kingsbridge, with a population of approximately 350.

The church of St Mary is a prominent landmark on land rising from 17 ft to 450 ft above sea level, between the Avon valley and the sea inlet from Salcombe to Kingsbridge. It is situated on the main A379 Kingsbridge to Plymouth road. St Mary's is the mother church of Kingsbridge, having existed in the 11th century.

On 17th December 1703, a storm occurred in the parish – the church and chancel were badly damaged as were the adjoining cottages. In February 1988 the church tower was struck by a thunderbolt, but the lightning conductor saved the building!

The Church House Inn nearby is a 16th century building in green slate. Today it has been extended, taking in several cottages, to give a modern interior.

The village has no school or vicarage, but at one time the Union workhouse stood at the border of the parish nearest to Kingsbridge. A wooden church hall forms the meeting place for the village, built by the incumbent prior to 1928.

The number of residences remained the same until after the Second World War, since when approximately 90 houses have been built on the south side.

Churchstow has always been entirely an agricultural community, with a blacksmith's and a small store only. Today farming is still an important industry, but many residents are of retirement age and the younger generation commute to nearby towns for employment.

Lower Leigh Austin Priory, which has been in existence since the reign of Henry II, has had a chequered history since the Dissolution of the Monasteries. It is being restored by English Heritage.

Coombe Royal, mentioned in the Domesday Book and rebuilt in Tudor times, is now a senior citizen's residential home. Its gardens in this warm and fertile valley are linked with those of Lower Coombe Royal and were laid out by John Luscombe by 1871. He was an enthusiast who corresponded with Kew and raised hybrid rhododendrons.

The Whitehall estate, until its sale in 1905, consisted of a family residence, Home Farm and three cottages together with 99 acres. Since that date it has been converted into several apartments, providing accommodation for retired people.

Clawton 🦢

Clawton is a parish and small village three miles south of the market town of Holsworthy in North Devon. The name is derived from the river Claw, a tributary of the Tamar, which flows through the village and is crossed by two small bridges of one arch only.

The parish church of St Leonard dates back to the Norman period, as is evidenced by its large stone font with cable decoration and carved stone heads.

There are Methodist chapels at Clawton Bridge and on the western side of the parish, as well as a thriving primary school established in 1876 which took the place of the penny school held in a cottage in the village.

The population of the village in 1086 consisted of 28 villagers, six smallholders with two ploughs and two pigmen. Lands in the possession of these people were Kempthorne, Fernhill, Tinacre, Kennicot, Leworthy and Eastdown. These are still working farms to this day.

Parts of the parish are more than 500 ft above sea level, affording outstanding views over attractive farmland as far as Bodmin Moor to the south-west and south-east to Dartmoor. Present-day farming is mostly dairy, with some beef cattle and sheep.

Clawton is fortunate to have an award-winning hotel within the parish, the Court Barn Country House Hotel which is situated near the church and the parish hall. It was previously a landed gentleman's residence.

Clayhanger

Clayhanger is a small village at the north-easterly tip of Devon. From miles away you can see the 14th century tower of its ancient church, which with the 16th century manor house of Nutcombe and the beautiful unspoilt scenery of its secluded valley, 800 ft above sea-level, are its most striking features.

Inside the church of St Peter are the very striking carved pew-ends dating from the 16th century, they include a man with a trident, and a harpy. Behind the altar is part of the ancient rood screen, and there is also an old oak alms box and a Norman font of Ham stone to interest the visitors.

The manor house of Nutcombe was owned by Thomas de Notcombe in 1620 and then by Richard Notcombe, sheriff of Devon from 1715–16. The memorials of the Nutcombes, and several other well-known families, form part of the aisle of the church, and on Richard's stone is inscribed, 'Who in an age both in principles and practice corrupt, kept his faith and his morals untainted'. Obviously someone much to be admired. In the large hall at Nutcombe Manor can be seen an elaborate plaster mantlepiece, copied by Elizabethan craftsmen from German and Flemish patterns.

Further down the valley can be seen an old water-mill, listed in the Domesday Book as Donicestone (1086) and later known as Doddiscombe or Dencombe. It is now a flower nursery.

There was a village school here from 1866 to the mid 1940s, and at one time it had 30 pupils. Farmer's children would walk across the fields from the age of five to 13, after getting up at five o'clock, milking a cow or two, feeding the poultry, bringing in the wood etc.

Up to 50 years ago the main occupations were farmers and farm labourers, with a scattering of fish-hawkers, carpenters, smiths and millers. There were at least two shops and two public houses. Now there are still a few farms, but most people work outside the village and several people have found Clayhanger the ideal spot for retirement.

A chapel for Bible Christians was started in 1892, but closed in the 1960s and is now a private house. Only two new houses have been built in the past 50 years, and Clayhanger remains relatively unspoilt.

Clayhidon

High on the Blackdown Hills, bounded on two sides by the Somerset border, Clayhidon is not a village but a collection of small hamlets and scattered farmsteads, a predominantly agricultural parish now, as it has always been.

The church of St Andrew has stood sentinel over the parish for more than 700 years. Built of local stone it gives an impression of the strength of the community and their worship throughout this time. A stone figure, clothed in a monk's habit, thought to be of Ralph de Hidon, the first priest whose name appears in the records in 1274, lies in a recessed tomb in the wall of the south aisle.

In the early 1860s George Brealey came to Clayhidon and founded the Blackdown Mission, establishing chapels in the surrounding area for the Brethren to meet. The original chapel in Rosemary Lane is still used regularly today.

'Applehayes', Clayhidon

Once the parish had five public houses, but now the number has shrunk to two. One, the Half Moon, in the shadow of the church, is thought to be unique in having a public right of way through the middle of it. Now on Rogation Day the church congregation make their way through the entry, thus ensuring its continued existence.

Applehayes, a lovely old farmhouse, retaining many delightful period features, was, during the early part of the 20th century, the home of Harold B. Harrison, a retired rancher from the Argentine. His passionate interest was art, studying at the Slade School. He had many friends amongst the Camden Town painters including Robert Bevan, Charles Ginner and Frederick Spencer Gore. They were invited to spend their summers here with him and now examples of their work, showing our landscapes, are exhibited in many art galleries in this country and overseas, including Plymouth and Exeter.

Details of a mill are given in the Domesday survey for the manor of Hidona, one of the earliest mills in this part of the county. Today there is still a Hidon Mill, probably very near the original spot. The house is a lovely example of a thatched cottage and buried within its walls have been found the original cruck frames, making it one of the oldest houses in the parish. Buried beneath the floor in the doorway was a collection of bones, a charm against evil spirits.

Many tales are told of the lawlessness of the people of the hills, cases of sheep stealing and counterfeiting, crimes which a scrutiny of the gaol records have proved to be true. However, it must be remembered that many families found it hard to survive the agricultural depression, particularly after the decline of the woollen industry, for many were spinners and weavers, as well as being small husbandmen or farm labourers, and like many other places the younger members of the parish drifted away to the nearby towns to find employment.

Now with the coming of modern transport and the motorway nearby, people can commute to the towns of Wellington and Taunton to work, and the lawlessness has become a spirit of independence in a small close-knit caring community.

Clearbrook

Clearbrook is a small hamlet situated on the edge of Dartmoor, about half way between Meavy and Yelverton. Its name is taken from the clear brook, which runs the whole way through the bottom of the long gardens at the back of the row of cottages, and is made up from drainage from the moor and from a myriad of springs. There is a population of approximately 160.

Strangers coming to the area must wonder why this little row of houses came into being, virtually in the middle of nowhere. The cottages were built and owned by tin miners, the first ones built in the 1880s.

In the 1890s a block of 'town' houses was built on vacant land at the lower end of the row, and one of them housed a post office and general store. At the rear of the building a bakery was built, which served all the surrounding district with bread, flour, and the ever popular saffron cake. The deliveries were made by a fleet of horses and carts, but this came to an end in 1916.

In the 1770s the Yeoland Console Mine was already in existence, and during its working life was purported to be the most productive mine in the area. It was the first to use a water turbine, the water for this being supplied from the Drake's leat situated on the hill above the mine, and drained into the river Meavy. The leat, which was constructed of granite and built by Sir Francis Drake in 1591 to take water from the Burrator reservoir to Plymouth, is still in excellent condition in this area, but is now only used for drainage.

The river Meavy runs through the hamlet and divides the two parishes of Meavy and Yelverton. On the Meavy side of the river are two 16th century miner's cottages, which are under a preservation order.

The Skylark Inn was just a small farmhouse in 1790, but was made into an alehouse for the miners' pleasure and recreation.

In 1901, Sir Francis James Elliott Drake gave a piece of land on which to build a reading room for recreation during the week, and a church on Sundays. It is now the Clearbrook community centre. A curate from Buckland Monachorum, in whose parish Clearbrook stood, used to come and take the services in the early days, but after Yelverton church was built in 1911, the vicar, or a reader would come from there. Church services are no longer held.

Clearbrook has a post office, but no shops of any description, and has a very mixed population. Being only 20 minutes from the centre of Plymouth, it is a very convenient residential area. There are three buses a week, which go directly to Plymouth.

Clovelly 🌿

This unique village is recognised world-wide from pictures of its famous cobbled street that descends over 400 ft in less than half a mile, with assorted cottages clinging to the cliffside colourful with shrubs and flowers.

Visitors to the village constantly wonder how those who live here manage to do so when no vehicles are allowed into the village. The answer is 'by hard work' – all goods, including furniture, are either carried in or tied to a wooden sledge and dragged down the cobbles, the empty sledges then having to be carried back up the street for the next trip. Local men have to be recruited to supplement ambulance crews to carry up a loaded stretcher – by the time they reach the ambulance they all need treatment! Fire crews practise in case there is a fire – minor fires have to be treated as serious because the old buildings include a lot of cob which burns easily.

Clovelly being a privately-owned village, all the cottages are let on a permanent basis. The population at present is around 175 with quite a large proportion of young families helping to keep the village school open. The children climb everyday up the cobbled street and up 'Wrinkle-berry Lane' (another steep climb) to the Victorian school building in Higher Clovelly – here they have magnificent views of Bideford Bay and the Atlantic Ocean, as long as the wind doesn't blow them over! Meanwhile their parents are at work, many serving the tourists in the shops, hotels or the new Visitors' Centre. There are a handful of fishermen left, lobsters, crabs, plaice and herring are still caught and sold locally or sent to market.

There is no accurate record of when Clovelly came into being but it is listed in the Domesday Book as Cloueleia. In the 13th century records show there was a settlement in the cliffside (clof – Old English for ravine) and people lived by fishing, especially herring. The manor was acquired by the Cary family in 1370 and was in their ownership until passing to the present family in 1738. In the 19th century Clovelly was a thriving port, with its own small yard building boats suited to local conditions – a 'picarooner' can be seen at Exeter Maritime Museum. Clovelly men lived from the sea, not only inshore and deep sea fishing but piloting, sup-plying ships lying in the 'roads', and servicing the boats that brought in limestone, coal and building stone. At the end of the 19th century 34 local men held Master's certificates. There was a lifeboat based in Clovelly from 1870 until August 1988 and the crews performed many rescues in the treacherous waters of the Atlantic. With such a strong seafaring tradition there must have been involvement in smuggling but few incidents are recorded. However, the practice of wrecking was widespread.

The most influential owner of Clovelly in recent years was Christine Hamlyn, a small formidable lady who controlled (and patrolled) the village for 52 years until she died in 1934. She cared greatly for her tenants and continued her parents' work of restoration of many cottages. Her initials and a date are carved in the plaster of these cottages, confusing visitors as to the age of the buildings – most have origins in the 1500s when cob was widely used. In 1929 she ensured the continuation of Clovelly as a living village by forming Clovelly Estate Company.

The most famous residents – the donkeys – are still kept here as a tribute to their deep involvement in the commercial success of the village. Originally used to carry fish from the harbour to the carriers' carts at the top of the village, they progressed to transporting lime, coal, mail, refuse, beer, milk and with the oncoming of the tourists, both luggage and people. They are now protected and today human donkeys do the work.

Clyst Honiton ✺

Clyst Honiton, originally Clist Honiton, referred to by some of the older inhabitants as Honiton Clyst, was once a small quiet backwater. With the advent of the Exeter airport, it is now an extremely busy village carrying the bulk of traffic to the airport and adjacent Business Park.

One special custom is the ringing annually on 26th November of a half-muffled knell on the eight bells of St Michael and All Angels. Edward Trapnell, who died on that date in 1716, left a sum of money for this purpose, which now amounts to 50p a year between the ringers. Connected with this is a small legacy to buy coal for the poor. This knell has been rung annually ever since that date with the exception of the war years when there was a ban on the ringing of church bells.

Once there were many traders in the village including two bakers, a blacksmith, two cobblers and a firm of thatchers. There is now one thatcher, a post office stores and two inns.

The parish church of St Michael dates from the 12th century and has a Norman font, though it was substantially rebuilt in the 19th century.

Clyst St Mary 🦢

The oldest possession of the village is its name, for Clyst is a Celtic word meaning 'the clear stream'. Roman coins were dug up in a garden at Milldown a few years ago. The bridge is thought to be the oldest surviving in Devon, first mentioned in 1238.

The existing Winslade manor house was built c1785 by Edward Cotsford (d1810) who had made his fortune in the East Indies. The house replaced one erected only some 50 years earlier by Theodore Taner, which in turn was built on the site of the medieval manor house dating back to the 1100s. After the death of the last owner (Rev Hamilton-Gell) in 1925, a break-up of the estate began. The house stood empty (although the grounds were used by the army during the Second World War) until sold as a private school in 1946.

It is probable that the earliest church of St Mary was Saxon, and that it was rebuilt in Norman times. A sketch in the vestry, dated 1799, shows the tower much as it looks today. The remainder of the church was rebuilt and altered during the 19th century. The somewhat remote situation of the church from the village is probably due to its originally having been built as a private chapel for the lord of the manor.

St Gabriel's Hospital (for twelve aged, blind or infirm priests) was established in the village in 1311, and occupied a site of about one acre, bounded on the south-west by Sidmouth Road. Two white pillars of Beer stone, which once carried an arch and were probably part of the main entrance to the hospital, can still be seen in the main road, and some of the houses fronting the main road contain parts of the ancient structure.

The character of the village has changed since the 1950s and Clyst St Mary now acts more as a dormitory village for Exeter. This has been brought about by the development of Winslade Park, the improvement of access to the village by the building of a dual carriageway taking the main Sidmouth and Exmouth traffic around the village and lastly, but probably most importantly, by the coming of the motorway. A large employer has moved into the village, buying the manor house from Winslade School. Although they have extended their office complex, every effort has been made to landscape it in keeping with the village environment. In 1983, the old vicarage was acquired by them, modernised and added to the complex.

The development of Oil Mill Lane, Manor Park, Frog Lane and the Cat and Fiddle give the village as diverse a selection of dwellings as the occupations of the people who live in them. The possible arrival of industry in Clyst St Mary coupled with the opening of the County Show Ground in 1990 may yet again alter the character of our village. Only time will tell.

Cofton 🌿

Cofton, or Cockton, takes its name from the stream, meaning 'red brook', the colour of the local soil. It is three miles from Dawlish and still has its own thriving shop, a flourishing school and two pubs. The three hamlets of Westwood, Middlewood and Cofton Hill, straggle up to a point that was once known as Gallows Corner, but at the foot of the hills lies Cockwood, a well-known beauty spot, now a conservation area.

When Brunel was building the GWR he described the area as 'the unfathomable swamp of Cockwood'. The coming of the railway brought great changes. Instead of a swamp there is now a beautifully sheltered harbour.

Strawberry Fair used to be an annual event in June. Baskets of fruit were spread out along the harbour wall and people came from far and near, some rowing over from Exmouth. They were encouraged to eat as many strawberries as they could for a nominal sum, washed down with copious draughts of cider. The Anchor Inn did a roaring trade, literally rolling out the barrels! In the place of this fair has come the Cockwood Revels, organised by the local boat club. This is held annually on the highest tide of the summer.

Cockle-raking used to be a popular occupation. Both men and women earned good money from the cartloads that went up to Exeter. One woman is known to have brought up five children on the proceeds. The numbers of cockles that can be gathered has declined greatly, because of pollution in the river.

For a time, the Plymouth Brethren held their services in local cottages. Baptisms by total immersion were carried out at the Cockle Steps. In 1888 a fine new chapel was built near the harbour.

The fertile valleys and steep hillsides of Westwood, Middlewood and Cofton Hill have long been famous for the excellence of the produce grown there. The never-to-be-forgotten scent of violets drifted from the fields to the lanes on damp evenings. By contrast the smell of rotting seaweed, used as a fertiliser, was not so pleasant! But times have changed. The cider orchards, plum trees, daffodils and violets have long since gone. Today the most widely grown crops are pinks, anemones, strawberries, lettuces and chrysanthemums – grown under glass or in poly-tunnels.

The church, dedicated to St Mary, has had an eventful history. It was built in the 13th century as a chapel of ease for the people of the district, and came under the care of the vicar of Dawlish. It seems that he neglected his duty to hold regular services in the chapel, and after a long and bitter feud, the parishioners attempted to murder him in Exeter Cathedral where he had taken sanctuary! For this foul deed they were excommunicated.

Finally, the church was restored from its ruinous state by the Earl of Devon in 1838, and in 1863 it became at last a parish church. Among the special treasures of the church is a mother-of-pearl chalice believed to have come from the Spanish Armada.

Colaton Raleigh 🌿

Colaton Raleigh is a small village between Newton Poppleford and Budleigh Salterton and is bisected by the A376. The name is Saxon from 'Cola's tun' (a large enclosed farm).

It has some cob and thatch houses but most of the more recent building is in brick.

The oldest house is Place Court, which was once a rectory of the Deans of Exeter, and it is surrounded by an ancient cob wall topped with thatch. The medieval house still remains, and tradition has it that Sir Walter Raleigh was baptised in the chapel there, which is dedicated to St Michael.

The land surrounding the village was bought in 1785 by Dennis Rolle, father of Lord Rolle of Bicton, for £72,000.

The WI maintains two 'gardens' which flank the main road through the village, one being in the old horse trough that was used by the village blacksmith. The smithy stood on the opposite side of the road, but it has now been demolished.

There is an interesting monument to Queen Victoria on the main road. The monument with its eight water taps was restored by the Parish Council in 1971 and the kerb is made of setts from Truro Cathedral forecourt. Sadly the water was turned off during a period of drought and has never been reconnected, and only five of the original taps can now be seen.

Coldridge 🌿

Coldridge is a village which stands on the summit of a high ridge and can be seen for miles around. The houses are gathered round an open 'square' from which there are wide views across to Dartmoor. In the village 'square' is the village green with its war memorial. The clock in the church tower was given by villagers in memory of those who gave their lives in the First World War.

The parish church of St Matthew stands at one corner of the village green. It is almost entirely early 15th and early 16th century, but there are distinct traces of Norman work inside. Its special features are a beautiful 15th century carved wooden rood screen and a carved oak pulpit of the same date; a window of 15th century stained glass which has recently been removed, overhauled and replaced; many late medieval floor tiles and wooden benches; some fine carved bench ends in the south aisle and south chancel aisle, including the prayer desk of Sir John Evans which is probably early 16th century; a parclose screen dividing the Evans chantry from the chancel; an early 13th century font. The church has a bell tower which houses six bells which are rung every Sunday. The church is always full of beautiful flower arrangements, courtesy of the ladies of the village. The churchyard has some of the largest yew trees in the area and a path of typical Devon cobbles.

Next to the churchyard is the old school house. The school is now the village hall. Opposite the green is the Post Office. The old bakery, next to the Post Office, is now a private house, and the old smithy is about to be converted into a private house. Petrol used to be available from the old bakery too, but the pumps have long since disappeared.

The village no longer has a shop or a pub, but it is rumoured that at one time there were seven of the latter!

Colyford 🌿

Colyford is a very old village on the Roman road from Dorchester to Exeter where it crosses the river Coly.

In 1341 a charter was granted to the Borough of Colyford and mayors were elected until the late 19th century. The Borough has a mace and insignia, but although it flourished for a time it had failed by the 15th century. However, it retained its status and was a 'rotten borough', returning two Members of Parliament until 1832. The custom of electing a mayor was revived in 1931. Each year, on a Saturday near the feast of St Michael, the mayor, burgesses and villagers beat the bounds of the old Borough, and the ancient Fair, dating from 1207, was revived in 1980. Until 1988 the fair was held at the 'Old Manor' – previously two farms, then a private house, a home for retired gentlewomen, and now an hotel.

Coly House at the western end of the village was the home of Admiral Impey and later of the Scarborough family. It is said that John Scarborough quarrelled with his brother, refusing to live in the same house or attend the same church – St Andrew's at Colyton. So John built St Michael's, and a house for himself – St Edmund's (opposite the post office). The Swan Inn was just across the road from John's new house, and when he found his workers calling there he sacked them and closed the inn. It is now a private house called Hillside. St Michael's church is now a chapel of ease in the parish of Colyton.

Colyford has two inns – the White Hart, near the river, and the Wheelwright, until 1933 the home and workshop of the wheelwright. Opposite the manor is the garage, opened 1928.

Toll gates stood at each end of the village. That at Boshill has disappeared, but near Coly House the tollhouse remains.

Besides the farms originally at the manor house there was Mount Pleasant Farm – now Yeoman's Acre, a guest house and restaurant, and Ship Farm near the river. Horriford Farm is very much alive and has been in the same family for some years. Springfield and The Elms occupy what was Dares Farm.

Although there has been a lot of development in recent years the village retains a lot of its old character, and several pretty cottages and houses are thatched.

Colyton 🌿

Colyton is situated on the river Coly, a tributary of the Axe, and two miles from the sea. The population is approximately 2,000, and the parish includes the neighbouring village of Colyford. The buildings are largely flint and cob with slate or thatch. At one time there were several mills using the river for water power. Perhaps the best known are Colcombe Mill, formerly operated by Mr Hann, and Coles Mill, owned by the Zealley family and milling flour within living memory. Water power is still used by Hamlyns Mill and Tannery. This is one of only three in the country producing high quality leather using oak bark for tanning.

The chief landowners were the Poles, Courtenays and Yonges. Colcombe Castle, belonging to the Courtenays, Earls of Devon, no longer exists but was occupied until Tudor times. Henry Courtenay fell foul of Henry VIII, was beheaded, and his lands confiscated. 'Twenty good men and true', local yeomen and traders, collected £1,000 – a large sum in those days – and took it to King Henry requesting the return of the Courtenay lands and this he agreed to do. Thus was formed the Colyton Chamber of the Feoffees, a body which still exists, and has done and still does much good for the community. They founded the grammar school in 1545, laid a water supply from a spring above the town, and also built the large town hall. They still meet regularly for charitable purposes. A memorial banquet is held annually, and a New Year party given to the retired folk of Colyton.

St Andrew's is a fine example of West Country Wool Churches. It was built largely of Beer stone, and has a medieval octagonal lantern built onto the Norman tower. The beautiful west window is one of the largest in an English parish church. In 1932 a serious fire almost destroyed the building, but it was carefully restored and a Saxon cross discovered in the foundations of the tower.

There is a good supply of shops, pubs and guest houses, and a primary school covering a large catchment area. Farming, the tannery and several small factories are the main employers.

A useful tram service connects Colyton with Colyford and Seaton. It runs on the old Southern Railway line closed by Beeching in 1963, and is very popular with visitors.

Combeinteignhead ❧

The village lies in a pleasant valley through which a brook meanders to the Teign, but the parish itself is very extensive, reaching the outskirts of Newton Abbot and taking in the hamlets of Higher and Lower Netherton. The original place-name meant 'valley in the Tynhide', the Tynhide being an outlying section of the Exeter-based hundred of Wonford consisting of ten hides (the 'hide' was a unit of land measurement). Tynhide later became 'Tinhead', which version can still be seen on the old parish boundary stones. The 'Teign' spelling is a corruption which attained official recognition in the first edition (1809) of the Ordnance Survey map.

The parish church, formerly without a patron saint, was recently dedicated to All Saints. It dates mainly from the 13th and 14th centuries, though it has a Norman font as evidence of an earlier building.

Among many attractive secular buildings the most distinguished is the Church House, presented to the parish in 1530 by John Bourchier, Baron Fitzwarren, who was related to Alice Fitzwarren of Dick Whittington fame. The upper floor was used for village functions and the lower floor was a brewhouse which sold ale to the locals. In 1789 a charity school was founded in the upper room and this was taken over by the School Board in 1874. After the closure of the school in 1932 the building fell into disrepair until it was restored and converted into two almshouse flats with a studio below in 1977–78. At the same time the garden was laid out for public use to commemorate the Queen's Jubilee.

There are two inns, the 17th century Wild Goose, formerly the Country House, which was a farmhouse until c1840, and the 18th century Combe Cellars beside the Teign, once known as the Ferryboat, a favourite resort for boat trips from Teignmouth and elsewhere. The vicinity was called Combe Cellars long before there was an inn here, the name being derived from the salt pans ('salaria') which once existed beside the shore. The place was formerly a notorious haunt of smugglers, but is now a popular venue for sailing, water-skiing and windsurfing.

The parish, with a population of about 400, has a post office stores, a garage, and a guest house called Coombe Hatch, while Netherton House, a Victorian mansion built by Arthur Reynell Pack, locally known as 'Squire Pack', is now occupied by an advertising agency. The outlying areas of the parish are chiefly devoted to agriculture.

A six acre field, beautifully sited beside the Teign near Combe Cellars, was recently bequeathed to the parish by Capt Hearn, a local landowner, and is used for cricket, football and other recreational activities.

Combe Martin 🌿

Combe Martin lies on the western fringe of Exmoor. The village street of one and three quarter miles is reputed to be one of the longest in England. Combe Martin was mentioned in the Domesday Book, when it was known as Cumbe or Comba (Celtic for valley). The 'Martin' was added later when the holding passed to Martyn de Tours. The river Umber flows through the valley to the sea, the name derived from the umber which used to be extracted from it.

The ancient ceremony of the 'Hunting of the Earl of Tyrone', banned in 1837 because of drunken and licentious behaviour, has been revived in recent years. The 'traitorous Earl' is hunted through the woods by 'Grenadiers'. When captured he is placed backwards on a donkey and led through the streets preceded by a hobby horse and a fool. At the beach the Earl is dispatched by the Grenadiers and his body consigned to the waves. The ceremony originally took place at Ascension, probably tacked on to an early pagan fertility ritual.

By far the most lucrative local industry was the mining of silver from galena, a lead ore with silver lodes. Combe Martin silver has been mined from at least the 14th century. In the reign of Elizabeth I a cup made from Combe Martin silver was presented by the Queen to the Lord Mayor of London. The mines were reopened on several occasions during the following centuries with varying degrees of success. The last attempt to reopen them, in 1875, was abandoned. Iron ore and manganese have also been mined in the area.

Limestone was quarried and some 16 lime-kilns existed to produce lime as a dressing for the soil. Some of the older houses still have floors made from lime ash.

In the fertile valley strawberries and potatoes grew well. They are still grown today and their quality is such that when sold in the nearby towns of Ilfracombe and Barnstaple they are labelled 'Combe Martin produce'. However, they are not grown in the quantities they were before the First World War when boatloads of strawberries left for Swansea market. The sea was the main highway then.

With a sheltered harbour, fishing must have always been a source of income. There are still one or two boats in the bay, mainly to take holidaymakers on fishing trips. Another product of the sea is laver, a form of seaweed cooked and eaten as a vegetable.

The growing of hemp produced other industries – a rope walk where ropes were made for the boats and hemp was also spun into shoemaker's thread. The land on which the hemp was grown is still known as Cobbler's Park.

The Pack O' Cards is a unique building built by George Ley to celebrate his success at the gaming tables. It resembles a card house with four floors to represent the four suits, 13 doors on each floor and, originally, 52 windows.

The parish church is very fine with a 13th century chancel. The dedication to St Peter ad Vincula (St Peter in chains) is a rare one. A North Devon jingle referring to their respective churches goes –

> 'Hartland for length
> Berrynarbor for strength
> And Combe Martin for beauty.'

Combe Martin seems to have enjoyed a chequered history of varying fortunes. It was a market town with an annual fair from the 13th to 18th centuries. While 18th century travellers seem to have found Combe Martin a pleasant and picturesque place, by the mid 19th century the village appears to have sunk into squalor. Charles Kingsley dubbed it a 'mile long man-sty'.

The present day Combe Martin is a pleasant village with a good community spirit. Its quiet charm and picturesque scenery are appreciated by residents and holidaymakers alike.

Cornwood

The local community is made up of two villages, Cornwood and Lutton, each with its own identity.

In 1212 the two villages were called Curnwod and Ludeton and the church, or most probably the church tower, which stands on the highest ground in Cornwood, was in existence at this time, surrounded by various groups of cottages, several farms and three big houses – Delamore, Blachford and Fardel. A fourth, Slade, was built later, in the reign of Edward I. The Methodist chapel was built in Lutton at the end of the 19th century.

Although the rapidly growing town of Ivybridge is on the parish boundary, and ever-expanding Plymouth is on the horizon (its night-time neon glow reminds some villagers that when war-time bombing set it alight it could be seen burning from as far away as Torbay!), this has always been an agricultural parish. However, in the last hundred years the growth and prosperity of the local china clay mines has given work to many of the local residents. For that reason the population has remained fairly steady, and this industry has become the life-blood of the community, ensuring the prosperity of the village school, the shop and the post office, not to mention the two local pubs.

Life in the village seems to have thrown up very few famous or infamous characters, instead it manages to hang on to a feeling of continuity down through the ages. This is best illustrated by looking up Cornwood in White's Devon Directory for 1850, where the names of families in the parish then, such as Northmore, Horton, Roberts, Phillips and Mudge are very much in evidence today.

During the Civil War the vicar of Cornwood, Henry Smith, a 'zealous Loyalist', escaped from Cromwell's men by climbing from a garret window of his vicarage but was later caught, his possessions plundered, and himself confined in Exeter gaol. A later description of the same vicarage, in the time of the Napoleonic Wars, recounts how 'during the fear of invasion a store of guineas was kept in the house, and everything was ready to send all the women into the heart of the moor'. No doubt similar feelings existed during the Second World War.

When Cornwood Agricultural Show holds its centenary it will be with great local pride. Although the format may have changed over the years, it has remained a genuinely 'local' show.

Cornworthy

Between Totnes and Dartmouth through narrow winding lanes rich with violets, primroses and bluebells in the spring, campions, vetch and cow parsley in the summer, is the lovely old village of Cornworthy. A village recorded in the Domesday Book as Corneorda, it paid 80 salmon yearly to the lord of Totnes.

On top of a hill at the west end of the village stand the ruins of a medieval gatehouse which is all that now remains of the Augustinian priory of nuns founded between 1205–1238. With probably never more

Cornworthy village

than ten nuns in residence, it also served as a retreat for noble ladies and in one instance as a 'schole' for two small girls. Today the gatehouse stands sentinel over the village, home to rooks, owls and jackdaws and overseeing once a year the village 'Pig Roast', where villagers and visitors get together to enjoy themselves and raise money for the village hall.

Tucked into the fold of the hill opposite the gatehouse is the church of St Peter, a 15th century building. It was entirely refitted in 1788 and is now one of the most delightful church interiors in Devon. There is a good canopied tomb of Thomas Harris, sergeant-at-law (1610) and Elizabeth his wife. The Rev Charles Barter was vicar here for 71 years, 1775–1846, the longest known tenure of a Devonshire living.

Next door to the church is the school which opened in 1866, attended by the children of the adjacent village Tuckenhay and the outlying farms in addition to the local children. It was closed in 1963. It is now the village hall and is used regularly by the villagers.

Part of the village and surrounding countryside is in a preservation area. Bow Creek, an arm of the river Dart, is a short walk away across the fields. Along its banks, thickly wooded in places with mature beech, oak and chestnuts and lovely views down towards Dittisham, are the remains of lime-kilns and a lime-burner's house. The limestone was brought across the river from a quarry near Stoke Gabriel. From quarries in Cornworthy, stone was taken by boat to Dartmouth to build the castle there in the late 15th century.

Cornworthy has a variety of architectural styles, including some thatched cottages. It has a public house and a shop/post office, a local farm provides the milk. A village bus driven by volunteer drivers takes villagers into Totnes twice a week.

Crediton ❧

Crediton lies in the very heart of Devon, steeped in history and legend. Its church of the Holy Cross is one of the finest and most impressive in the county, and is owned by the people of the town. At the time of Henry VIII's suppression of the monasteries he destroyed the collegiate buildings, but by public subscription the people purchased the church, for £200. Twelve Governors were appointed to care for and maintain the building. This arrangement continues to the present day, and to be made a Governor of the church is the highest honour Crediton can bestow.

Over the years Crediton has known periods of prosperity and of recessions. It was a centre of the wool industry. The three-storey cottages in East Street are said to have been weavers' cottages, where the weaving was done in the topmost rooms. At one time there were many shoe factories, and at least two tanneries, one of these being in Newcombes Meadow. It is certainly true that in the 1700s the thatched house, now known as White Cottage, adjacent to the Meadow remained empty for a considerable time, as the smell was unendurable. In this house the officers in charge of the prisoner-of-war camps during the Napoleonic Wars were billeted. The lane outside the house, which was a muddy one leading up to the green at the top of Crediton, became known as Belle Parade, as it was here the officers paraded in their best uniforms to impress the local belles.

Although many old and interesting houses still remain, and there is an extensive conservation area, much of the old town was destroyed by two disastrous fires, the worst being in 1743 which destroyed the greater part of the West Town, with great loss of life. This fire is said to have been started by two young men, who had drunk too freely the previous night, being left in charge of the spit-roasting of the family dinner.

Crediton today is a thriving place with many housing estates and an industrial estate. The latter is on Lords Meadow, where once Charles I reviewed his troops. Despite the growth and prosperity the community spirit still flourishes. To go shopping in the long, straggling but delightful High Street is a pleasure not to be missed. Here one is sure to meet friends, and the shopkeepers still attend to their customers with courtesy and personal interest, in fact they too are friends.

A little way past the Ship Hotel is an archway over which appears 'Dart & Francis, Ecclesiastical Art Works'. Although no longer there the work of this firm is to be found all over the world. Another famous name is that of Helmores, believed to be the oldest firm of auctioneers and estate agents in England, founded 255 years ago.

Croyde

There has been a community in Croyde since prehistoric times. Excellent examples of Stone Age tools have been found. Fields known as 'Blood Hills' where perhaps battles were fought are still named on farm deeds.

Croyde became part of the parish of Georgeham. The beautiful Saxon church there is where early Croyde dwellers worshipped, and indeed, at the present time is still 'the church'. When compulsory education was introduced in the 19th century, Croyde children had to climb the hill to Georgeham.

82

Stretches of unbelievably yellow sands and blue sea hide cruel rocks and dangerous currents. But the sea can turn grey and roar when south-westerlies whip up to storm force. Rolling waves attract international surfers in the summer and foolhardy ones in the winter, so it is very reassuring to have close by an RAF sea/rescue helicopter service, a skilled coastguard team and an inshore RNLI lifeboat. It is a dangerous coast as the rhyme reminds us:

'From Mortehoe Point to Hartland Light
A sailor's death both day and night'

The fierceness of the early settlement turned to cruelty in the dreadful work of the 'wreckers' in the 18th century. Grisly stories are told of passengers left to drown, some with legs broken by a 'wrecker', to prevent their escape, after being relieved of their valuables. Smuggling was also rife. Tobacco and rum from the Caribbean found its way into many a farm cellar.

Croyde has Dartmoor to the south, Exmoor to the east and sea on the north and west, and so has been geographically isolated for hundreds of years. The opening of the first turnpike road making vehicular traffic possible must have had a similar impact as the first railway to nearby Braunton. This 'progress' was the start of tourism. Edwardians came. They took apartments in farmhouses. Whole families were cared for for 2/6d a day. There was no 'Promenade', so beloved by strolling Edwardians, but a beautiful part of what is now the coastal footpath towards Baggy Point served this purpose. A whale was washed up on the rocks at about this time. Some of its bleached bones are still by the pathway, now owned by the National Trust.

And now the link road to the M5 has brought caravan parks, cream teas and people. People arrive pale from inner cities and depart tanned and relaxed; people who love our village and return year after year.

Cruwys Morchard

Cruwys Morchard is a very large mid-Devon parish on a wet and windy plateau 750 ft above sea-level, dropping steeply down to verdant valleys. A watershed, its streams feed tributaries of the Taw and Exe. It is an area of isolated farms and cob-walled cottages, including the tiny hamlet of Way Village, the larger slowly-growing one of Pennymoor and half of Nomansland.

The A373 Tiverton to South Molton road was cut in the 19th century as a toll road. The toll house with its watch-window, now bricked up, still stands at Mudford Gate. All other roads are no more than narrow lanes meandering up and down and round about. At the centre just off the A373, the manor house, church and parish hall stand alone.

The name comes from two old words; Cruwy meaning cross and Morchard, the great wood. Since the 12th century the family named Cruwys has occupied the manor house, which is mainly Georgian with a medieval core.

The large church of the Holy Cross is a Grade I listed building of charm and tranquillity. Rebuilt after the fire of 1689, it has an unusual plastered barrel ceiling and a fine screen of the same Queen Anne period. Notice the farm names on the pews and the pull-out apprentice seats in the south aisle; outside there is a sundial above the door, the parish stocks and an 18th century revolving lychgate.

The third building in this leafy setting, the parish hall, is in complete contrast. Built soon after the First World War, it is asbestos-walled, damp and draughty. Nevertheless it is in constant use.

Congregationalism took a firm hold here in the 19th century. The first services were held in a cottage at Way Village before the chapel there was built. This is still used for worship. Pennymoor and Nomansland are also 'Continuing Congregational' churches.

For years the two blacksmiths shops beside the pubs at Pennymoor and Nomansland were favourite meeting places for the locals where parish topics were debated. Alas the hearth at Nomansland is now cold, the smith has retired. An itinerant smith now shoes many of the area's horses.

At the northernmost end, on the A373, the aptly named Nomansland lies at the junction of three parishes; Witheridge, Thelbridge and Cruwys Morchard, with a section in each.

There is no shop, post office or doctor's surgery in the parish but there is a garage selling petrol, papers and a few groceries. There is one public phone box; and two public houses, the Mount Pleasant at Nomansland and the Cruwys Arms at Pennymoor. The latter is the place where the packhorses once broke their journey between the two great moors. Much of the social life of the parish is centred on these two inns with their skittles and darts teams.

Culmstock 🐝

Culmstock is a pretty village of over 800 inhabitants which straddles the river Culm at the foot of the Blackdown Hills.

It was once a thriving woollen cloth-making centre, an industry which continued well into the 19th century. The mill, with its magnificent water-wheel, still stands, although now divided into residential flats: there are also some old cottages where fittings for looms can still be seen.

The fine old five-arched bridge dates back to the 12th century, but today's heavy lorries greatly tax its strength.

The village supports a primary school, a village hall, two inns, a butcher's business, a post office, a general store, a garage, a Baptist church, a Methodist church and a Church of England church – the latter of Saxon foundation.

A feature of the church of all Saints, of which the village is justly proud, is the yew tree growing from the top of the tower, the roots running in the interstices of the masonry, which is believed to have been there for 250 years. It does not appear to damage the stonework and during years of drought the villagers valiantly carry water up the tower to keep the tree alive.

The unique Beehive Beacon Hut sits atop Culmstock Beacon Hill, which has recently been designated an 'area of outstanding natural beauty'. The earliest record of the beacon hut is in Elizabethan times, when it was used to warn of the approach of the Spanish Armada, and although there is no evidence, it is assumed that it is of a much earlier period.

Noteworthy characters connected with Culmstock included Frederick Temple, who lived in the parish and taught in the Church Sunday school before becoming headmaster of Rugby school, Bishop of Exeter, Bishop of London and eventually Archbishop of Canterbury; and R. D. Blackmore, who wrote *Lorna Doone* whilst resident at the vicarage where his father was curate.

Although the village is largely rural and residential and, to some extent, a dormitory to Tiverton and Wellington, the inhabitants are active with a Parish Council, Parochial Church Council and many village organisations.

The beauty of Culmstock is that it is still an unspoilt village with the land, its fields and hedge boundaries, its farms and buildings much as they were 150 years ago and many old houses unchanged – at least from the outside!

Dalwood 🐚

Dalwood, a small attractive village with a population of about 500, lies some three miles west of Axminster, on the edge of the Blackdowns, in the valley of the Corry brook. Until 1842, when the county boundaries were adjusted, Dalwood was in Dorset.

The right to hold an annual fair was granted by Edward III in 1345. This lapsed for a time in the 19th century, but is now firmly re-established as one of the jolliest annual events in August.

St Peter's church is a small and charming building which can be dated, by its Perpendicular style, to the early 15th century, but there is said to be earlier work in it. There is a tradition, firmly believed in the village, that the Tucker's Arms, the old thatched inn, was built to house the men who were building the church.

One of the treasures of Dalwood is the little Baptist chapel at Lough-wood. Built in the mid 17th century it now belongs to the National Trust and has been skilfully rethatched and restored. Inside you will still find the original pulpit, box pews and baptismal cavity, which lies under the floor. Once deeply hidden in thick woodland, it was the ideal meeting place for dissenters. Also, being situated on the county boundary, it gave scope for rapid escape from persecution into either Devon or Dorset according to need.

On the extreme edge of the village there used to be an Admiralty signal station, a relic of the Napoleonic wars of the early 19th century when communication between Plymouth and London was by semaphore. This is still remembered by the name Telegraph Cottage.

Part of the parish boundary follows the line of the Roman road from Dorchester to Exeter. In some places it is marked by a double hedge on a 5 ft high bank. Some stretches of this hedge are thought to be over a thousand years old.

Dalwood has always been mainly a farming community. Though many of the farmhouses are modern, the farms themselves are old, probably dating back to Saxon times. Burgh, for example, now Burrow Farm, is mentioned in a document of 1369. Today you will find there the beautiful and widely known Burrow Farm Gardens.

The village used to have many more trades than it does now. There was a corn mill by the Corry until 1909 with, at one time, a malt mill and a woollen mill beside it. Weaving, tanning and soap boiling were once important. Before the Second World War there were two carpenters (one also being a wheelwright) who operated a saw-pit by the Corry. There were two shops, one including the post office, and three shoemakers.

St Peter's church, Dalwood

Today, apart from general farming, there are two intensive poultry rearing units, a large piggery, a flourishing coach firm and a caravan and camping site. There is still a shop and post office, a school (with swimming pool), and a reading room (1904) where billiards, snooker and darts are regularly enjoyed by the men and boys. The village hall (the original school) is a Victorian building owned by the village and constantly in use for all activities.

Dartington 🦢

As a typical Devon village Dartington must come as a disappointment initially to the casual visitor, for it has no village square surrounded by thatched cottages, with the pub, general store and village shool at its centre. But if you know where to look, however, it does possess all of these features and more.

The old manor encompassed four and three quarter square miles of wooded and agricultural land with its farms and hamlets linked together by trade, industry and religion. Dartington is known to have had a priest in 1152 and it is believed there was a church at the site of Dartington Hall long before that was built.

The Cott Inn at Dartington is said to be one of the oldest pubs in England, and plied its trade by refreshing the passing traders of wool, tin and hides as they trod one of the oldest trade routes in the country between Totnes and Ashburton. The inn and the surrounding hamlet after which it was called are named after Johannes Cott, a wealthy merchant.

Dartington prospered during these years. Many names in the parish registers today can be traced back to medieval times – despite the effects of the depression during the second half of the 19th century when village populations declined and the route of the highway was altered to its present course.

In 1878 the foundation stone of the new church was laid in a more central position in the parish, and nearer the parsonage, and the church was moved away from the Hall (though the 14th century tower remains today and services are still held there).

The arrival of Leonard and Dorothy Elmhirst in 1925 saw a great upturn in the fortunes of the Hall and surrounding area. New businesses were begun – cider mill, saw mill and tweed mill, farms were resurrected, a new school was founded and an arts centre established, drawing its artists and performers from around the world.

Dartington's population has increased greatly during the 20th century. The Elmhirsts had over 50 new cottages built and the council has estates at Beacon View, Redlake, Tolchards and Newman Crescent (in conjunction with the Hall).

A village hall was built in 1925 as a memorial to men of the parish who had fought in the First World War. Nearby, in 1927, the Guy family opened their grocery shop and still run it today, though the garage they also established is now owned by Harrisons of Totnes.

Sadly, the 'Estate' has declined in recent years, the mills no longer exist, and the famous Dartington Hall School closed. Employment locally has been hard to come by. A small business park has been established on the old sawmills site, and life is returning to that area again. The Cider Press Centre displays and retails craftsmen-created wares and is a great attraction for visitors. But some visitors are disappointed, and frustrated, when they discover that the Dartington Glass Works are not here, but at Torrington, North Devon!

Dartmouth

At the estuary of the river Dart stands a castle built in 1480, to guard the entrance of the harbour. At that time a chain stretched from it across to Kingswear Castle opposite.

Nearby is Bayards Cove with its cobbled quay, which was the setting of the TV series *The Onedin Line*. Moving further along into the town is the Butterwalk, built in 1630, with eleven granite piers which support the living accommodation of the four shops underneath.

In the centre of the town stands the parish church of St Saviour of 1372. The mother church of Townstal, called St Clement's, stands in a commanding position on the hill. At Townstal many of the townspeople are employed on the industrial estate.

In Royal Avenue gardens, with its blaze of colour, stands an elegant bandstand and a memorial to Thomas Newcomen, inventor of the early steam engine, who lived in Dartmouth.

The Embankment, which is half a mile long, is divided into South and North, the North Embankment being a complete contrast to the commercial part of the South Embankment, which runs along the river Dart, well known for its boat trips to Totnes. The richly wooded banks are a sight to be seen, at high tide stretching down to the waters' edge.

Naomi James came ashore here with thousands cheering her in June 1975, after 30,000 miles and 272 days sailing solo around the world.

The Britannia Royal Naval College nestles on the hill, where royal visitors attend at the passing out parade of the cadets. Here also more local people are employed.

Further along the river Agatha Christie's house is situated, where she wrote many of her famous novels.

Dartmouth is famous for its Royal Regatta, established in 1834, held annually at the end of August with its sailing and rowing events. It gets its 'Royal' from Queen Victoria, after she came to Dartmouth in 1856. There is an influx of visitors to the town during the Regatta, and a good time is had by all with spectacular firework displays. After this three day event, when all the visitors have left the town, the locals say they settle in for the winter and the peace and tranquillity returns.

Dawlish 🦢

Dawlish is well-known for its red sandstone cliffs, which look attractive against the sea and countryside.

The shopping area and town were built around Dawlish Water, or The Brook as it is now known. The site of the present gardens and Brook was a swamp, until raised and laid out by a Mr Manning in about 1800. Old Dawlish is of very ancient origin and not much alteration was made until the 18th century. The cottages were mostly built of cob with thatched roofs.

Larger houses started being built about 1793. The first of these was Bridge House. Barton House was the largest and had a big estate, including much land south of the Brook. It occupied the whole site of the present Barton Crescent. Ashcombe Towers and Luscombe Castle are on the outskirts of Dawlish. Ashcombe Towers is the home of Sir Ralph and Lady Rayner and at Luscombe Castle the Hoare family have been in residence since 1797/8 to the present time. A large house named The Rise was built in 1802. Caroline of Brunswick, then Princess of Wales, stayed there in April 1806. It is now run as a holiday and nursing home by the Sisters of Charity. In 1805 a bath house was built near the sea; it brought the first of the holidaymakers to Dawlish, as it was popular at that time to take the 'waters'.

The parish church of St Gregory has been in existence from 1148, by Church records. One entry in the parish accounts reads '1689 Paid to the hellier for mending the church roof when it was blown up by the wind £1 5s 0d.'! The Church House was nearby and in ancient times was used as an hotel for visiting parishioners from far away, offering refreshments, drinks and also wedding breakfasts. A lot of people were saddened when the daughter church of St Mark was closed and demolished. The land was sold to developers.

The main industries of Dawlish are agriculture and the tourist trade. A lot more fishing used to be done from Lyme Bay. Flowers were sent to Covent Garden from nurseries around here, among them the famous Devon violets.

The coming of Brunel's railway and the change to the narrow gauge track in 1892 made a great difference and opened up a lot more trade for Dawlish from all over the country.

The small coves, caves and over-hanging cliffs in this area were ideal for smugglers, and many a barrel found its way to Dawlish beaches. Smuggler's Inn is still open for business on the Dawlish–Teignmouth road!

Denbury 🌿

The village of Denbury is now a quiet place which people 'happen upon', it being fairly remote from the main routes. It was not always so.

The name is Celtic and derives from 'Defnas burh' meaning 'the fort of the men of Devon'. The fort referred to is a very visible Iron Age hill fort, about 500 ft above sea level to the south-west of the village. The oval top is crowned with good, mixed woodland which makes it an even more conspicuous landmark from every direction. There is evidence to suggest that the Celtic Dumnonii held out here against the Saxons coming up the Teign estuary. Incidentally, the ramparts make an excellent home for badgers and they have burrowed into and through the bank making a complex network of tunnels over many years.

Denbury was fortunate to be granted a licence to hold a three-day fair, once a year on the feast of the Nativity of the Blessed Virgin Mary, and also to have a market every Wednesday. The fair first started in 1285 on 8th September, but in 1757, because of changes in the calendar, it was moved forward ten days. The fair was very important socially to all classes and was looked forward to as a time of great festivity. Much business was also done, especially in the sale of cheese. An older couple from the village were chosen to play the roles of Old Mother Denbury and Old Father Denbury. There was a procession and 'chairing' of this couple and they would preside at the fair, Old Father Denbury bearing a scythe.

The people of Denbury must have felt a great loss when the fair came to an end in 1866 due to a disease of cattle called Rinderpest. The fair did take place in later years but sadly seems to have been forgotten now, the only reminder being the name of the site on the outskirts of the village – Fairfield Farm.

Entering Denbury from another direction, fairgoers would have passed a large flat area of land called the Great Field. In the 1930s flying became popular and this large flat field was ideal for use as an airfield. Villagers remember enjoying airborne circuits of the area for a nominal sum and watching aerial displays by 'Cobham's Flying Circus'.

Just before the Second World War, the same airfield was converted to a military camp. Many regiments served there and many men including Americans, passed through the camp. The village felt the impact of this dramatic influx of young men!

In 1967 the camp changed hands from the War Department to the Home Office and gradually the old wooden huts were converted into the modern buildings of HM Prison, Channings Wood. There is a pleasing link with the past however, as the civilian address of the prison is Greatfield.

Great excitement was felt round the village when Denbury Down was put up for auction by a local farmer: would the purchaser conserve this historical site? After a thrilling exchange of bids, Devon County Council bought the site. The people of Devon are now the owners of Denbury Down. It seems that we have come full circle: Denbury is once more 'the fort of the men of Devon'.

Diptford

The village of Diptford lies along the left bank of the river Avon, which flows from Dartmoor to Bantham and in which trout and occasionally salmon swim. Once the railway from South Brent to Kingsbridge ran along the river valley and through the woods which, then as now, are full of snowdrops, daffodils or bluebells. At one spot, where a railway pillar remains, dippers have nested for over 20 years. Downstream is an old packhorse bridge and from its hump one might see a kingfisher darting by. Here also are the remnants of lime-kilns.

Diptford was spelled Depeforde in the Domesday Book. The ford was probably near the old millhouse of which only the water-wheel survives. The church, and most of the village, is on high ground overlooking the deep ford. The church has one of the oldest medieval broach spires in Devon.

Opposite is the old church house, where worshippers from a distance were sheltered between services. Next door is the village hall, a wooden building, erected in 1920, as a war memorial and a place of relaxation 'for the men of the village'.

In 1851 the population was 747. Now it is some 450, scattered over a large area. When the villagers beat the bounds, the distance covered is 17 gruelling miles.

Most of the working population are dairy farmers although many sheep are raised and some corn grown. The professional sheep-shearer's services are sought from as far away as Norway. He and an engineer in the parish have invented a device for the simplification of fleece packing and have thereby won an award.

The centre for Pony Riding for the Disabled is managed entirely voluntarily. Over the years the village has been presented with a playing field, tennis court, and a cricket pitch. On a sunny afternoon it is bliss to sit watching the cricket while listening to the flowing river and watching the sheep on the hillside.

The post office is only open three days a week. There is a hairdresser, an electrician, a plumber and a builder, but there was a time when the village was completely self-supporting, when the population was swollen by the quarrymen. The largest slate quarry was at Larcombe. When eventually the quarries were worked out, the quarrymen left for Delabole or the colonies. This exodus caused the demise of the village inns, and also the end of the breed of fighting cocks, the Diptford Greys. (They are still reared but fortunately no longer for cockfighting.)

Several of the scattered farmsteads are old, with walls of weather-beaten granite. Tucked away in one valley is Crabadon Manor, a medieval house. Diptford Court, once the Court for the district, is now a fine farmhouse with an imposing gatehouse. Three Domesday manors, Beenleigh, Curtisknowle and Fareleigh still exist in name and situation.

Dittisham 🦋

Dittisham lies on the west bank of the river Dart, about three miles from Dartmouth, a small settlement which was included in the Domesday survey as Didashem, the homestead of Deedas.

In the church of St George the beautiful carved and painted pulpit dates from the 14th century. This escaped being damaged by Cromwell's men but the chancel screen of about the same date was badly damaged. It is thought the damage may have been done by an unruly mob which plundered the rectory, turned out the rector, John Strode and his family, and burned all the church registers. In 1933, the 600th anniversary of the restoration of the church, a beautiful carved reredos, choir stalls, altar rails etc were dedicated and a fund was opened for the restoration of the chancel screen, which was finally restored in 1955 by a firm in Exeter.

The church is situated on rising ground some distance from the river. Cottages climb up from the river on one side and from the creek on the other. Between them is a peninsula known as Gurrow Point where, in about 1934, some developers planned to build houses all round with a country club in the middle. However, there was only spring water here that time and when they had built about twelve houses, they were told that if they built any more they would have to bring water across the river from Paignton, which they declined to do. After the Second World War 14 council houses were built, then six council flats. During the following years new houses have been built in various parts of the village but no estates. The water meadows in the centre of the village, from the river up to the church, were saved from developers in 1960. Dittisham Court is no longer a farm, the house having been divided, the barns converted and houses built in the grounds.

Years ago men worked on the local farms and two boat-loads of workers went down the river every morning at 7 o'clock to the boat yards in Dartmouth. Now there are many more retired people and not as many workers, though the building trade is well represented and busy. There is still work on the farms and salmon fishing on the river. Near the church is the post office and a very good shop and the Red Lion pub, while near the river is the Ferry Boat Inn.

Doccombe 🌿

The little hamlet of Doccombe lies some two miles east of Moretonhampstead on the road to Exeter. It consists of two or three farms, a collection of cottages and an old millhouse.

Within living memory it has had a sub post office, a pub, a small shop and half a dozen working farms. The post office closed, the pub has been a private house for several decades and the working farms have largely been bought for the houses; the fields being sold off or rented out for the grazing.

There is now a tea rooms in a row of thatched cottages and the Mill House is a comfortable guest house with a thriving trout farm.

But the main claim to fame of Doccombe is its connection with the murder of Thomas a Becket in 1170. One of the knights who committed the murder was William de Tracey, who owned much land in the area and gave his name to the nearby town of Bovey Tracey. William de Tracey died, in 1174, in Italy but before his death, in expiation of his part in the murder, he drew up a charter granting the manor of Doccombe to the prior and convent of Canterbury Cathedral 'for the love of God, and the salvation of his soul and the souls of his ancestors, and for the love of the blessed Thomas Archbishop and martyr; the income to be used for the clothing and support of a monk to celebrate the masses for the souls living or dead'. Doccombe continued in the possession of the Church until its sale in 1860.

Dolton 🦢

The village can be easily missed, as it is just off the main Exeter–Torrington road – which is nice for the residents, who number around 600.

Farmland surrounds the village although the community is a pleasing mixture of young and old; some employed locally in the two resident industries, Boughton Transmissions and H. Turrall's fly fishing factory.

Dolton is fortunate to be self-sufficient. There are shops supplying groceries, a butcher and delicatessen, greengrocery, electrical goods, a post office, hairdresser and a 'chippy'. A doctor's surgery is also held in the village twice a week. Perhaps the village's most important 'claims to fame' are its three pubs!

The village school, dating from the 1850s, has been remodelled to encompass the growing number of village children. St Edmund's church is adjacent to the school and contains an ancient Saxon font believed to have been part of a stone cross.

Within the parish is a thriving trout fishery at Stafford Moor. There are several ancient farmsteads with names like Iddlecott and Cherubeer, mentioned in the Domesday Book. Stafford Barton is a former residence of Dolton's squires and contains a superb carved ceiling. The ancient title of 'lord of the manor' was recently purchased by the Lavis family of Stafford Barton to ensure it was retained for the parish of Dolton.

The parish is bounded on the west by the river Torridge and a long stretch of the river and adjacent 140 acres of woodland is now the Halsdon Nature Reserve, looked after by the Devon Nature Trust.

A modern legend refers to the Jubilee Cake made in 1977 by the ladies of the local WI. Made large enough to allow everyone to have a slice, when completed with marzipan and icing, it was found to be too large to be removed from its room of assembly! In order for the cake to be carried round the village by four strong local men, the door frame had to be removed. The cake even had a poem written about it!

A new estate of some 70 houses on the fringe of the village has in no way detracted from the central core of thatched houses. The added population has integrated well with village life and ensured the survival of many organisations in Dolton.

Dunchideock ✤

Dunchideock is a roughly heart-shaped parish, nestling in a valley on the east side of the Haldon Hills, five miles south-west of Exeter. The estuary of the river Exe is five miles away to the east just north of Starcross and Dawlish. The population is around 230 people.

The village hall, which was once a school is, in this sprawling village, the nearest point to its community centre. The school was closed in 1959, and there are no shops, but the 13th century church is a prized and active gem. There is mention of Dunchideock House in the Domesday Book, although nothing of that date is now visible in the dwelling, and the oldest cottages in the village vary in age from 1300 onward. Some are thatched.

The remains of what was once reputed to be the largest house in England, are now known as 'The Lord Haldon', a residential hotel. It was built by Sir George Chudleigh in 1735 and purchased by Sir Robert Palk (Lord Haldon). It contained over 400 rooms, and the estate then covered thousands of acres of forest and moor. All that remains is one large corner of the original building, once the servants' quarters, coach house and stabling.

It was Sir Robert Palk who built the prominent landmark, known as Haldon Belvedere, or the Lawrence Tower – a folly standing high on the hill overlooking the village, commanding splendid views on a clear day. It is still possible to pay to go up the tower during the summer months. When Sir Robert had the tower built in 1788, it was with the intention of commemorating his friend, Major General Stringer Lawrence, who commanded the British Armies in India for 20 years. The little bridge built across Webberton Lane near the entrance to the hotel was erected to make it possible for King George III to travel directly from Haldon House to the tower.

The church is built in local red sandstone on the site of an older church dedicated to St Michael. The rood screen and parclose screen were originally carved in the 15th century but have been restored and are deserving of especial attention.

The oldest dwelling in Dunchideock is on the left as you leave the church gate. This is known as the Priest's House, now modernised into two cottages. It ceased to be the rectory in 1791 when the living of the parish was amalgamated with that of Shillingford St George.

Along the ridge fairly close to the Lawrence Tower, some Neolithic remains were discovered and, after excavation, some postholes of a dwelling. Various flints are now in the Rougemont Museum in Exeter. It is pleasant, when strolling along the road in front of the tower, to recall the ancient transportation of salt along the ridgeway, which caused the road to be known locally as 'the Whiteway'.

Dunkeswell 🐝

Dunkeswell is a high village, 800 ft up in the glorious Blackdown Hills to the north of Honiton, and it is not unknown for it to be cut off by snow.

Long low farmhouses and thatched white cottages with pretty gardens abound in the village and are hidden up outlying lanes, and the Madford brook romps to meet the Madford river in its wild little valley where if you are lucky you may see a deer. The school has long since closed and is now a well-kept village hall which is the centre of lively community activities. The newly-thatched pub, The Royal Oak, has darts and skittles teams, and there is a thriving football club and an Aero-club.

Dunkeswell still has its post office, housed in a wisteria-clad thatched cottage, with an owl on the roof so realistic as to cause passers-by to stop and look again!

In 1201 the 'manor of Donkewell' was granted by Lord William Brewer to the Cistercian order for the foundation of an abbey. Now only a ruined gatehouse and traces of walls remain. The monks' fishponds now form part of a beautiful nature reserve and holiday complex, aptly named 'Fishponds'.

Two miles away from Dunkeswell Abbey lies Dunkeswell village itself, with its church of St Nicholas, rebuilt in 1868 but with a Norman font, one of the oldest in Devon, carved with crude figures, among them the unlikely figure of an elephant. The tower was rebuilt yet again after the Second World War and now houses six bells which are regularly rung.

Off the road to Honiton lies Wolford, once the home of John Graves Simcoe, the first Lieutenant Governor of the province of Upper Canada. He purchased the estate, which then included much of the village, in 1784. In 1966 the chapel was given to the State of Ontario by its owner and it is now maintained by the John Graves Simcoe Memorial Trust, and visited by many Canadians each year.

Those who return to Dunkeswell now find a changing and expanding village. Although the centre is essentially the same, an explosion of new building on the outskirts will quadruple the population. This promises the return of a village shop, a doctors' surgery, maybe even a school and a bus, and the village is trying to absorb and welcome the influx of new residents just as it did the Americans in the 1940s.

Some things don't change however. In 1953 the old custom of 'Old Twelfie' was revived and it continues to this day. On Twelfth Night, a group of wassailers go from house to house singing a traditional Wassail Song in return for food, drink or money. The evening's revelries end with the wassailers conducting a midnight ceremony of chasing off the evil spirits from the apple trees to ensure a good crop.

Dunsford 🦋

Dunsford is in the lovely Teign valley between Exeter and Moretonhampstead, within the Dartmoor National Park, and is surrounded by wooded hills and rolling farmland sweeping down to the river.

Dunsford's name has varied only slightly. Its origin, Dunns' (ie cattle) ford, refers to cattle summered on the moor which were brought down for fattening, over the river where stepping stones mark the old ford. Dunsford had an annual cattle fair until at least 1930.

A church was dedicated here in 1261 but only fragments remain. The present church, St Mary's, was completed by 1455 and restored between 1840–50. It is reached by steep steps and a cobbled path, and its square granite tower stands high above the houses – mostly of cob, and many still thatched. There is a piece of ancient cross in the churchyard, which was moved there after an observant visitor spotted it in the village street being used as a wheelstop. It is thought to have stood at St Thomas's Cross, where the Cheriton Bishop road leaves Dunsford.

The church has some ancient glass, and an impressive Jacobean monument (1610) to Sir Thomas and Lady Ursula Fulford, in the 'Fulford pew'. The manor of Dunsford was purchased by the Fulfords in 1544, after the Dissolution of the Monasteries. The family still lives at Great Fulford, a majestic Elizabethan house built around a square courtyard and set amid parkland.

Dunsford has its own school, which adds much to the life of the village. There is also a village hall, post office and shop, surgery, garage and two pubs. The Royal Oak is in the village centre, the other at Steps Bridge, the famous beauty spot alongside the river Teign. This nature reserve, in Dunsford and Meadhaydown Woods, is run by the Devon Trust for Nature Conservation, and owned by the National Trust. Wild daffodils bloom in their thousands each spring.

In 1973, eight bungalows were built for elderly residents, and there has been other building since – generally well integrated – which has helped school numbers and the village's social activities. About 500 people over 18 live in Dunsford now, and there are about 250 houses in the parish. Development has altered the proportion of residents involved in agriculture and local industry, though the area around still largely depends on mixed farming. The iron mill is now also a museum, though some specialist agricultural tools are still made there, for thatching for example. The handsome water-wheel driven from the leat has been restored. This leat also runs under the small Baptist chapel; a trap door gives access to it, as it was used for baptism.

East Allington ❧

East Allington is off the beaten track and far removed from the mainstream of local and national events. During the Saxon period Aetha was the major landowner, in the northern part of the parish to which he gave his name, Aetha's tun. In the Domesday Book it was recorded as Alintona.

The plague, which in the 14th century decimated so many towns, villages and hamlets, also took its toll in Alintona, which by default allowed the de Faleputtes to move into the manor house. Their estate and fortune increased and by the 15th century the de Faleputtes were considered wealthy enough to attract in marriage the son of the prestigious Fortescue family. The Fortescues remained as lords of the manor until the middle of the 19th century.

The village cottages spread southwards along the valley floor from Fallapit House. After the Reformation the church of St Andrew was built on the far hillside of the valley. Before long a cluster of cottages appeared around the church and as the old ones around Fallapit crumbled a new village nucleus emerged.

In the middle of the 19th century the Fortescues sold their estate in East Allington to William Cubitt (later Lord Ashcombe), the celebrated architect and builder. He enhanced his manor house, and at his own expense rebuilt and refurbished the church to save it from disintegration. Next he systematically demolished older cob dwellings and rebuilt the present terraced cottages. It was during this period that Allington received the prefix 'East'.

East Allington was one of the six villages evacuated during the Second World War to enable the Allied Forces to practise for a final invasion of Europe, which it was hoped would finally turn the tide towards victory. Luckily, being on the outskirts of the D-Day rehearsal area, most of the houses were relatively undamaged and the residents of the parish were able to return after a period of seven months.

From time immemorial the village has been predominantly agricultural. Only in recent years have the inhabitants moved away from the land to lighter, better paid, jobs in the surrounding local towns. As more and more work on the farms is done by machinery even less of the population will earn their living from the land. The large number of new houses that have already been built, and many more planned for the future, will inevitably turn East Allington from a rural agricultural village into a dormitory for the nearby towns.

East Budleigh ✥

East Budleigh is an ancient village, settled by Saxon invaders in around AD 700. It became known as East Budleigh to distinguish it from West Budleigh, the name once given to an area between Tiverton and Crediton. Budleigh Salterton, which lies two miles south-west on the coast, was part of East Budleigh parish until 1894. Today East Budleigh has a population of about 800.

The village is dominated by All Saints' church, which stands at the top of the High Street. Visitors to the church notice especially the beautiful carved pew ends which date from Tudor times. One of these pew ends bears the coat of arms of Sir Walter Raleigh, East Budleigh's most famous son. He was born at Hayes Barton, a fine Tudor farmhouse in Hayes Lane, about a mile from the village, and is said to have been educated at the ancient cob house, now called Vicar's Mead (also in Hayes Lane, near the car park) which was formerly the vicarage.

On the walls of All Saints' church can be seen several memorials to the Rev Ambrose Stapleton and his family. He was vicar here for no less than 58 years, from 1794 to 1852! He was a popular preacher and a kindly man who helped the poor, but he is chiefly remembered for his involvement in the smuggling trade, reputedly allowing his vicarage to be used for hiding barrels of brandy.

On 1st November, All Saints Day, there is much excitement in the churchyard when, from the roof of the church, the vicar and sexton throw buns down to the schoolchildren. This unusual custom is said to commemorate the landing of that Protestant hero William of Orange at Torbay in November 1688.

A more recent annual event is Raleigh Sunday. In alternate years in July, East Budleigh and HMS *Raleigh* (the Royal Navy training centre at Torpoint, near Plymouth) visit each other. When it is East Budleigh's turn to be the host there is a church service, followed by lunch in the village hall, with games and sports in the afternoon.

Below the church, the High Street with its cob houses, many with thatched roofs, runs down to the Budleigh brook. This winds its way through the lower part of the village past the village hall, behind the post office, the school and the gardens' of the Middle Street houses. It reappears in Lower Budleigh to flow alongside the road past the Rolle Arms, under the main highway A376, and on to the river Otter. In Lower Budleigh many attractive little bridges cross the brook to reach the houses on the other side.

At the north-eastern end of the village at the end of Vicarage Road stands Salem chapel, built in 1719 by nonconformist Congregationalists. It is thought to be the only cubiform chapel of that period still in use as a place of worship in the country and is now used by the Church of the Assemblies of God.

Since 1945 there has been considerable new building in the village, largely of bungalows which are popular with the many older people who have chosen to make East Budleigh home in their retirement. Most of these houses are on higher ground and have fine views of Woodbury Common.

East & West Putford 🌿

An unspoilt, widely scattered, mainly dairy farming community in north-west Devon, Putford nestles in a wooded valley, almost equidistant from the towns of Holsworthy and Bideford. The parish is divided into East and West by the infant river Torridge and consists of the hamlets of Colscott, Sessacott, Thriverton and Wedfield, the bartons of Cory, Field Irish and Julians, Churston Manor, a number of charming white and stone-built cottages, several with traditional thatched roofs, a medieval church and a Methodist chapel. Both parishes were in existence in 1086 and are recorded in the Domesday Book as Poteforda and Potiforda.

In the centre of a cluster of mature trees stands the beautiful, grey stone 14th century church of St Stephen. It was fortunate in managing to avoid the church restorers of the 19th century. The original oak beams with carved wooden heads, are in the north transept ceiling and there is a stoup or stone bowl which, in pre-Reformation times, would have held holy water. The tower once contained three bells, two of which were dated 1713 and 1729. These have been re-cast in recent years to make the current peal of six bells.

Other notable properties in the parish are Churston Manor, built by

Sir Nicholas Prideaux on land purchased from the Vigures family in the late 16th century, and Cory Barton. Cory is, in all probability, the oldest house in the area. Built around 1485, it spans some 500 years and is still in use as a working farm.

The inhabitants of the parish, whilst widespread and few in number, are friendly and, as is to be expected in a rural area, mutually supportive. Sport, of course, plays an active part in Putford's social life. The skittle alley supports six (four men's and two ladies') teams to do battle in the local North Devon leagues, and there are also two football teams in the area.

East & West Worlington 🐝

Attractively situated on south-facing hillsides to the north of the Little Dart river, the two villages form the centre of the parishes of East and West Worlington. Until 1885, when they were united for civil purposes, West Worlington was in Chulmleigh and East in Witheridge Hundreds.

Many of the houses are still thatched and each village has its own, originally 14th century church, both dedicated to St Mary. East church was extensively restored in the 19th century by the Earl of Portsmouth, but West church has retained many of its Elizabethan characteristics, including its crooked spire, originally of oak shingles. Sadly, in 1976 it was struck by lightning and severely damaged by fire, but thanks to much local generosity, it was restored in 1977.

In the west of the parish was Affeton, formerly a separate parish. The original castle was built of Drayford stone (from a small hamlet to the east). By the 15th century the village and church at Affeton had gone, probably due to the plague. Affeton Castle was sacked three times during the Civil War in the 1640s and only the gatehouse remains as the home of the Stucley family.

Many of the farms have long lanes because, during the Napoleonic Wars, new, straight roads were cut to take out timber for the ships needed to fight 'Boney' and the old roads were used less and allowed to degenerate into farm lanes. As in so many rural areas the population has decreased from over 700 in the 18th/19th centuries to about 250 in 1989. At one time the thriving community consisted of many rural occupations, including cobblers, blacksmiths, thatchers and others. The only pub, the Stucley Arms, closed in the 1930s. Opposite it stood the parish poor houses, which also housed the dame school (until 1875), a library and a cheese-making school for the local girls.

Now at East Worlington, the old tithe barn has become the parish hall, and the elementary school, built to replace the dame school, is a lively primary school, with a playgroup. Also in East village there is a small shop and post office, and the recently restored parish pump. There are two Methodist chapels at each end of the parish, which were built in the 18th century.

As yet, although there are some holiday cottages and a caravan park, the parishes are still predominantly engaged in farming, and continue to maintain their rural charm.

Exbourne 🌿

It is easy to pass by Exbourne without exploring it as it lies just off the A3072. Its leafy and compact appearance is evident on the skyline driving from Sampford Courtenay towards Hatherleigh.

St Mary's church is the dominant feature and parts of it date back to the 13th century. It is mainly 15th century and was extensively restored by the Victorians. The church has a good peal of bells, restored in 1931, and a group of village bell-ringers has started to ring these again.

Just past the church in the churchyard are the remains of the old almshouses, previously the church house. The stone from these was used to build Exbourne school. This fortunately is still thriving and is one of the smallest schools in the county.

The Methodist church at the lower end of the village was built in 1932 on the site of the former Lethbridge Arms, destroyed earlier in a terrible fire. This replaced the Bible Christian chapel in the High Street, now converted to a house.

To the east of the church is the manor house, built in early Victorian times on the site of the ancient Saxon manor. This at one time owned a substantial amount of land in the parish but the estate was finally broken up following the death of Sir Roper Lethbridge in 1919. The manor garden is, however, still the perfect setting for the church fete.

The old Holmeswell pump, restored to commemorate the Queen's Silver Jubilee in 1977 is located in the road below the church. This apparently provided the best water in the village, although there were several other wells. It is situated next to the old wheelwright's shop, where electricity was first generated in the 1920s.

It is difficult to compare the quietness of Exbourne today with the hustle and bustle of earlier years when it was more self-sufficient. In 1851 there were three grocers, three butchers, a poultry dealer, three bakers, a

Exbourne village

post-master, two innkeepers, plus local craftsmen and farmers. Now there is just one pub, a post office and garage. Guy's Bakery in the Square, which baked excellent bread and cakes, sadly closed in 1982, having operated since the 19th century.

Many properties were originally thatched and there were seven resident thatchers in 1851. A lot of the cottages have subsequently been reroofed in slate.

Exminster 🌿

Exminster, as its name – the church beside the Exe – suggests, was once a secluded little hamlet. It is situated on the west bank of the broadening estuary between the historic City of Exeter, four miles to the north, and the popular coastal resort of Dawlish, eight miles to the south. In 1984 the village was bypassed by the A379 and this is named Sannerville Way, after the village near Caen in Normandy, with which it is 'twinned'.

It remained a comparatively small village until the late 1950s when a certain amount of residential development commenced – Glebelands, Gissons, Westfield and Crockwells.

The County Structure Plan makes provision for a further 500 houses into the 1990s, some being built on the hospital land which became available when the Exe Vale hospital closed in June 1987.

The Priests' House is the oldest building in the village. Already in existence in 1583 and originally the vicarage, it was used until 1702 when the second vicarage (The Manor) was built. The present vicarage was built in 1962.

The church, parts of which date back to the 13th century, is dedicated to St Martin. Most of what is seen now is 15th/16th century.

A house stood on the site of Church Stile, belonging to Jane Wills, in 1583. A later owner, Margaret Taverner, left £3,000 in her will of 1629 to the poor of the village for 2,900 years. In 1869 the house was bought for use as an industrial school for delinquent boys, sold in 1954 and divided into flats.

The almshouses were described in a deed of 1702 as a church house for the accommodation of paupers. The adjoining houses were also church property. These are now privately owned, being Days House, the Almshouses, Rose Cottage, and Clematis Cottage which has an interesting plaque referring to an unrecognised school run by an ex-head of the village school.

The Turf Hotel was built in 1829 when the canal was extended to five miles in length with a basin and tidal lock. It was the only pub in England with no road access and beer was delivered by boat.

Frogmore & Sherford 🌿

Frogmore lies on the road between Kingsbridge and Torcross. You don't really notice the village as you dodge and weave down the busy road. But if you turn right, over the bridge, and look down the creek, a sense of peace and well-being returns.

When the tide is in, boats and swans bob up and down on the water. It is beautiful. While sitting on the bench here, close your eyes and imagine how it used to be – a small port, barges coming and going, coal wharves and stores, limekilns and a blacksmith's forge.

Sherford is found by taking the first turning left, out of Frogmore. The village, mentioned in the Domesday Book, lies one mile up this quiet lane. The lane itself is a ribbon of history – on the left of the valley, woods hide the long disused quarries which provided building stone for farms, cottages, houses and the church. They are now a home for an abundance of wildlife.

Once, this valley would have been clothed in cider apple blossom. Only at Stancombe, an historic Manor house (now an award winning holiday cottage complex), do you find a recently planted orchard. Cider is made and sold here in the renovated Pound House.

Some farm buildings have been very carefully converted – one houses the workshops of a wooden toy and plastic table giftware maker, and further along, a round ended building perilously perching on a high bank beside the road was a pound house, where some locals remember a donkey going round and round crushing the apples. Now, it is a cabinet and chair maker's workshop.

The school, built in 1879 for £400 and closed in 1933, is now a private house. Then, you enter the centre of the village where once was found The Malt Scoop pub, the blacksmith's, the poorhouse, the pound for stray animals and a bakery – all private houses now. The church alone stands relatively unaltered.

Its Rood Screen was removed for safe keeping during the evacuation of this area in the Second World War. While being renovated before replacement, the painted figures of apostles were found under the whitewash.

The two villages have a few real local families left. Recently they shared their memories, old photographs and anecdotes, and allowed photographs to be taken of sites and things of interest for an exhibition in the village hall. Locals, newcomers and visitors remembered or got a glimpse of what village life was like, and this is now a start of a village archive.

Georgeham 🦚

Georgeham, a village of around 600 inhabitants, lies in a gap in the hills which rise steeply from the sea behind Baggy Point, eight miles from Barnstaple and one and a half miles from the North Devon coast with its lovely sandy beaches. It is an ancient village, mentioned in the Domesday Book, the name Hama meaning settlement or water meadow.

The 13th century church and many of the original thatched cottages are clustered around the stream which runs through the valley and here there has been virtually no new building for centuries. George was added to the name following the dedication of the church to St George, but even today the village is commonly known as Ham.

The 14th century square tower now houses eight bells which are regularly pealed by a team of local ringers. In the tranquillity of the churchyard is the headstone to Sergeant John Hill, who fought at the battle of Waterloo.

The village has been home to many authors including Henry Williamson, whose most widely known work is *Tarka the Otter*. The Henry Williamson Society was formed in 1980 following his death and members, now numbering 500, return to the village every year to visit the timber writing hut he built for himself at Ox Cross. The author is buried in the churchyard just above Skirr Cottage, where he lived for several years.

Stories of the past abound in the village. HMS *Weazle*, an anti-smuggling vessel, was wrecked off Baggy Point in 1799 and nine of her crew and one woman passenger are buried in the churchyard. A stone by the lychgate remembers PC Creech, the village constable who was stabbed by a drunk outside one of the local pubs, at the end of the last century. The murderer succumbed to his drinking and died on the day he was due to be tried in Exeter.

Georgeham has a thriving village school, a general store with post office, a much used village hall, a Baptist church and two public houses. Many traditions remain, two of which are centred around the marriage of local girls. A shotgun is fired before the bride leaves her home to ward away evil spirits. After the ceremony there is no way from the church until her groom has paid a ransom to local farmers, who place a rope across the road and stay there until the money is handed over.

Gittisham 🦢

The first written reference to the village is in the Domesday Book, where it is spelt Gidesham.

The Bronze Age people came from far and wide to bury their dead on Gittisham Hill, one of the largest Bronze Age burial areas in Devon.

Rev Richard Polewhele in his history of Devon published in 1797 describes Gittisham as follows: 'The village is delightfully situated and is esteemed the cleanliest in the county. It is not large, but consists of many trim cottages, and the people are remarkably neat in their houses and themselves.'

Sir Nicholas Putt bought Combe, the largest manor in the village in 1614. He was a Sheriff of Devon and an active loyalist. In 1644 a party of Cromwell's soldiers came to the village to arrest him. They smashed everything in the church that they considered Popish including the statue of St Michael which is known to have been there, and they broke the stained glass out of the windows. Some of these fragments came to light in a box in the timber yard at the beginning of this century and were rescued by Mrs Marker and set in the north east window of the church. Sir Nicholas Putt was ill in bed at the time of his arrest but was carried off to London. This was too much for him and he died en route at Axminster.

On Shrove Tuesday all the village children go Tiptoeing. They visit all the houses in turn, knocking on the door and singing: 'Tip tip toe, tip tip toe. Please for a penny and away we'll go.' It is not known when this custom started.

Joanna Southcott, the 'prophetess', was born in the village in about 1750 and the Rev Marker gave her extra schooling realising the child was exceptional.

The Tom Putt apple, named after Thomas Putt (1722–87), a barrister who perfected it, is still cultivated in the village.

Within living memory there was a cobbler, a wheelwright, a coffin maker and a blacksmith in the village and earlier a candle maker. He is commemorated in the name Tommy Wax.

Goodleigh

Today's mingling of thick-walled, 16th century cob cottages, opening directly onto the main street, and the new, white-walled houses set discreetly back behind green hedges, shows Goodleigh's willingness to yield to outside influences, yet still retain its own individual character. This happy, casual, friendly mix forms the fabric of Goodleigh village life. It is in no way a bustling village but, like a beehive, it hums with activity beneath the surface.

In essence Goodleigh has changed little since its early beginnings. Arable and dairy farming and grazing land for sheep have been predominant, but apple, and more especially cherry, orchards brought unlikely fame to Goodleigh until the 19th century. In the 16th century, the vast mazzard orchards, with their luscious, black cherries, brought villagers flocking from miles around to enjoy the harvest of fruit and the merrymaking that followed. The high fertility of Goodleigh land, which made its orchards famous, was probably due to the numerous springs which fed the land and also a lake, today no more than a boggy hollow. This lake must have been a boon for the vast majority, though not for the local miscreants who found themselves receiving more than their fair share of its contents, on the end of the ducking stool!

Nestling in the folds of sheep-strewn hills, 'up hill and down dale' would be an accurate description of Goodleigh, with land falling away sharply on its southern side and rising up suddenly and dramatically on its 'northern face' up which, Sherpa-like, worshippers climb to the lovely old church of St Gregory. Here, like a guard, it has stood for 700 years.

Close by the church is the old schoolhouse, where today's young children are still taught, just as their parents and grandparents were before them.

Skittles is a game that remains popular, with several teams and two skittle alleys to cater to demand. One of these alleys is an added attraction at the New Inn, Goodleigh's only pub, and the other is at the rear of the village hall, a light, airy building, of which Goodleigh is rightly proud.

Peter Newell, well-known local artist and sculptor, has his studio here and his classes, in both painting and sculpture, have added an extra depth and dimension to the village.

There is no self-conscious, picture postcard prettiness about Goodleigh, but an honest and appealing simplicity whose beauty lies in its landscape, and the undulations of which the houses seem to form a natural part, like the outcrops of stone seen on a hillside.

Great Torrington 🌿

Approaching Great Torrington on the main Exeter road, one sees the spire of the parish church of St Michael and All Angels towering over the town, and the steep side of Castle Hill in spring ablaze with yellow gorse bushes and then, in June, becoming carpeted with pale green bracken.

The place itself is truly ancient, having merited an entry in the Domesday survey in 1086. It also took an active part in the Civil War, when the church was blown up in 1645 with 200 Royalist prisoners inside. One of the oldest public houses, The Black Horse, was supposed to be where General Fairfax was housed during his campaign. Other ancient buildings include Palmer House, where a Mrs Palmer, sister of Sir Joshua Reynolds lived, and where he often visited in company with his friend Samuel Johnson.

Torrington is fortunate in being surrounded on three sides by common land, which was given to the town in the 12th century and was subsequently protected by Act of Parliament in 1889. This common land adds a beauty to the town with its 365 acres and 20 miles of footpaths, topped by a well placed golf course, and with the river Torridge wending its leisurely way below the town, past the Dairy Crest factory and so on to Bideford.

At one time several men were employed at the Marland Brick and Clay Works while their wives would be employed at home in the glove-making trade, a much needed boost to the weekly wage. The machines, treadle type, were provided by the factories, of which there were three in the town at one time, employing in excess of 600 workers. It has been known for mother to be using the treadle with one end of a rope tied to it, with the other end attached to a cradle to keep baby quiet! With the more general use of electricity small electric motors were fixed to the treadles making the whole operation much easier.

Apart from the Milk Marketing Board's Dairy Crest factory and glove-making, a terrific boost was given to the town when Dartington Glass decided to come here. The expert Swedes came over and recruited local people to learn the trade, which has grown and flourished, attracting hundreds of visitors over the years.

Halberton 🌿

The large parish of Halberton extends from about two and a half miles east of Tiverton almost to the Somerset border.

The village consists mainly of one long street (Higher Town) with a lane turning off to the church, and Lower Town to the south. These two parts are divided by the mill stream and pond which is said to be supplied with warm water and never freezes. There are a number of interesting houses in the village including The Priory, which is said to have housed a small number of Augustinian monks from about 1154 to the Dissolution of the Monasteries.

The church is dedicated to St Andrew and is built of red sandstone with many characteristics of the Decorated style of the 14th century. There is a Norman font, a richly carved 15th century pulpit and a massive rood screen of the same date.

Quite a long stretch of the Grand Union Canal, goes through the parish, looping north of the village, and the area has been designated a Country Park. Trips on the horse-drawn barges from Tiverton make popular outings.

A quarter of a mile from the village is the now defunct single-track railway, closed in the 1960s and which, until 1924, was used for carrying limestone and sandstone from the quarries at Holcombe Rogus and Westleigh to Tiverton.

Between 1862 and 1872, Halberton had an illustrious vicar, Canon Edward Girdlestone, who became known nationally because of his fight for better conditions for farm workers. Eventually the Canon organised the migration of between 400 and 500 local people – a good many of them with families – to other parts of the country where better paid work was available.

More recently, W.T.C (Tommy) Shapland was a stained glass artist of considerable note, having been responsible for the great west window in Chester Cathedral, some windows at Southwark and Peterborough Cathedrals, and many churches throughout Britain and overseas. He died at the age of 47 in 1972.

At the end of the last century, when the public houses were open all day, some of the more well-to-do villagers drank large quantities of beer and whisky (then 3/6d a bottle). One 'hostess' of the New Inn was in the habit of reading a chapter from the Bible to her customers on a Sunday evening, presumably to produce a sobering effect!

In 1907 the Parish Council unanimously passed a resolution protesting against the sale of Sunday newspapers in the village as having 'a bad and pernicious influence upon public morality, and as affecting the moral tone of the rising generations'.

In the same year expressions of gratitude were being made about the local policeman, PC Tooze, for the energy he had shown when dealing with tramps who, instead of pestering for food and money as before, hurried through Halberton at 5 miles an hour as if afraid of the plague. Among the tramping fraternity PC Tooze was known as 'The Body-snatcher'!

Harbertonford

To most people the village of Harbertonford is a garage and a nasty bend on the A381 between Totnes and Dartmouth or Kingsbridge. Those who slow down a little (and the villagers would appreciate that!) might glimpse the church, the mill, and the ford area from which the village derives its name.

Originally the village was just a part of the parish of Harberton, but came into its own when the river provided power for the mills which grew up along its banks. It was really put on the map when the 'new' road from Totnes to Kingsbridge was built, including the bridge which replaced the ford as the means of crossing the river.

The imposing building behind the church was until 1956 a woollen mill which employed in its heyday around 100 men, women and children. It has been reduced in size in recent years and now awaits the planners' decisions as to its future. Of the other mills only a couple survive. Hill mill, which was an edge tool works about a mile upstream, is now a tranquil restaurant and hotel, and the other, Crowdie mill, has been completely renovated and once more produces stoneground flour and can be seen working.

The church and the old school buildings stand nearly opposite one another on either side of the main road. The school was built in 1848 and was used also as a place for worship prior to the construction of the church in 1859. After a brief spell as a pottery the old school buildings have been converted into a home – the old clock has been preserved, and is lovingly wound to keep good time.

Harbertonford bridge

Over the last decade or so the village has seen a lot of changes with cottages being renovated and modernised yet for the most part still keeping their character. One area of new homes was named Packs Close in memory of the gentleman who kept his threshing machine on the land for many years earlier this century. The Maltster's Arms really was owned and run in its early days by a maltster, and Brewery Cottage was the site of a thriving brewery which served several villages. In spite of its strong links with the past – a wander around the church and its graveyard will reveal many names still represented in the village today – the village is alive. It has two shops, one including a post office, and a well known restaurant. The old stepping stones which formed the original ford have long since gone and in recent years the area around has been grassed to provide a recreational area used by residents and visitors alike.

Harracott ❧

Harracott is a small hamlet in the parish of Tawstock approximately one mile inland from the A377 Barnstaple to Exeter road, about five miles from Barnstaple. The main cottages and two of the farms are situated between two sets of crossroads. What was once a blacksmith's shop is now a car repair workshop. The old inn where wrestling took place many years ago is now a thatched residence by the name of 'Signpost Cottage'. There is no existing shop but a telephone kiosk remains in working order.

Set apart from the main part of the hamlet is Trinity church, a chapel of ease to Tawstock St Peter's which was built by the late Rev Sir H B Wrey 9th Bart MA, rector in 1844 but was sadly closed in the 1960s and has since been converted to a dwelling, the outside appearance remaining the same. The organ, however, was shipped to Lundy Island and installed in their church.

Opposite the church is a bungalow which was originally built as a school in 1860 for 60 children. To the south side of the church is a hall given to the village by a member of the Wreford family as a men's reading room, but which in recent years has become the village hall. An open round house exists in the village where cattle feed and 'street lighting' now exists, which keeps the through traffic's speed down to 30 mph. Villagers not working on the land or retired commute to Barnstaple.

Hawkchurch

The village, some 500 ft above sea level, stands on the eastward banks of the river Axe. The earliest recorded mentions of Hawkchurch, which was originally in Dorset, are in the history and records of Cerne Abbey.

The rectory house as we know it today replaced a much older thatched building. As a young man, the writer Thomas Hardy was apprenticed to a firm of Weymouth architects and he was engaged in overseeing the building. His notes as to how the drains were to be laid and various comments as the work progressed make interesting reading – finally he says 'Rector well satisfied'.

Some idea of the population at the time of high production and labour intensive periods was shown by an 1801 census – 124 houses were occupied by 150 families with a total population of 679, 117 being employed in agriculture and 108 in trade manufactures. Over the years the population fell.

The church was intensively repaired and parts rebuilt in the years 1860–62. Thomas Hardy was again employed by the architects. Many traces of Norman–Saxon work were retained with a new chancel added. There are ancient carvings on the bases and capitals of the pillars.

The main business of the village is still agriculture, with a flourishing corn merchants and a firm which specialises in farm buildings and roadways etc.

In the past many people were engaged in the growing of flax, making of twine and rope spinning. An ancient leather-bound book shows cottages (now gone) in the Langmoor area, each with its own twine-spinning walk and pits for retting the flax.

There were three wheelwrights, four blacksmiths, nine cordwainers, two thatchers, three butchers, a tailor, a potter, a carpenter, two clothiers, two flax dressers, a mason, a miller, three bakers, a mariner, and seven twine spinners. There was once a brickworks, a tile and pipeworks on Wyld Court, a tucking mill, a dye works, and a tannery. A table tomb in the churchyard records an Aaron Stark, 'Tobacconist of this Parish'. Tobacco was reputedly grown here.

The village street cottages and the church walls were planted with climbing roses by the Rev John Going at his own expense – hence its name 'the Village of Roses'. The Rose window behind the font is his memorial.

Haytor Vale 🌿

Haytor Rocks can be seen from as far afield as Torquay and Dartmouth. They do not form the highest tor on Dartmoor but are certainly the best known.

Not so well known is the village of Haytor Vale, lying in a valley below the Rocks and Haytor Down. A survey in 1566 refers to the hamlet as 'Idetor', a name subsequently corrupted to 'Hey Tor' or 'High Tor'. The village belongs to the large parish of Ilsington, second only in size to Lydford in the County of Devon.

Haytor Vale did not become a village until the early part of the 19th century. There are records, however, of a few farms in the area from the 13th century, most of them still in existence today. One of the attractions for present day visitors to the area are the quarry remains and the granite railway on Haytor Down. It was this industry that was direcly responsible for the development of the village.

At one time, labourers at the quarry lived in huts in the shadow of its workings but George Templer of Stover, who opened up the quarries in 1819, saw the need for better living conditions for the men and built a row of cottages and an inn for them in what is now the Vale. Two families lived in each cottage, the tenants in the front half paying 1s/6d per week and the tenants in the back half paying 1s/3d!

The quarries did not prosper after 1860 and were last worked in 1919 when granite was provided for the Exeter war memorial. During the 19th century an iron mine was worked in the Vale and its remains are still to be seen by any visitor straying beyond the main lanes of the village. Indeed some of the houses in the area are built over mining remains.

Over recent years the village has grown and there are now 80 houses in its environs though a casual visitor would be hard put to it to find them all, well hidden as they are in the surrounding countryside.

There are also four hotels in the village, three of them of some historical interest. The Bel Alp, now a country house hotel, was built early in the 20th century for Dame Violet Wills, the tobacco heiress. The Moorland Hotel, built on the site of small tea rooms, became famous for its association with Agatha Christie. *The Mysterious Affair at Styles* was one of the novels she wrote whilst holidaying there. It burned down in 1970 but was finally rebuilt and reopened in 1984. It now also houses a flourishing craft centre.

The Rock hostelry, originally built for the convenience of the quarrymen, has won a 'Pub of the Year' award and now attracts visitors from all areas.

Heanton Punchardon 🌿

Heanton Punchardon in North Devon is on the seaward end of a sharp east–west ridge.

Heanton's church, St Augustine's, is 15th/16th century with a fine tower, and has many monuments to the Basset family who lived at Heanton Court by the river Taw from the 15th to the early part of the 19th century. Heanton Court, partly demolished to build Watermouth Castle, is now a public house.

Wrafton, also part of the parish, has a long history of farming and the sea. Ships would bring limestone from the island of Caldy in South Wales to the quay, where there were three lime-kilns in operation.

Wrafton boasts a famous thatched public house, The Williams Arms (named after a local landowner) dating back to the 16th century.

In Heanton churchyard lies the grave of Edward Capern, the 'Postman Poet', who was born at Tiverton on 21st January 1819 and who died on 4th June 1894 at Brookdale, Wrafton Road, Braunton (which is now known as Capern House).

Royal Air Force Chivenor is situated in the parish and the church commands an interesting view over the 700 acres of airfield.

The village of Chivenor is situated in the heart of the station and provides a focus for the many community activities of the RAF inhabitants. The Fiddler's Green is a delightful old farmhouse which has been converted into a pub, community centre, playgroup and sports centre. Next door are a paddock and stables which provide room for several horses. Various other old farmhouses in the road provide character for what is essentially a modern development, although the RAF has been at Chivenor since 1940. It was in those days known as Barnstaple Airport and operated civil flights to Lundy, the Channel Islands, Bristol and Cardiff.

RAF Chivenor's role is to train pilots in the art of air combat and ground attack, using the Hawk TMK1 and TMK1A aircraft. In addition to its two squadrons of Hawks (Nos 63 and 151) it has a small flight of two Search and Rescue Helicopters which are very active around the Devon coast and over the moors. The RAF is very popular locally because of the large amount of community work undertaken by RAF Chivenor. In 1988 it raised over £35,000 for charity, and the mere presence of the 'North Devon Air Force' gives an annual boost to the local economy of around £10 million.

Hennock 🦜

Hennock, a parish and a village, has a population of about 230 and is situated on a hill 600 ft above sea level overlooking the beautiful Teign valley, close to the Kennick and Tottiford reservoirs, a local beauty spot.

Entering the village at Five Lanes, a green lane leads from this junction to an ancient beacon at Bottor Rock, a one-time Bronze Age settlement.

The village shop/community post office was built in the 1870s by a Matthias Joll. He raised the funds to build these premises by selling his drapery wares around the local parishes. Matthias Joll participated greatly in the community and played a clarinet in the parish church before an organ was installed.

In the older part of the village the Palk Arms public house, named after Sir Lawrence Palk, a wealthy landowner of the parish, makes up one side of what was formerly the village square. It was the alehouse and its immediate neighbour 'Union Cottage' was the cider house.

The thatched rectory is of great historical interest, with parts dating back to medieval times. It hides behind a high stone wall, which adjoins a gatehouse and tithe barn which is the village hall.

The parish church of St Mary, built of granite in the 1200s, has its original medieval font and an old oak rood screen depicting the saints, one of the most beautiful screens in Devon. A flower festival is held on alternate years within the church.

Past the parish church is a row of cottages, some of which once housed miners, and 'Longlands', a listed ancient building mentioned in the Domesday Book. This was formerly a farmstead, but is today a Field Study Centre. Just above Longlands is the Wesleyan chapel, once used as a light industrial unit but now a private home.

The character of this end of the village altered when rows of cottages, built for the mining boom, were cleared to make way for new housing built in the 1950s.

Lead, silver, copper, tin and iron ore mines were formerly worked in the parish. The mining industry had a stimulating effect on the village with rapid population growth in the years of the mining boom. Between 1801 and 1831 the population of Hennock increased from 537 to 747 and by 1861 with the peak of the mining industry, it rose to 1,004. By 1891 there was a little mining of iron at Great Rock but by then the population had dropped to 685. Great Rock Mine, a micaceous haematite mine, was acquired by Ferrubran Manufacturing Co in 1902, in whose hands it remained until its closure in 1969.

Teign Village, lying below Hennock, was built in the early 1900s by the Teign Valley Granite Co to accommodate the workers in the local quarry.

Hennock is once again a quiet agricultural area, with no real industry apart from a quarry and concrete works near Trusham. Many of the present inhabitants commute to Exeter, Newton Abbot and Heathfield to work.

Holcombe Rogus ✁

Holcombe has its mention in the Domesday Book, when it had 1,000 acres and was worth £10. Several of the surrounding farms are still known by their Saxon names – Freathingcott, Kytton, Turnham – but there is little else to remind us today of those early times.

The present small Perpendicular church was built mainly by the succeeding lords of the manor, the Bluetts. They have their family chapel there, with ornate alabaster and marble effigies and their coats of arms. They also built much of Holcombe Court, a fine Tudor country house which lies in its walled grounds in the lea of a wooded hill commanding the village.

A great deal of the village retains the look it had throughout their days. There are quiet hints of history – the Court has carving done by Spanish prisoners from the Armada, an ancient courtroom, and a nebulous ghost which worried the American servicemen billeted there during the Second World War. The large Court Pew in the church was carved by Dutch refugees in the 17th century. The old Priest House in the Court grounds has been fully restored by the Landmark Trust. The long tenure of the Bluetts lasted until the mid 19th century.

Holcombe Rogus was never a large village, the present population of about 490 is much the same as it was in Tudor times. The Industrial Revolution brought a sudden increase in the early 19th century, when the long-standing chair industry in the village reached its peak, with over 5,000 chairs a week being completed. These chairs were famous over the West Country and were carried by the new railway. The Grand Western Canal was started at Holcombe, and the stretch from here to Tiverton was in use carrying limestone for some years. This length is now a Countryside Park and its beauty and tranquillity can be enjoyed by everyone. The nearby quarries are flourishing still.

The village has moved gracefully into the 20th century. It has a thriving school and village amenities. Though the agricultural background is still strong, residents now come from different places and have different occupations, but there is still a continuing sense of identity and comradeship – and it has won the Best Kept Village Competition for small villages for four years running!

Holne 🦋

Holne may be reached by a beautiful road from the A38 at Ashburton, or by the road over the moor from Tavistock through Hexworthy; worth sampling in summer, but not recommended in winter, as Dartmoor fog and snow must be respected. The village itself is compact, but the parish boundaries are wide, from the river Dart and Hembury Castle, to way out across the moor, including Venford reservoir.

The church of St Mary was mentioned in the 13th century and there would have been a settlement here much earlier, as tin and copper were 'streamed' in the vicinity. Holne would have provided food and shelter for travellers on the packhorse tracks from Bronze Age times.

As is customary in many moorside villages, there is an inn, The Church House, beside the church, to provide for those attending services whose farms were miles from Holne. Built at much the same time as the enlargement of the church, it now provides food, drink and shelter for inhabitants and visitors. There is also Holne Chase Hotel, in a beautiful setting by the river, and several houses and farms offer bed and breakfast.

There was a flourishing forge and smithy beside the churchyard, which has a Dole Stone, from which charities were distributed. Now the forge has become a cafe, and sells pictures by local artists and a range of 'tourist' goods. Local needs are served by the village store and post office, a vital service in such an isolated village.

The only other public building is the school, which has become the village hall, housing a variety of activities.

Hembury Castle is an Iron Age fort, made credible by the Dartmoor National Park's partial restoration; and there are interesting hut-circles on Holne Moor, some of which have been excavated and studied. In the next valley, of the Mardle, there was tin and copper mining and a flourishing flint implement 'factory' from even earlier times.

Charles Kingsley was born in the old vicarage in 1819, while his father was curate here for a short time. He is Holne's only claim to a famous inhabitant. No-one could call Holne noteworthy, but it is a charming and friendly place.

Holsworthy ✒

Holsworthy is in the northern part of Devon close to the border with Cornwall, with a market charter going back to the 12th century. Every Wednesday there is an influx of people from the surrounding villages to visit the shops and the street and cattle markets.

Notices on the approaches welcome you to the 'Port Town of Holsworthy'. A thousand years ago it became a Port Town, an enclosed area giving safe 'harbourage' for travellers, their goods and stock.

A major event early in May is the annual Agricultural Show, started in 1886 and still thriving today. At the beginning of July there is St Peter's Fair. On the eve of the fair the portreeve and the Court Leet meet for a humorous session in the Memorial Hall and then proceed in turn to each of the inns for the ale tasting – an old custom to pronounce the ale good for the fair and to signify this by hanging a branch of ivy over the door.

The Pretty Maid Charity was set up by the Rev Thomas Meyrick who gave money to produce £2.10s.0d annually to be 'given to the young single woman resident in Holsworthy being under 30 years of age and generally esteemed by the young as the most deserving and the most handsome and most noted for her quietness and attendance at church'. Another charity – Specotts Charity – was given by Peter Specott in 1665 to Edmund Prideaux and other trustees to be used for the poor of Holsworthy and Black Torrington. With £180 they bought 16 acres of land and the income from the rent is applied 5/9ths to the poor of Holsworthy and 4/9ths to Black Torrington on the first Monday in the New Year.

The name 'Holsworthy' originated from Harold's Worthy, as it was previously land owned by King Harold. Further royal connections are indicated by the names of several inns – the White Hart, the Crown & Sceptre and the King's Arms. The Earls of Stanhope held the manor of Holsworthy for several centuries and they generously gave the town the recreation ground, the Church school and the Great Bell. The estates round Holsworthy were sold in 1910.

Today, Holsworthy is a bustling town but people rely on their own cars for transport. The railway was opened in 1879 but was closed in the 1960s. There are still two very impressive viaducts on either side of the town. The railway in turn had superseded the canal which was responsible for transporting sand, coal and other freight from Bude Harbour. The sand, being very rich in shell material, was spread on the poor culm measure soils of the area.

The present hospital, still known to many in the town as 'Dawfield', was built in a field owned by a Mr Dawe. It once served as the workhouse. Today it is being replaced by a modern hospital between the industrial estate and North Road.

Hope Cove

Hope Cove is a coastal village, and forms part of Bigbury Bay where ships, for centuries, have sheltered when storms lash the Channel. Indeed, the name Hope comes from the old Icelandic word Hop, meaning bay or inlet. Outer Hope and Inner Hope are united by a road built after the old road fell into the sea. The cliff path, or a walk across the sands, are pleasant alternatives.

From earliest records, the main source of income was fishing. At one time there were huge shoals of mackerel and pilchards to be caught. The first little bay below Bolt Tail is known as Pilchards Cove, no doubt named when there was a flourishing pilchard fleet at Hope Cove. This was disbanded when the pilchards came no more. Today, just a handful of local fishermen take their boats out, mainly for crabs and lobsters, for which the village is famous. They are greatly relished by visitors and locals, and some are sent far afield.

Farming was another means of earning a living, and provided odd jobs for fishermen in the winter when fish were scarce. The fertile red earth sustained cereal and root crops, and grass for the dairy herd, beef cattle and sheep. Seaweed was collected from the shore to be used as fertiliser. Little has changed today, except for modern farming methods and machinery.

There have been many ships wrecked on the rocks at Hope Cove and neighbouring coasts, some very famous ones. These brought to the public eye the exceptional bravery of the Hope Cove lifeboatmen, supported by the coastguard team. Various awards were made to individual members, including one to the father of a long-established village fishing family, who joined the first lifeboat crew at the age of 18, and served for 47 years, until the Lifeboat House closed in 1930.

Near to the Lifeboat House, is a small single-storey building, originally a rest room for the fishermen, known now as the reading room. A daily paper is placed there every day. Opposite, take a step back in time in the little square, with its thatched cottages and cobbles, and small Victorian chapel (Wesleyan). The old barns, once used as a cinema, have now gone, but have been replaced by a family house.

Inner Hope is sheltered by Bolt Tail, a steeply rising promontory, with the outlines of an ancient Iron Age fort still visible. The tail is washed by the sea, and the rocks revealed at its end are said to be the remains of a jetty built by the Danes.

The hub of village life is at Outer Hope. Clustered round an original thatched cottage, are the post office cum general store, two inns, a restaurant and cottages. Seaward is the Shippen, a rock where the outline of gardens is still visible. The beach and harbour, once filled with fishing boats, have few now. Small boats and yachts at holiday time take their place. Hope Cove Weekend is held in August, when stalls and events for all ages raise money for charity.

Landwards on the cliff, tiny St Clement's church looks out to sea, her cross a spiritual guide to mariners. Built as a chapel of rest for older folk, it was later used as a school. A family service is held there every Sunday.

Horrabridge ꧁

The river Walkham runs through the centre of Horrabridge, and has always been the centre of village life. Many hours are spent on the bridge, as it overlooks the salmon leap. Horrabridge is the only village on the banks of the river Walkham, which rises 1,750 ft up on Dartmoor. Horrabridge did not become a parish in its own right until October 1950.

Water was taken from the river in the past for indutrial use. There was a thriving woollen worsted industry in the 1800s, and tin and copper mines using the river were the main reason for the village growth. Horrabridge had two mills (now private houses), the one beside the bridge using the river to drive a water turbine for a DC generator which provided street lamps and light to nearby houses. During the First World War the street lamps were half blacked-out and switched off at 7.30 pm. Nowadays the river is used more for leisure – fishing and swimming and the occasional 'Duck Derby'.

It was in the 16th century that Katherine of Aragon passed through Horrabridge at 16 years of age on her way to meet Henry VII and his eldest son Arthur, with whom a marriage had been arranged. She had landed at Plymouth where the nobility and gentry of the neighbouring counties crowded to do honour to their future queen. She then went on towards London via Horrabridge, Okehampton, Crediton and Exeter.

There is a wide variety of wild life along the river Walkham including kingfishers and herons. Downstream from 'Magpie' or Bedford Bridge there is a beautiful walk through woodlands and open glades where the

Walkham and the river Tavy meet, known as Double Waters. From here the two rivers, now joined, make their way to the Tamar estuary and the sea at Plymouth.

Iddesleigh 🌿

The village stands on a south-facing slope with a fine view of Dartmoor, ten miles to the south. The farmland in the parish is mostly grassland with many hedgerow trees and several acres of deciduous woodland. The scene has changed little in the last 100 years. In common with all rural Devonshire, the population halved between 1850–1950, since then it has remained stable at just under 200.

The parish of 2,900 or so acres is bordered to the south by the river Okement and to the west by the river Torridge. The village is mostly cob and thatch cottages set around the green.

Dominating the western edge of the village is the parish church of St James. The present building dates from the 15th century. Behind the organ is a cross-legged effigy of a Crusader, thought to be of Henry de Sully.

The Rev Jack Russell, the famous hunting parson, who was the originator of the Jack Russell terrier, was curate from 1830 to 1836.

In 1664 Hugh Stafford of Exeter owned land in the parish, as did Sir Francis Northcote. The two families intermarried and for the next

The Duke of York, Iddesleigh

200 years owned 2,000 acres of the parish. Of this lineage Sir Stafford Northcote rose to great eminence and was given a peerage in 1885 after being Foreign Secretary and Chancellor of the Exchequer. Although not residing in the parish he took the title 'The Earl of Iddesleigh' because of the land ownership. He died in 1887 and his family sold most of the farms and land between 1910 and 1919.

The Iddesleigh Men's Friendly Society is one of only two remaining active in Devon. It was founded in 1838 as a means of providing sick pay and funeral benefits long before National Insurance schemes came into being. 'Club Day' is now held on May Day bank holiday. Members are still expected to wear a blue ribbon during the day or pay a fine of 5p for non-compliance.

One aspect of farming life which plays an important part in the community is the Farms for City Children project. This is an educational charity set up in 1973 to give city children direct experience of living and working on a farm. A thousand children a year come from all over England to the pioneer farm at Nethercott House. Nethercott was built in 1871 by William Arnold, one of a family who farmed in the parish for 800 years.

Another large house in the parish is Ash House. The Mallet family lived there for nearly 350 years until 1875. The present owners are co-founders of the Rare Breeds Survival Trust and have set up a centre for endangered breeds of domestic animals. Currently they run the Ashrose Angora Stud of some 500 pedigree goats and a herd of Highland cattle.

Instow 🦞

Instow is situated on the estuary of North Devon's two major rivers, the Taw and Torridge. Instow was mostly developed by 1838. It was a time when sea bathing had become a fashionable health cure and when it was announced in the press that there were newly created baths at Instow, the wealthy were encouraged to visit the new resort.

Since the beginning of this century many changes have been made in Instow. New houses have been built and many of the 'names' of Instow have disappeared, leaving only a few of the original families. Instow was once known as 'baby land' as many hundreds of people came at weekends with their children and during the summer holidays so many people came that the London and South Western Railway had to erect a halt at the sandhills to cope with the crowds. Many of the visitors who were bound for Appledore on the opposite bank of the river disembarked at Instow and continued the journey by ferry. The ferry men waited at the station entrance to ply their trade.

The Yacht Club, formed in 1905 and now housed in the old railway station, has seen many changes. Many years ago, following a disagreement among members, a breakaway club was formed and although both clubs had the same class of boats, the North Devon Club had its boats painted white and the Taw & Torridge Club's boats were painted bright yellow.

The North Devon Cricket Club, founded in 1823, is one of the oldest in the country and many great names have played there, in fact many overseas teams play there now.

Instow House was the property of the Rev John White, and when his daughter, Mrs Orphot, died All Saints chapel was given to the village as a memorial to her by her husband. The parish church, dedicated to St John the Baptist, dates from the 14th century. The font is Norman.

The village hall was built in 1911 and until recently was called the Rifle Hall, as it was built so that there was somewhere for young men to be taught how to shoot in preparation for the First World War. The hall was owned by the Tapely estate but a few years ago the estate generously gave it to the parish, since when it has become known as the parish hall.

The present-day appearance of Instow owes much to the Christie family of Tapely Park which owns a large part of Instow and most of the agricultural land surrounding the village. Tapely Park is an elegant red brick and stone house just outside the village with beautiful Italian gardens open to the public. The Christie family is very well known as they are the owners of Glyndebourne in Sussex, of opera fame.

Yelland adjoins Instow and most of the old village remains but it was never very large and has become swallowed up by modern homes and estates. The manor was famous for its pottery but the village is now best known for its splendid garden centre.

Inwardleigh 🎵

Inwardleigh, so named for Inwardus, a thane who held the manor of Leigh at the time of the Norman Conquest, is a peaceful backwater nestling in the heart of the county.

Lack of historically recorded events would suggest the parishioners were adept at keeping a low profile. With the installation of a turnpike gate at the Folly hamlet and later upgrading of the road, Inwardleigh became bypassed, enabling it to retain its natural charm.

Dominating the scene is the ancient church of St Petroc with its fine cobbled path and breathtaking views of Dartmoor. An idyllic setting for many pretty weddings and baptisms, the latter being performed at the old Norman font, it is enhanced by the pleasant churchyard which provides a peaceful resting place for loved ones.

The spiritual needs of the community are well served, not only by St Petroc, but also the Methodist chapel at Folly Gate and Baptist chapel at Oak. Meanwhile the redundant Wesleyan chapel at Waytown enjoys an unusual new lease of life, as a workshop for 'Dormouse Crafts'.

A rural area, agriculture forms the main livelihood, sons carrying on the farming tradition, indeed some families can trace their line back many generations. Today it is largely dairy farming and Inwardleigh is justly proud of its delicious Curworthy cheese, with its gorgeous black wax coat, named after the farm of its origin. Pioneered by *The Farmers' Weekly* the production has since been taken over by John and Rachel Stephens of Stockbeare. If you have never sampled Curworthy cheese you have missed a treat.

With the need to diversify other projects have developed, as wide ranging as sawmills for timber, to the conversion of barns for holiday flats. A tasteful example of the latter is The Granary at Westacott, which still retains its old stone steps and brickwork around the windows.

The advent of the motor car, not surprisingly, saw the establishment of Cleave's Garage and petrol pumps at Folly Gate, while the blacksmith has inevitably given way to the agricultural engineer. Also situated at Folly Gate is the parish hall, site of many parties, coffee evenings and whist drives.

No sketch of Inwardleigh is complete without a mention of the Crossways Inn, a popular 'watering hole' with locals and visitors alike. It also accommodates the skittle and dart teams.

Ipplepen ᘛᘚ

Ipplepen is a village of great antiquity situated midway between Newton Abbot and Totnes and about six miles across country from the popular Torbay area. The village is surrounded by a network of lanes and bridleways intended for packhorses and pedestrians.

The famous story *The Hound of the Baskervilles* originated in Ipplepen. The author, Conan Doyle, was a frequent visitor to his friend Mr Bertie Robinson at Parkhill House. He was driven in a horse and carriage to Dartmoor to gather material for his book by the groom (Harry Baskerville), hence the title of his book.

Harry was born and lived in a cottage which is still in existence in the village. He retired to Ashburton but returned to visit his friends when he was well into his nineties. He was a regular visitor to the Ipplepen Cottage Garden Society's show, held every July since 1890. This is a great village day when families and former residents return to renew acquaintances.

The first of May was celebrated at the village school in bygone days, when the children would sing and practise

First of May ducking day
Second of May sting nettle day
Third of May Kissing day
Fourth of May courting day

Another ancient custom is revived at intervals of time of beating the parish bounds, when someone young taking part in the walk is selected and bumped on the boundary stones.

The main employment in bygone years was farming and quarrying. There are limestone quarries and a marble quarry. Only one quarry is worked today and that is mechanised. Today most people commute to Newton Abbot and the Torbay area and some even to Plymouth and Exeter for their employment.

There are a number of manor houses still occupied by private families. One house, known as Old House still has the remains of the 'village clink' on their property.

The old village was very compact, built around the ancient church of St Andrew, which stands out very boldly on commanding ground with good views over Dartmoor and the surrounding countryside.

The population has trebled with the building of many new estates. With this has come a new village primary school and medical centre. The village hall is fully used by the community. The Parish Council own a recreation ground catering for football, bowling, tennis and a children's play area, as well as a separate ground for cricket. Ipplepen is known as a friendly village and long may it remain so.

Ivybridge 🌿

Nestling amid the southern foothills of Dartmoor lies Ivybridge. It has not always been a town, but the sprawling new estates which encircle old Ivybridge and house the workers of Plymouth, the industrial estates to the south and west and the new shopping complex and sports centre have all played their part in elevating Ivybridge from the sleepy Devon village it used to be. Yet the character of the old village is still there to see.

Ivybridge was, is and always will be dominated by the river Erme which flows through the centre of the village, having gathered on the slopes of Dartmoor ready for its short journey to the sea. In years gone by it provided power for local industry. The huge paper mill sits neatly beside the river and has played its part in the affairs of the village for years.

Ivybridge is of course, much like the rest of Devon, linked closely to agriculture, but it sees a much more diverse side of farming than do most towns and villages. On the outskirts where the river slows and meanders toward the sea there are rich grazing pastures that produce the milk and meat for which Devon is famous. Yet just a few short miles back up the hills to where the Erme starts its life, the soil is thinner, the climate is harsher and moorland sheep and cattle graze where no others can survive.

Ivybridge has always been guarded by its Beacon, a large bracken and granite covered hill which stands to the east. The Beacon has given Ivybridge its character. Its roots are set unshakingly in the Devon soil yet it is close enough to the harshness of Dartmoor to give it a strong heart. Every year Ivybridge holds its 'Beacon Race', a raw lung-bursting affair which sees hordes of masochists running and tumbling down the sides of the hill and down into the town to the finish line. It is designed to give instant acclaim to the winner and pain to everyone else!

There are some who understandably mourn the loss of the days when Ivybridge held cattle markets in its streets, when its railway station was open to load those cattle onto wagons and take butter and cream to the markets of Plymouth, but the spirit of the old village lives on.

Kelly & Bradstone

Kelly and Bradstone are two separate parishes very closely linked with one another. Social life in most forms is shared, the village hall being host to diverse activities.

Bradstone is thought to have got its name from the broad stone, 11 ft by 6 ft, which is now upright in the hedge of a field behind the manor house. Tradition has it that it may have been an altar stone or part of a cromlech since it is pierced by a round hole through which the spirit is supposed to escape after burial of the body. The church is dedicated to St Nonna, with the Tudor manor house of the Cloberry family close by. The latter has a lovely early 17th century gatehouse. One Oliver Cloberry was notorious, being called before the Star Chamber on more than one occasion for robbing people returning from market and causing affrays in the church.

The word Kelly means a wood or a clearing, which is not difficult to imagine, the countryside being richly wooded to this day. Kelly House, a Tudor and early Georgian mansion, is where the Kelly family have lived for nearly 900 years, alongside which is the church dedicated to St Mary.

Tithe Barn at Kelly

In between the two World Wars Mary Kelly had the idea of forming a Dramatic Society which might include all the people in the parishes. After some opposition, acting not being considered quite 'the thing' to some of the older farmers, plays were produced each year on Ascension Day in the tithe barn at Kelly, which had been used by the family for theatrical occasions for many years. This became a Great Day in the year. Plays were mainly of the morality type such as *Pilgrim's Progress* with practically all families partaking, plus one or two from neighbouring parishes.

There are no shops, public house or public transport, but initiative and energy continue unabated. A Country Fayre, a Flower Show that has a staggering amount of entries for a small place, a concert in the church now and again and many other activities bring back many old friends to the villages.

Kentisbeare & Blackborough 🌿

Kentisbeare, an attractive East Devon village, is situated on a tributary of the river Culm in fertile farming country beside the notable Blackdown beauty area.

Some of Kentisbeare's oldest farms are listed in the Domesday Book, one of which is Wood Barton (formerly Hewisa or Wode). The remains of its timbered communal hall dating from the 12th to 14th centuries are still visible. Another ancient house is the Priest Hall, a medieval church house, containing many original features, which stands beside the parish church of St Mary. The early history of the church is uncertain, although it is likely that it was of Anglo-Saxon foundation. The greater part of the church was rebuilt by John Whytyng who lived at Wode in the first quarter of the 16th century, and the beautiful wooden screen and some very fine stone carving date from that period.

Later several shops and workshops were to be found in Kentisbeare, even after 1945. A blacksmith's, a bakery, a butcher's shop, tailor's and grocer's were all active here. The remains of the cobbler's workshop for instance is still to be found at Moorhayne Cottage. Presently the village has a thriving primary school, the Wyndham Arms public house, and a post office with village shop. Clubs and societies are well supported and the cricket and football teams are locally renowned.

On the eastern edge of the parish of Kentisbeare, Blackborough lies on a west-facing scarp of the Blackdown Hills. From here on a clear day there are magnificent views over Kentisbeare towards Exeter and Tiverton, and the higher ground beyond.

Blackborough's church, All Saints, celebrated the 150th anniversary of its dedication in April 1989. Blackborough Beacon provided the focus of the 'Armada 400' celebrations in July 1988.

Although Blackborough has a number of clubs and societies of its own, the two villages combine for many activities. The Church of England school in Blackborough closed in 1948 and since then all the children of the parish have travelled to Kentisbeare for primary education. Blackborough has no post office or shop, but does have a recently modernised village hall, which Kentisbeare lacks. However, Kentisbeare possesses a very attractive reading room holding up to 45 people, and many folk come 'down the hill' to take part in various club meetings and social activities here.

Kenton 🐛

Kenton village has changed considerably over the years. It was once a thriving, independent community where employment was based on farming the surrounding countryside and which supported numerous local tradesmen. Not so long ago, a trip to Exeter was a major excursion to be undertaken perhaps once a year. Now buses pass through the village every 15 minutes, making little of the journey to Exeter, and there is only one shop and post office. However, The Dolphin and The Devon Arms still survive, supplying villagers and visitors alike with refreshment, as they have done down through the ages.

It is hard to believe, but at one time ships sailed up river to Kenton and in the mid 16th century cargoes of salt left Kenton for Rochelle and ships returned with French wines and spirits. Kenton even sent two ships to fight against the Spanish Armada and also supported the fishing trade off Newfoundland.

Although Kenton was reputed to have been served by over 100 pumps and wells, these were of no avail when, on 16th April 1856, fire swept through the village, destroying half of the properties. Since they were built of cob and had thatched roofs, they were soon consumed by the flames which were fanned by a strong breeze.

All Saints' church, having been constructed of stone, survived. Reputedly built on the site of a church established cAD560 and dedicated to St Petrock, the present building is thought to date from 1360–1370. The carved and painted rood screen in Kenton church is of particular interest, having panels depicting 40 saints and prophets, as is the 15th century pulpit, which is said to have been carved from a single oak trunk.

This pulpit had, for a time, been replaced, but was rediscovered, in pieces, in a cupboard in the schoolhouse, and subsequently restored.

Powderham Castle was built by Sir Philip Courtenay between 1390 and 1420. It was damaged during the Civil War, but has since been restored and altered. It is the home of the Earl of Devon, a direct descendant of Sir Philip Courtenay, but the many features of furniture and structure can still be seen on summer afternoons when the castle is open to the public.

A notable one-time resident of Kenton was Richard Polwele, who wrote his *History of Devon* whilst he was curate at Kenton in 1793. In more recent times, Stanley Lake is said to have invented traffic signals, which were the fore-runners of our present day traffic lights.

There was a time when villagers had the choice of hiring a horse-drawn cab, travelling by train (having first reached the station at Starcross or Exminster) or going on foot. In those days Kenton had no electricity, but was lit by gas from its own gas works. Kenton even boasted its own fire engine. During the Second World War a stalwart of Kenton's Home Guard captured a German pilot who had landed by parachute at the top of the High Street!

Kilmington 🌿

The Roman road from Axminster to Honiton passed through Kilmington, in fact the main road followed its route through the village until the present road was built about 150 years ago. Katherine of Aragon would have passed through the village on her way from Plymouth to London, to marry Henry VII's son, Arthur.

A beacon was built to the north-west of Kilmington in 1563. The churchwardens' accounts show that the bell-ringers were paid in 1588 for a special ringing of the bells to celebrate the defeat of the Armada.

Some old tradesmen's buildings still exist – the Old Smithy, the Old Forge, the Old Bakery, the brush factory and the butter factory (now demolished). In 1900 there were two bakers, two blacksmiths, two tailors, three shoemakers, two butchers, a coach builder and two sawyers. There was a village shop and a post office, first at the Cross then at Mustons before moving to the present site.

Through the ages there have been houses at Coryton near the site of the timber-built Saxon manor house. An elegant mansion was erected in 1756 but partially demolished in 1953. At the turn of the century, as well as the Coryton mansion there were four large houses in the Shute road adjoining the common – Heathfield, Goscot (Little Park), Bywood, and Eaglemont (Greenhayes).

The church (St Giles'), originally built in the 14th and 15th centuries, was largely rebuilt (except for the tower) in the 19th century and reopened in 1862. There has been a school since 1862, when Mr Tucker of Coryton Park gave the land for the building of a poor house. The present village school dates from 1867.

An interesting feature of the village is the presence of numerous subterranean springs in the Shute Hill area. The most notable is Kate's Well. The water is piped to the corner of the road where the Street meets George Lane (Newtons), where it runs out freely for anyone to use. Tradition says that this water has healing properties particularly for eye ailments and that Kate's Well derives its name from St Katherine, patron saint of the blind. One reason for this theory is the presence of a very ancient cottage on the opposite side of the road to the spring, which was believed to have been occupied by a priest whose duties were concerned with dispensing water from the holy well. However, this ancient cottage (now in the garden of Wayside) is in fact the parish house given to the village by Robert Weston, lord of the manor in 1266 'to sell ale upon for the mayntenance of the chapell'.

Kingskerswell 🌿

Kingskerswell lies mid-way between Newton Abbot and Torquay. The earliest known record of the village is to be found in the Domesday Book, which shows the settlement to have existed in Saxon times, when the manor was held by Edward the Confessor. In 1086 it had a population of 270 and the only animals mentioned were 120 sheep kept on the King's land. Kingskerswell was one of the Devonshire manors retained by William the Conqueror and his successors as part of their royal domain.

In March 1267, Sir Roger de Maclis made a great impact on Kingskerswell by obtaining the grant to hold a weekly market on Tuesdays, and an annual fair on the Feast of St Giles. The market was probably held along a roadside, not far from Dacca Bridge, across which both buyers and sellers would pass. This market still existed in the early 17th century, when it was held on Sundays – it is thought pressure from Puritans resulted in its closure.

The church, built before Domesday, was probably originally of timber with a thatched roof – a long building to include chancel and nave, but no aisles. Situated on the southern side of the wide valley, flooding was avoided. Close by was a grain mill, and some buildings connected with the mill still stand, while the mill leat runs outside the churchyard wall.

During the late 18th century, pottery, cider and brewing became new industries, all of which for a time were highly successful.

Early in the 20th century the third road system in Kingskerswell was constructed and became of the highest importance. Planned to follow the line of least resistance, avoiding flooding and steep gradients, this road must negotiate the transverse ridge carrying the St Marychurch Road into Kingskerswell. A tunnel was made in this ridge, known as Kerswell Arch. The Arch remained in position for over 60 years. Finally traffic became so dense it was useful no longer and in 1964 it was demolished and a steel/concrete single span bridge is in its place. Today, only the people using the railway to Torbay, would see the medieval part of the village – the thatched houses and beautiful church of St Mary, all now in a conservation area.

Naturally the village has expanded over the years – the population is now around 4,180. The playing field occupies part of the once flat marshy valley, and the village football and cricket teams are well known in the area.

The grain mill known originally as Whitepot Mill, now called Whitpot, for years was run as a delightful tea garden, but is now a private residence.

There is a library and a health centre. Recently a new primary school was built, and the old one has been bought to be used as a community centre.

Kingsteignton

Although much development has taken place over the last 20 years, Kingsteignton still has a few mementoes of its past thousand years. An open space called Berry Meadow still exists. In Saxon times a bury meant a fortified place and was for protection against attack. Now the only attack comes from visiting bowling teams! Vikings raided the village in 1001 and left a souvenir in the form of a Danish ship, found 900 years later buried under eight feet of mud. Archers improved their skill on open ground still called the Butts and sharpened their arrows on the worn sandstone of the church wall.

In the late 17th century Kingsteignton ball clay was used to make tobacco pipes. It soon became famous for being of a very rare type for the making of fine china. As this trade improved two canals were constructed for the sole purpose of conveying the clay to the river and then on to Teignmouth and the docks. This was transported by barges called lighters and beside the now filled-in canal stand the ruins of the lighter-men's cottages. In 1791 no less a personage than Josiah Wedgwood came to Kingsteignton to buy clay for his potteries in Stoke-on-Trent. The village is justly proud that today ball clay is being exported all over the world.

Thatched cottages stand at the old edge of the village, known then as Townend. Three mills still exist although none is used today as such and the water that turned the wheels all those years ago still runs through the village. Unfortunately it is seldom called by its former name of Fairwater. One must fall into the brook to be termed a true villager! Once there was a terrible drought, or so the story goes, and a ram was sacrificed on the bed of the stream. The water started to flow again and from then on a ram roasting fair has been held every year on Spring bank holiday. A ram is still roasted and the brook still runs!

With its growth have come some 20 shops, two post offices and five public houses spread over a wide area. A good bus service, health clinic, two schools and a bank, all these are, of course, the advantages of this expansion. But there is also a real danger that this ancient village thriving even at the time of the Domesday Book, will be swallowed up by its large neighbour, Newton Abbot.

Kingston 🐑

It was in the year AD836 that Aethelwulf, king of the West Saxons, whose son was King Alfred, took to himself the coastal strip of land between the rivers Erme and Dart in South Devon. Hence Kingston, the King's settlement, a village nestling near the Erme estuary, in a lovely area now designated as of outstanding natural beauty.

Nothing of course remains from those very early days, except some natural landmarks delineating the parish boundary. Most of the village farmhouses date from the 18th and 19th century, but many incorporate parts dating from 300 years earlier. Farmhouses and cottages are built of local stone or cob, and are either thatched or roofed with slate. Since the 1960s many new houses have been built, and many of the old stone barns have been converted to dwellings, although the population still remains at around 300 souls.

The school, which educated children between five and eleven years old not only from Kingston but from neighbouring villages as well, was closed in 1966 and has now been converted to a private house. The 15th century church of St James the Less, stands on its slightly elevated site overlooking the equally old Dolphin Inn, and the much more recent village hall, built originally as a men's reading room in 1912.

Kingston has always had a close association with the sea. Years ago many of the village men earned their living from the sea, laying crab and lobster pots off nearby Wonwell beach (the pots made from willows grown for the purpose), catching mackerel and bass and any other fish the unpolluted water would provide. Wonwell is now a very popular bathing and wind-surfing beach. Before the days of motors villagers would use donkeys to carry their fish up from Wonwell, and to haul loads of seaweed and sand to act as fertiliser in their gardens. Ships anchored off the beach would bring coal for the village, fertilisers for the farms, and limestone which was burnt in the kilns which may still be seen on either side of the estuary.

Not so long ago there was a working carpenter and wheelwright in the main street, and a blacksmith whose forge lay on the edge of the village. He was kept busy shoeing farm horses, hunters and ponies. Going back further in time there was a second inn in the village (a house now stands on the site) and a general store, butcher's shop and bakery. Now there is just the Dolphin Inn, a combined shop and post office and a private hotel.

Kingston has always had a strong community spirit. A modern tradition is the Village Fair, held annually on the first Saturday in August. All the village organisations take part, and the centre of the village is thronged with people.

Kingswear ❧

Kingswear is a small village situated on the eastern bank of the river Dart, on the opposite side to Dartmouth. It is thought that the name of the village is connected with the farm Kingston and may also refer to the remains of a system of weirs at Waterhead.

In 1847 the present church was built, replacing a simple 15th century building but retaining the Norman tower which is still preserved.

In the 12th century people began to move down from the hills surrounding Kingswear and Dartmouth to build harbourside houses and wharves in order to conduct trade with France and other European countries, and later to spread to the USA and Newfoundland. Much of the trading was connected with the fishing industry. There is evidence that smuggling took place during this time, which probably accounts for the Coastguard station at Mansands, which now seems to be very remote.

The house which is known as Kittery Court has figured in much of the village history. On this spot existed wharves and warehouses. The family of Champernownes figured largely in the promotion of trade, and their name is very prominent in the village of Dartington. The name Kittery has endured and is famous as the earliest township in the State of Maine, USA. There are a number of houses in the same area as Kittery Court which date back to the 17th century and the house known as Ravenswell in Beacon Road has the date 1651 built into a wall.

In 1864 the railway came to Kingswear which must have changed the area. In order to build the station and the adjacent hotel many of the old buildings had to be demolished, and the slipway also had to be considerably widened. To the south of the slipway Tudor buildings were pulled down and new buildings erected.

The river Dart was very busy during the First World War, and again in the second conflict. General de Gaulle and the Free French had headquarters in Kingswear. There were a number of aerial attacks and one serious attack on the Noss works a short distance up-stream when 40 people were killed.

The railway line from Kingswear to Paignton was closed in the 1960s. Fortunately a private company took it over. It is now a big attraction for visitors during the summer months especially as the engines are steam.

Tourism must now be one of the principal activities. A great number of pleasure boats ply between Brixham and the river Dart. It is also a venue for yachtsmen and several marinas are situated on the river. Quite a number of fishing boats use the quay on the Kingswear side, catching crabs and lobsters mostly. There is not much industry in Kingswear apart from the Noss works where boat building and repairs take place.

Lamerton

Lamerton is a scattered parish of some 550 people situated three miles north-west of Tavistock. It is recorded in the Domesday Book as Lambertone, which it is understood means 'a grazing place for lambs by a river'.

The 14th century St Peter's church was burned down on 19th November 1877 and rebuilt, in the Perpendicular style, at a cost of £6,000. One of the oldest inhabitants, who used to teach in the school, says that draught from a broken window caused the oil lamp keeping the organ dry to flare, thus catching the church on fire. Today the church is seldom filled, but an elderly villager remarked that when he was a lad in the First World War, if he did not get to church early he didn't get a seat, although the church accommodates about 300 people. By the church entrance is the medieval priest house which was once used as the parish poor house. In 1782 the parish vestry resolved that its lower storey should be used for a parish stable and the upper part should be used for vestry meetings.

During the 18th and 19th centuries mining was the main industry of this area but by the end of the 19th century mines generally became financially unviable. However, one villager remembers working over the spoil heaps of Collacombe Down mine during the First World War for zinc, ore and ochre. This was then taken to Morwellham Quay and down the Tamar to Plymouth. Before the coming of the mines Lamerton was largely agricultural but today, though there is still much farming, most people commute to work in the neighbouring towns.

There are several large old houses in Lamerton. Two of them, Collacombe and Willestrew, were Saxon estates. Collacombe, which was rebuilt in Elizabeth I's reign, was the home of the Tremaynes from the 14th to the 17th centuries. A feature of this house is a large transomed window containing over 3,000 panes of glass. There is a monument in the church to the five brothers of Digory Tremayne which was erected in 1588.

Venn House is a Tudor building and was at one time the home of Sir John Spear, the MP for Tavistock in the early 1900s. Nowadays Venn is a home for retired people. The fine avenue of trees, which is now the way into the village from the main road, was once the carriage way to Venn.

Landkey ✍

The village of Landkey lies three miles to the east of Barnstaple. Its name is derived from Llan De Kea meaning 'Church of the blessed Kea'. St Kea, a monk from the great abbey at Glastonbury, brought the Christian faith to the area, and the parish church of St Paul probably occupies the site of his cell and oratory.

The church, which is a Grade I listed building, was built in the second half of the 15th century and contains a 13th century font and three stone effigies, all that remain of an earlier building.

The church also contains several impressive monuments to the Acland family. The Aclands are the oldest surviving landed family in the county. The name Hugh De Accalen, now spelled Acland, first occurs in a deed dated 1158 when they were landowners in an area of North Devon. At one time in the 19th century they had accumulated an enormous estate of practically 40,000 acres, but their huge estates have passed mainly to the National Trust.

Acland Barton stands well up out of the Landkey valley at a height of 400 ft above sea level. There is no branch of the Acland family which does not stem from the tree which took root at Acland Barton.

The original house was completely rebuilt in the 16th century, with its own domestic chapel licensed by the bishop, to save the family the muddy walk down 'Akkers Lane' to Landkey church.

As well as the parish church, Landkey has a Methodist chapel, a village hall, a village school, two shops and a post office. Of the original five pubs only two remain and the bakery situated at Town Mills closed a few years ago. The mill wheel is the only one that still turns out of a total of 13 along the leat. Until mains electricity came to the village the water-wheel provided electricity for the mill machinery, the bakery, the mill house and Town Mills bungalow. The mill house was built in 1659.

The area is a farming community, mostly small family farms not employing much outside labour. The local quarry has a local workforce, but most of the people in the village earn their living in Barnstaple. With its close proximity to the North Devon Link Road a certain amount of housing development is expected to take place, but it is hoped that Landkey will not lose its village identity.

Lapford 🌿

Lapford is a village of some 950 people, situated mid-way between Exeter and Barnstaple. It has a winding main village road which climbs for 250 ft from the river Yeo, and has a mixture of ancient and modern dwellings. The village pub, with its open fireplace and beams, dates from the 16th century; many of the cottages and farms are at least a century older, and there are the buildings of two corn mills together with their leats. In contrast, there are modern developments of varied character.

The manor of Lapford, then called Eslapaforda, was once owned by Queen Matilda, the wife of William the Conqueror. In the time of King Stephen it passed to the de Tracey family, one of whom, William, was a murderer of Thomas a Becket. As a penance for his crime, he enlarged the Saxon chapel in 1180, and the resulting church was dedicated to

St Thomas of Canterbury. It has 15th century carved bench ends and a beautiful 16th century screen.

Near to the church is the village hall, built after the First World War and much extended and improved since then. It is the centre of many village activities, and a doctor's surgery is held there each week.

Although in common with other Mid Devon villages Lapford might seem rather isolated, it is relatively well served by public transport. There are regular trains to Exeter and Barnstaple from the station, at which passengers have to flag down the driver. Main road coaches run past the station, and another coach service passes through the village itself. One of the more outlying farms has its own landing strip, which accommodates light aircraft.

There is a Congregational church and a Plymouth Brethren chapel in the village, with everyone uniting for special occasions such as a carol service at Christmas.

A ghostly footnote: An old Lapford legend tells that at midnight in Revels time, 'Our Tom' has been seen, dressed in robes and mitre, riding slowly round the church and then down through the village. Not a sound of hoof-beats to be heard nor a sign of hoof-prints to be found!

Lee 🌿

Lee is a small coastal village, three miles west of Ilfracombe with a population of approximately 200.

There is National Trust land to the east of the village known as The Torrs, and to the west are downs known locally as the Old Golf Course. Winters are usually very mild, though gales are frequent. It is not unusual to find fuchsias flowering in the garden at Christmas.

The church of St Matthew and St Wardrede was consecrated in 1835. It is Neo-Gothic in style and is a fine example of a small early Victorian church. The woodwork includes an oak pan pulpit and carved choir gallery, all being much older than the church itself, having probably been collected from old buildings by the Squire.

Adjoining the church is the old school room, the foundation stone of which was laid on the 21st June, 1859. It is now used as a craft shop. The school bell came from the *Europa*, wrecked off the coast in 1858.

The thatched Old Maids Cottage, now a private residence, has for many years been associated with the poem of '*The Three Old Maids of Lee*'. There has been a building on this site since the late 17th century.

The Grampus Inn, originally The Old Farm, was in the past known as

Old Maids Cottage, Lee

Nether Warcombe. It is about 400 years old and probably one of the oldest buildings in the village. Until 1972 it was run as a farm and tea gardens.

The Old Post Office is dated 1706. The day Queen Victoria died, there was a terrific thunderstorm at Lee. Mrs Taylor, the postmistress, was taking down a telegram telling of the Queen's death, using the most primitive equipment, when she was struck by lightning in the left eye and so blinded. After this she would have nothing to do with the telegraph, so the post office was transferred to new premises.

The present post office and lychgate was formerly The New Inn run by Martin Richards, the son of Hannibal Richards who came to Lee in 1789 and settled at The Gwythers which he ran as an inn. He was said to have been a notorious smuggler and wrecker. His tombstone can be found in the Ilfracombe parish churchyard.

Above The Gwythers stands the Manor Hotel looking down on Southcliffe Hall on the opposite side of the valley. This was completed in 1898 and was built because of the animosity between Canon Tugwell (who owned Southcliffe) and Charles B. M. Drake-Cutliffe of The Manor (now Lee Bay Hotel). The latter built his new manor house at a higher level so he could look down on Canon Tugwell!

The Old Mill dated circa 1560 was a corn mill. It is a listed building which ceased operating in the 1890s. Latterly it was used as a tea house,

141

but is now a private residence. On the opposite side of the bay stands the Smugglers Cottage (formerly the Beachside Tea House), built of local stone; this is also a listed building and bears the date 1627.

The wild and rugged coastline has witnessed many shipwrecks, of which the most notable were the *William Wilberforce*, the *Lochlibo* and the *Europa*, and in the 18th and 19th centuries was the scene of much smuggling, mostly gin and brandy.

Littleham (North Devon)

Littleham was first recorded in the Domesday Book as Liteham, and was about one-third of the size of Bideford at that time. The village is three miles from Bideford and can only be reached through narrow lanes. It is not on the route to anywhere else.

It is a straggling village with the church set apart from the houses. It is not particularly pretty although there are a number of old cob and stone cottages, once thatched but now with slate roofs. The beauty of the village is in the wonderful views towards Dartmoor, which seems to rise up in the background on clear days, and Exmoor which is nearer and usually clearly visible.

The village has grown with new houses springing up in all parts of the village. Despite the growth there is now no shop or school and even the post office closed in 1987.

At one time the community must have been fairly self-sufficient with farming as its main industry. There were three blacksmiths, two shop-keepers and two publicans working in the village.

During the last century, Littleham was known for its brewery. Apps ale could be purchased for between one shilling and one shilling and six-pence a gallon. This ale was made from locally grown hops and mineral spring water and was said to 'possess medicinal properties of a most valuable nature'.

The lane leading from the village past Apps is still known as Wagon Road. Part of it, an unusually straight stretch of the lane, was built by the brewery and was a private road used only by the brewery wagons. It must have been along this road that a man, seeing smoke rising from the brewery on the 15th March 1885, galloped all the way to Bideford to fetch the West of England Fire Brigade.

The church history is interesting. The first Rector was recorded in 1310. There is evidence of an earlier church and the north transept is thought to be all that remains of it for on the wall is a fresco said to be of the church's patron saint, Swithin. It has been dated at about the 12th century. The church roof has a definite bend in it, at the top of its crucifix shape. This bend it seems was deliberate and depicts Christ's head on the cross. The church was beautifully restored in the 1890s by the Rev Morse who paid for the work himself. It is now one of Devon's most beautiful church interiors and it is extremely well cared for and loved by all the villagers.

The churchyard is also one of the prettiest to be found. It is noted particularly for its wealth of wild flowers which are being conserved with great care. Within the church are two beautifully hand made books with paintings of all the churchyard flowers. This has been created by one of the many talented artists and craftsmen of the village.

Littleham (South Devon)

The church dominates the village of Littleham, near Exmouth, and has existed since Saxon times. There is a scratch dial, known as a mass clock for telling the time of services, dating from the 13th century. The north aisle was added by a local family in 1528. An act of open penance took place in the church in 1805 when a woman was condemned to walk barefoot wrapped in a white sheet, from the lychgate to the church where she was excommunicated. Her crime is not known.

In the churchyard is buried Lady Nelson, wife of Admiral Horatio Nelson, as well as her son Josiah Nesbitt and his children.

The Plough Inn, a famous old cider house, was demolished in 1896 to make way for the graveyard behind the church, and thatched cottages known as Violet Cottages, said to have been the haunt of smugglers, were demolished in 1930. A small car park now stands on the ruins!

Pratts Hayes House, now belonging to the National Trust, was once a reed farm of willows and has connections with Sir Francis Drake's family. Green's Farm, also an old farm, is still being worked and stands on the route of the old path fields from Exmouth to Littleham. Back in the 1920s and long before, by the bridge over the village brook, was the blacksmith's shop run by a Mr Bill Hillman.

Smuggling is reputed to have been a local occupation, the loot probably being brought in from Sandy Bay and Rodney Bay nearby and it is said, buried in Bonds Lane (now renamed Gore Lane), which runs off Maer Lane leading directly to the seashore.

The old forge is no more and Tithe Cottage, newly thatched, is now a restaurant and serves cream teas to holidaymakers and locals on their way to a grand holiday complex on the cliff top nearby, which was once Lee's Farm. There is a very good museum of country life showing a great deal of what went on in Littleham many years ago.

A large housing estate stands where once were fields and trees and the railway which ran from Exmouth and connected with the main line to London is no more. Where the station platform and railway lines once were are now private houses and sheltered bungalows for the elderly. But the life of the village is still vigorous and although it could now be called a suburb of Exmouth it retains an individuality of its own.

Little Torrington & Taddiport 🎐

The parish, twelve miles inland from Bideford, is bisected by the busy A386 to Plymouth. The traffic speeds by, unaware of the two lively villages of Little Torrington and Taddiport. These, set in countryside which still has areas of permanent ley and old oak woods, retain much of the 'feel' of pre-war days. Most important is the continuation of community spirit, shown not only when someone is ill, but also by the large sums of money raised for the church, the new Victory Hall and local charities.

The traditions and standards of parish involvement have been handed down through the years: the How and Broad families go back six generations.

There is a long list of those who have helped make Little Torrington such a pleasant place to live. They include John 'Ganger' Martin who left school at the age of eight and went 'up the Bally Moor', to work at Petersmarland, and went to church every Sunday. He was also a charitable man, who gave 20 acres to Torrington hospital, and if a clayworker Petersmarland, and went to church every Sunday. He was also a charitable man, who gave 20 acres to Torrington hospital, and if a clayworker was sick, would send a bit of beef to the family.

And there was Granny Rooke, always called to help with a childbirth, and who became the unofficial local midwife. She also helped the undertaker lay out the dead. Wearing the black skirt obtained from the village Christmas charity parcel, Emily Rooke would sit in place of honour on the horse-drawn hearse.

Taddiport lies to the north of the parish. Though only separated from Great Torrington by the river Torridge, it has always been a self-contained and close knit community, right back to its 14th century origins as a leper colony. Much of village life still centres round the 14th century chapel of St Mary Magdalen.

144

In living memory, much of the village was thatched. There was a pound, a sawpit, smithy, carpenter's shop, pub and infants school. Only the shop/post office remains. The old ladies in black, with their white starched aprons, would hang over the hatches (half-doors) in the sunshine, chatting and watching the passers-by.

Until the opening of the Torrington & Marland Railway in 1881, all the clay from Petersmarland came by pack horse through the village, firstly to the Rolle Canal and then to Torrington railway station. People remember the stream of carts going to Sandfords Dairies, or collecting lime 'hot' from the kilns just the other side of the river. The timber waggons passed regularly to and from Bideford, with Mr Copp lolling fast asleep while his six great horses plodded steadily up the steep hills.

Up to the 1960s, there were still about twelve charity houses. Taddiport was not a wealthy community. They collected their blankets from the rectory each autumn (first there got the thickest!) and gratefully accepted their 'poor' parcel from the Brookes-Leeds at Christmas. However, people helped each other, and no orphan ever went into a Home. Despite all, large sums of money have been raised for the general good: electricity was brought to the village before Torrington; the strip leper fields were purchased by public subscription in 1970, and the old infants school is now a fine village hall.

Liverton 🦐

Liverton village is one of three in the parish of Ilsington, and recently it has grown dramatically due to new housing developments. However, the old part of the village remains essentially the same, having grown up around some small farms and an iron foundry.

The foundry itself has seen many changes. For many years it was a thriving pottery, complete with 'bottle' kiln, making a variety of items including traditional-style blue jugs and Toby jugs. In 1980 the pottery, which had employed many generations of villagers closed down, and the site was to see yet another change. It is now owned by a firm making soaps etc, and is once again employing local people.

The village has only a few thatched cottages but it does boast its very own master thatcher. One or two cottages go back to the 16th century. In 1879 a school which had been in the village was moved to a new building some three quarters of a mile away, on land owned by the church. This building still stands today and provides education for some 160 pupils.

Every third year Liverton hosts the parish Flower Show. It is held at the football ground and is an event which draws residents of all three villages together. The show has been running since the 1920s.

The village has its own football team, and furnishes several members to the parish petanque team. This rather unusual pastime is due to the link with Brasparts in Brittany which began several years ago and has gone from strength to strength ever since.

Loddiswell

Loddiswell lies some three miles north of Kingsbridge.

Through the ages the river Avon, or Aune, provided power for three grist and tucking mills, which accounts for the woolcombers, serge makers and weavers that are all named in the parish records. The church, mainly 14th century, is dedicated to St Michael.

A number of the inhabitants today travel to Kingsbridge and Plymouth to work in shops, factories and offices, but there are still family-occupied farms. There are builders, carpenters, plumbers, haulage contractors, garden centres, a vineyard, together with a home bakery, shops and the very necessary post office.

North of the village is Blackdown Camp, better known as the Rings. This is considered to be an Iron Age fortified settlement, but may prove to be even earlier. It consists of a motte and two baileys protected by a rampart and deep ditch, the latter being built by the Normans on the earlier earthwork. The whole of this was given to the parish by the generosity of the Peek family in 1988.

Richard Peek left Devon and walked to London to find his fortune, and is known by the Peek family as 'The Little Dick Whittington'. In London he worked in a tea warehouse and learned the business. He brought two brothers from home to join him and later the Peeks set up their own business and became one of the foremost teabroking firms of their time. Arthur Brooke, founder of the Brooke Bond tea company, learned his trade in a Peek warehouse! Richard Peek became Sheriff of London in 1832 and later retired to Loddiswell, his native parish. He founded a school in Loddiswell and the family also built a number of churches in the area.

There are a number of charities in Loddiswell. In 1591 Sir Matthew Arundell founded a charity 'For the use and behoof of the parishioners that shall be there from time to time'. The lands and tenements which he left have been since sold and the capital invested for parochial purposes. The village hall and the playing fields have both received money from this source, and when water was piped to the village the Arundell Charity provided the finance. The 1988 Peek gift of the Rings has been vested in the Arundell Charity.

The most popular charity, however, is the Phillips Charity, in which senior citizens have a very personal interest, for on St Stephen's Day at midday a little ceremony is enacted. The feoffees of the charity assemble in the parish church, the bell tolls, and senior citizens come forward and stand on Richard Phillips's tomb in the chancel. Here they are given a small sum of money by the chairman of the feoffees.

Loxhore

Loxhore, or Locca's Bank as the Saxons called it, is bounded by small rivers fringed with mixed woodland. The bulk of the land is pasture.

Of the three hamlets, Lower Loxhore has always been the biggest. Now mostly residential, many of the people commute to Barnstaple, but during the last century William Delve made and mended shoes here and Nicholas Cook produced hoops for wheels and barrels. Today's ranch-style houses and modern bungalows contrast strongly with the 16th century Rose Cottage and its elderly neighbours.

Loxhore Cott, once a collection of shepherds' huts, straddles the old Barnstaple–Lynton coachroad. At the turn of the century Mrs Agnes Garnish pulled pints for travellers at The Foxhunters' Inn, while horses were once shod in the forge opposite. Now the pub is the Lodge, guarding the back entrance to Arlington Court, and the forge has become a welder's workshop. Down the lane John Prescott had the wheelwright's shop, now a private dwelling, and two doors away Minnie Kidwell sold sweets and 'pop' to the children.

Loxhore Town earned its name in medieval days, when a collection of cottages clustered round the church. Today only their lumps and bumps remain in Cotty Field. South Town Farm, stone-built in the 17th century with neat outbuildings set around a spotless farmyard, is like others in the district, but whereas it is still a going concern, the adjacent North Town Farm provides holiday accommodation for summer visitors.

The church is dedicated to St Michael and All Angels, and has its roots in antiquity, although records go back only as far as the mid 13th century. In 1952 the Comer-Clarke family helped to refurbish the inside by providing oak for the pews from their own woods. In the churchyard, two headstones rest back to back. Apparently, Phoebe and Elizabeth never saw 'eye to eye' in life, and their relatives decided to continue the vendetta after death!

Spring means Chapel Anniversary, when a service is held on

147

8th February to commemorate the founding in 1840. The building was enlarged in 1925, with the original part becoming the schoolroom.

Men spreading lime on the grass, using lorries and tractors, are at their busiest early in the year. Their vehicles are kept in the biggest quarry on the roadside, opposite the site of the ruined Ivy chapel. This quarry supplied stone for runways at Chivenor air base during the Second World War, the 20 or so members of 'Quarry Flight' being billeted locally.

Summer means cricket, on a newly prepared pitch created from the village school field. The school was built in 1843, accommodating up to 80 children but rarely seeing more than half. Work at home was so much more attractive than book-learning! Closed in 1954 as a school, the building was eventually taken over to become the village hall.

One custom worth noting started in 1378: on the first of November, the tenant of a half-farthing of land at Loxhore Town was expected to pay his rent of one rose by the Nativity of John the Baptist.

Borough Farm at Loxhore Cott

Lustleigh 🎋

The manor of Lustleigh was recorded in the Domesday survey, as were the names of several local farms. In the centuries since then a rural community has lived simply and peaceably in the beautiful valley of the Wrey brook, ploughing the small fields, tending pigs and poultry and cultivating productive vegetable gardens. Many inhabitants never left the village at all and a visit to Exeter was an unforgettable experience. Before wheeled traffic became practicable, sledges were used for transport in the narrow, steep-sided lanes.

The coming of the branch railway line at the end of the 19th century opened up opportunities for travel further afield. At this time the board school was built. Before then village children had been educated in the old vestry, a small granite building within the churchyard, endowed in 1825 by one Parson Davy, himself a local character. He constructed a printing press and with the help of a maidservant printed a 26 volume *System of Divinity*.

The church was built in the 13th century, but a Celtic tombstone is evidence of an earlier religion worshipped on the site. The carved Devon screen was erected in Tudor times and decorated with pomegranates, the emblem of Katherine of Aragon. The craftsman who carved the small heads along the top of the screen must have had a sense of humour, for the faces of those looking towards the chancel are smiling while those looking towards the nave are all scowling. On 'Plough Sunday', when intercessions were made for a fruitful harvest, it was the custom for a local farmer to bring a wooden plough into the church to receive a blessing.

Social and economic change has affected Lustleigh, as is the case with many other villages. There is no longer a railway, village school, local policeman or resident nurse. But the local doctor holds a surgery in the village twice a week and the district nurse comes by car from nearby Moretonhampstead. Children are collected by mini-bus to be taken to school at Bovey Tracey; a panda car brings a helpful police constable when needed.

Riding ponies now graze where oats once grew. Cider orchards are neglected since the cider factories find it more economic to import fruit from the Continent. But it is still possible to find trails of hops to decorate the church at harvest festival, and the summer Flower Show is an important event in the village calendar.

Alders fringe the field where cricket matches are played on summer afternoons. Time was when parties from Lancashire mill towns camped in this same field, and cut bundles of alder wood for clog-making.

Lydford 🦚

In the 9th century, of the four moorland burghs created by Alfred the Great, one was sited on a hill overlooking the river Lyd; less than a mile distant the river was forded by a track, thus the simple name, Lydford.

The settlement grew to sufficient importance to warrant burning by the Danes in AD997 – doubtless a side excursion following their mayhem at Tavistock Abbey. A mint was operating at Lydford 1,000 years ago, a temptation to any Viking worth his salt and their pillage contributed to more of our coins being in Stockholm Museum than are held locally or in London.

Wealth came with the tin and through its stannary court Lydford was both a power in the land and unto itself by the exercise of Lydford Law, summary and cruel, for 'in the morn they hang and draw, and sit in judgement after'. This law was enforced at the castle, a grim stone prison on a Norman mound set a short distance from earlier Saxon and Norman earthworks. The last execution was recorded in 1650.

At the time of Domesday Lydford was credited with '28 burgesses within the walls and 41 without', a tidy settlement for the 11th century. The village church is dedicated to St Petroc and the first wooden building was a victim of the attack in AD997. 1237 records a stone building, enlarged and sympathetically improved over the centuries, culminating in today's mellow church. The tower has a peal of six bells and also serves to house and preserve the old stocks. A tale is told that on a certain wintry occasion a parishioner felt so positive that the weather would preclude any service, that for warmth she temporarily housed her goose and goslings in the pulpit. But the faithful arrived and the co-operative clergyman preached, legs astride in order not to disturb his feathered flock, only to be rewarded for his charity by some painful pecking.

St Petroc's was the final destination of the old Lychway across the moor, over which the dead were carried for burial in consecrated ground. When the weather was severe it was not unknown for the corpse to be salted down and suitably stored until conditions improved. The grave of George Routleigh in the churchyard is better known as The Watchmaker's Tomb, as this was his trade. To quote from his graven epitaph '. . . integrity was the mainspring, and prudence the regulator of all the actions of his life.'

Lydford Gorge, a beauty spot now in the care of the National Trust, was originally in the ownership of Mr Radford, the benefactor who was also responsible for giving the village its first free water supply to standpipes in the street. In the 17th century the gorge was reputedly home to a band of robbers, all red-bearded and rejoicing in the name of Gubbins, who finally disappeared 'as a result of intemperance and interbreeding'.

In 1660 this was described as a 'mean and miserable village' and by 1802 rated no higher than 'a poor decayed village with a few ragged cottages'. The picture today is much happier. One great benefit is the village school, which celebrated a centenary pageant in 1978. The first 'public' building was the freehold gift by Mr Radford in 1919 of the reading room, to be renamed the War Memorial Institute. The large village hall was an endowment in 1929 and has served the village well for countless social and sporting activities.

Lympstone ✣

At Lympstone's heart is a Saxon village, grouped in a sheltered little valley, with water and fishing and fields, protected by hills behind and in front, independent, hard-working and kindly, a good community. Until fairly recent times, Upper and Lower Lympstone indicated respectively the farming and fishing people, hinged on the centre of church, mill and manor.

There was considerable ship-building along the estuary, right up to below Nutwell – the old harbour before the railway came. A number of wealthy mariners built their houses in the village. The liberal-minded Sir Thomas Putt of Gittisham, who died in 1721, allowed his tenants to buy their freeholds at his death. This probably accounts for the large number of houses built in the village from then onwards. It would not have been permitted by the large landowners in many places. There are a few 17th century houses, mostly added on to and altered, but in the late 18th century and early 19th, a number of attractive places were built for visitors.

The advent of the railway in 1860, with its 30 steam trains a day, and consequent soot, drove the well-to-do from the centre of the village, but provided Lympstone with premises for every kind of trade and commerce. Indeed up to the beginning of the Second World War, the village was practically self-supporting, with a working mill, cider-making, dairy, slaughterhouse, as well as shoemakers, dressmakers and many little shops.

The parish church of the Nativity of the Blessed Virgin Mary received this dedication in 1409. The tower is said to have been used by both sides

151

View of Lympstone

in the Civil War (whoever was in possession at the time) to sight their guns firing at ships trying to relieve Exeter. The church was much restored about 1860.

From the late 17th century, there has also been a very strong Chapel history. Starting with the Gulliford meeting house and graveyard, tucked away at the end of Meeting Lane, and serving originally the Unitarians from Woodbury, Topsham and Exmouth as well as Lympstone, later a Methodist school and church played a large part in the village.

The present primary school was opened as a Church school as a private memorial early in the 19th century. Fortunately, having Royal Marine quarters in the village, the school still flourishes. Indeed, there are still many whose families have lived and worked in Lympstone for generations and hopefully this combination of old and new folk will continue to provide the present inhabitants with an unusually pleasant place to dwell.

Probably the best known landmark in the village (now appropriately in

153

the excellent hands of the Landmark Trust), the Peters' Tower, was built a little over a hundred years ago, near the lime-kilns, in memory of Mrs Mary Anne Peters of Harefield (now St Peter's school), who cared for the poor of the village.

Malborough 🌿

Most people driving between Kingsbridge and Salcombe will have a fleeting memory of the village of Malborough. The most likely impressions are that of a church whose spire is a landmark for many miles, a narrow stretch of road leading on to a sharp corner and the feeling that one has suddenly been hit by the full force of a south westerly gale!

However Malborough is more poetically but equally accurately described in an old directory as 'a parish pleasantly situated on an eminence commanding an extensive prospect and banded on the south by the open sea between Bolt Head and Bolt Tail, three and a half miles south-west of Kingsbridge'.

The old village is mainly to the south of the main road and besides the ancient parish church (All Saints) there are many picturesque thatched cottages and interesting old farm buildings. As with most South Hams villages there are also many newer houses and the population inevitably rises during the summer months when many second homes are occupied.

However, Malborough's modern claim to fame lies in its village hall, the largest in the South Hams and used extensively by many organisations not only locally based but from far and wide. Its building was the culmination of many hard years of fund raising and was made possible through the efforts of a courageous few who had the foresight to buy the village playing fields after the Second World War as part of the 'Welcome Home' Fund.

It is a most interesting and perhaps regrettable sign of the times that the focal point of the village has gradually moved over the years from the church to the village hall. It was reported in 1870 when the church was restored that 'the opening services were attended by large congregations, all the seats were occupied and many had to stand – a large marquee was erected and some hundreds of people sat down to lunch'. At the opening of the hall just over a century later it was equally attended by some hundreds of people, but in the somewhat different atmosphere of Carnival Day.

154

Manaton 🌿

Manaton, with its village green nestling beside the church, has been described as the most picturesque of all the Dartmoor villages. It is certainly one of the most attractive, and contains within its parish borders sweeping views of rock-strewn moorland, mixed with delightful secret places, havens of wildlife where human presence is seldom to be seen.

Mentioned in Domesday records, the earliest settlement is many centuries older, and the name of Manaton itself possibly comes from the existence of an ancient and massive stone enclosure, now destroyed. This stood close by the village green which, until recent times, was the hub of village activities. Here, within the compass of a few acres, stood the church and its handsome church house, the school, the Half Moon Inn, a shop and post office, a farmhouse and a scattering of granite-built cottages.

The church of St Winifrid has a typical granite interior dating from the 15th century, with waggon roofs and carved bosses. The fine rood screen bears the scars of vandalism from earlier times, with saints and martyrs being, literally, defaced. It contains a splendid window designed by Frank Brangwyn, apprentice to the famous William Morris.

Neadon Upper Hall, recorded in Domesday, deserves special mention as a unique example on Dartmoor of a building in which living accommodation was arranged above the animal stalls. Elsewhere, ancient farmhouses of the 'longhouse' design typify the moorland dwellinghouse – long, low granite walls, with windows hiding beneath deep thatch. In the tiny hamlet of Water, barely half a mile from the village green, granite cottages provide a glimpse of times past – here the communal water pump still draws sparkling water from deep beneath the ground!

Langstone and Hound Tor Farms are other Domesday manors, each of great interest and antiquity. Near Hound Tor lies a deserted medieval village, a whole community forever lost save for the sad remains of many buildings.

In more recent times the famous novelist and poet John Galsworthy came to live at Wingstone Farm, Manaton. World-famous for his series of novels, *The Forsyte Saga*, he was well-known locally for his generosity and interest in community life. The collected volumes of his works are known as the 'Manaton Edition'.

Though bleak and barren in winter, the moorland landscape in spring and summer gives way to rolling hills bright with yellow gorse and purple heather. Everywhere tumbling streams course through deep wooded valleys, growing in size and energy on their journey to the sea. Nowhere is their presence more spectacularly revealed than at Becka Falls. Here the Becka Brook cascades over and between massive boulders, finally descending in a roaring waterfall. At their best after midwinter rains, the Falls attract many thousands of visitors during summer months.

Also of great interest to visitors is the enigmatic column of stone known as Bowerman's Nose. This natural rock formation stands imposingly upon a lofty hill, looking for all the world like some petrified sentinel forever gazing across to the rugged hills of high Dartmoor. Not far distant lies the Bronze Age enclosure of Grimspound. This remarkable prehistoric site contains the remains of 24 hut-circles, once the homes of Dartmoor's earliest settlers. Few who visit this impressive monument will fail to reflect upon the lives of those who lived here those many thousands of years ago.

Marwood 🕸

Marwood parish is just to the north east of Barnstaple, in quiet wooded hilly country. It is made up from the scattered hamlets of Bittadon, Middle Marwood, Milltown, Muddiford, Guineaford, Prixford, and Marwood itself with its ancient parish church, dedicated to St Michael. There is a sundial above the main door which dates from the 1700s and shows the approximate times in the principal capitals of Europe and at Jerusalem. Sadly, the beautiful Elizabethan church plate must be stored safely in the bank.

A constant pleasure is Dr Smart's Marwood Hill Gardens, situated on both sides of the Marwood valley, sloping down to two lakes and planted with beautiful trees and shrubs and many rare and unusual plants. It is always open.

Marwood has a strange legend associated with it. The story goes that on her way to the local fair, alone, and wishing that she had a companion even if it were the Devil himself, a young girl called Mary was overtaken by a handsome stranger who asked to join her. She agreed, spent the evening with him, and he took her home. He came to the house to fetch her on several following evenings. Her parents were puzzled and worried because he would never come into the house. But one day Mary's mother saw that the handsome stranger had cloven hooves and, horrified, she slammed the door on him, with Mary still inside. Taking a lighted candle she went, by the back way, to the church to ask the priest for help. The priest assured her Mary would be safe as long as it was not known whether the candle the mother was carrying had burned out or not. So together they walled it up behind the rood screen in the church. As the last brick was put in place the Devil vanished. It seems that poor Mary never married and that, in the end, she went mad. It is said that, much later, workmen found a partly burned candle – bricked up at the back of the rood screen!

Mary Tavy & Peter Tavy 🌿

Mary Tavy and Peter Tavy are twin villages, which grew out of ancient settlements either side of the river Tavy. They each have a church, St Mary's and St Peter's. These are a mile apart, and are joined by a bridle path, with a bridge over the river, known as 'The Clam', an old name for a bridge.

Mining was the main industry until the 1920s, and many remains of the old workings are still scattered about the area. Devon United, a copper mine, ceased working on the Peter Tavy side of the Tavy in 1925. Wheal Friendship, in Mary Tavy, was at one time the largest copper mine in the world, later producing arsenic, which was exported from Morwellham. This was at first taken there by packhorse, but then John Taylor, who was the mine manager, had the Tavistock Canal constructed in 1817. The arsenic flues which snaked up the hillside to Wheal Bennets can still be seen, but are now almost covered by gorse. Wheal Betsy engine house is a prominent feature on the moorland, close to the A386 main road. This was part of the extensive workings of an old silver and lead mine, utilising the Cholwell Brook to work the many water-wheels. Women worked on the surface, breaking up the ore. They were known as Bal Maidens. Bal is an old word for mine, and there is still a Bal Lane.

The many leats and water courses, which were used to work the mine machinery, are now utilised to work the power station. This was one of the first rural areas to enjoy the benefits of electricity, and visitors can nowadays be shown around this rare feature.

William Crossing, the famous writer on Dartmoor, lived for many years in a cottage, now known as 'Crossing'. He wrote his famous *Guide to Dartmoor* there, as well as many other books. He was a familiar figure, walking the lanes, and gathering tales from the villagers. He and his wife are buried in Mary Tavy churchyard.

Celebration bonfires are lit at the top of Gibbet Hill, and all the people climb to this high point to take part in national events. This is where they

The engine house of Wheal Betsy, Mary Tavy

used to hang wrongdoers in the old days. The sight of the corpse, left hanging from the gibbet, must have deterred people from stealing sheep, or becoming a highwayman. The prisoners were kept in a cage at the foot of the hill, on the Brentor road, now known as Iron Gate.

Lady Howard, notorious for murdering her husbands, is said to travel up through the village at midnight, in her coach made out of their bones, with a black hound following behind. She has to pick a blade of grass from Okehampton Castle, and take it back to Fitzford in Tavistock, until there is no more grass left at the castle.

Peter Tavy has the beautiful 'Tavy Cleave' and 'The Coombe'. The old inn is world famous, and there are some delightful old houses clustered round the Colley Brook, which worked two lovely old mills.

Hill farming is the main occupation in the two villages, with the inhabitants having a common right to graze cattle, sheep, ponies, and in the old days geese, which would have been taken to the famous Tavistock Goose Fair.

The little hamlet of Horndon is where the pub with the unusual name of The Elephant's Nest is situated.

Meavy

Meavy lies in a valley of the same name. Close by is a ford with stepping stones on the monastic route from Plympton Priory to Tavistock Abbey. One of the crosses, which marked the way, still stands above the ford. Large vehicles still use it because the nearly 200 year old bridge is narrow, frail and awkwardly sited. A similar bridge at the other end of the village was washed away in 1909 and replaced by an iron monstrosity.

Not far from the iron bridge is the small manor house of Meavy Barton. Little sign is now left of its 16th century origin. Descendants of Drake once lived here and owned their own mill. This was fed by a branch of the leat promoted by their illustrious ancestor to serve Plymouth. Drake's leat has been dry since the water in Burrator Reservoir drowned the intake from the Meavy river. The mill house was once used as a general store and post office – alas, now closed.

Some 100 yards from the mill is the village green on which the ancient Meavy oak just survives, supported by iron beams. It is probably about 500 years old, but an oak at the village of 'Mewi' is recorded in the Domesday Book. A young tree stands ready to take over. The village cross, under the old oak, has been restored using parts of the original. There is a separate war memorial.

Beside the green are St Peter's church, the Royal Oak Inn and the old rectory. Cnut the Dane is said to have given the villagers leave to build a church here, but the present structure dates from Norman times. It was largely rebuilt in the 13th and 15th centuries. The Drake door in the south wall, added in 1705, allowed the Lady Chapel to be used as a family pew.

The Royal Oak Inn by the church is thought to be unique in Devon in being owned by the parish, the rental contributing to the parish rate. Originally built in the 12th century as a church house, it was rebuilt in the 18th century. Though recently extensively renovated, it still keeps its old world atmosphere. People spill out of it on summer days onto the village green, where Meavy Oak Fair is held each June.

Opposite the pub is the much used parish hall, part of which was the old school. After the Second World War it was extended as a practical form of war memorial and further enlargements have taken place since, a store in memory of Loveday Trahair, who did much for the parish over many years, being the most recent.

Close to the school is the old blacksmith's shop, strategically placed at the crossing of the Plympton to Tavistock road and the route from the village to the 19th century tin mining area.

There is still some farming in the area, and several of the old families commemorated in the churchyard have descendants living and working locally. Though the village itself is small, the parish is extensive and has seen much modern building, particularly at Dousland.

Membury 🦢

Membury is a small village lying in a valley 400 ft above sea level, under the guardianship of its ancient hill fortress, Membury Castle, the 'Stone Fort', whose ditches and ramparts are still there.

The church is some 700 years old, and was the scene of a skirmish during the Civil War, when Roundheads were put to flight by local Royalists. On the ridge above the church is a small Quaker burial ground from the days when there was a Quaker community in the village, followers of J. Smith, born at Lea Hill Farm. They used the cottage now called 'Quakers' as their meeting place, and when the soldiers came to arrest them, would hide in a cave in Whitehall woods.

Membury is a farming village, with sheep everywhere and the cry of lambs echoing from hill to hill. Challenger Farm, the 'Cold Slope', lies above the village and Godworthy Farm on its hill to the north. Yarty Farm stands over the ridge by the parish boundary on the river Yarty. In another valley lies Membury Court, where in earlier days the travelling judge held his court, and where the remains of an old chapel stand, and the foundations of a Roman villa.

All through the parish there are hedges full of primroses and violets in spring, then bluebells and stitchwort and campion, and later tall foxgloves in crimson ranks. Overhead buzzards circle lazily on the look-out for their prey, and deer skip silently through the woods below.

Not so long ago there was a resident witch, and a ghostly lady whom it is unwise to meet in June walks in Furley, a nearby hamlet.

The village school lies next to the church, anxiously cherished by the population as the numbers of children fall. The pupils decorate their corner of the church at Christmas, Easter and Harvest Festival, and take part in the Family Services with happy enthusiasm.

There is a pottery and a trout farm, a toy and candlemaker and a basket weaver. Several people make cider, and until recently there was a thatcher, now retired, but still captain of the bell-ringers.

The village shop not only sells nearly everything needed for daily life, but acts as a centre for the exchange of news, impromptu committee meetings, the buttonholing of Parish Councillors or churchwardens and the general business of WI, History Society or parish hall.

Milton Abbot 🕮

For centuries the fortunes of Milton Abbot have been closely tied to the interests of the Russell family. After the dissolution of the great abbey in Tavistock in 1539, Henry VIII gave lands and possessions including Milton Abbot to Lord Russell, the ancestor of the Dukes of Bedford.

Milton Abbot is a small attractive village midway between Launceston and Tavistock. In the Domesday Book it is referred to as Mideltona, perhaps because of its position between the two historic towns.

Strolling round the village you will be intrigued by the well-built grey stone houses. These were erected early in this century by the 7th Duke who planned a model village for his work people. The architect was the famed Sir Edward Lutyens and the stone was quarried locally. The Duke's ancestor, John, was responsible for building Endsleigh Cottage in 1810. Chosen by his wife Georgiana, the land slopes down to the river Tamar and has been described as the most beautiful in England. The house and land is now cared for by a charitable trust.

The church of St Constantine stands in the centre of the village. Built in the 15th century, it has a handsome west tower with six bells. The priest's door opens into the large seat, supplied with a fireplace, which is apportioned to the Duke. The large Victorian vicarage which stands below the church was built in 1838 for the Rev Sir Vincent Love Hammick. The nurseries on the upper floors would have been fully occupied by his 14 children. A Wesleyan chapel was also built at this time and is still attended.

On the outskirts of the village stand two ancient manor houses, Leigh

Barton, and Edgecombe. Leigh was the original house of the deLiga family and at some time owned by the abbots. It is still occupied today and the land extensively farmed. Edgecombe was the seat of the ancient family of Edgecombe, who resided there from the reign of Henry III.

The older inhabitants of this village have seen many changes from candlelight to electricity, from horse and cart to motor cars, from home-spun entertainment to television, and the mechanisation of farming. In 1953 the death of the Duke who had cared for, and employed, almost everyone in the village, was the greatest turning point. They also tell entertaining stories of the Cherry Fair when stalls lined the roads and the travelling entertainers came. The young lads could earn a few pence by polishing harnesses or pumping the bellows for the blacksmith. There were fireworks at Edgecombe, garden parties at the vicarage, and harvest suppers in the vicarage rooms over the stables. There were cream teas, saffron and seed cake, and each year a different farmer's wife poured the tea.

White's Directory for 1850 lists five public houses, though only one exists now. One well-remembered innkeeper was Granny Collins of the Kings Arms who was well into her nineties. She wore an elaborately decorated bonnet for church on Sundays when she escorted the Duke to his pew.

Entertainment today revolves round the WI, the Cricket Club (founded in the 1850s) and the Milton Players who produce a yearly play.

Modbury 🦢

Modbury is built on the slopes of a valley and consists of four main streets intersecting at right angles. It lies five miles south-east of Ivybridge. It used to have a supply of water from the lovely sounding Silverwell. Many houses still have access to their own well supplies of fresh spring water.

In February 1642, the Royalists Sir Ralph Hopton and Sir Nicholas Slanning with 2,000 men were attacked and defeated by the Parliamentarians from Plymouth under Colonel Ruthven. There is still a lane behind the church called Runaway Lane after the Cavaliers.

The church of St George standing at the top of the town is built in the Gothic style of the 13th and 14th century, re-erected in 1622 with a spire of 134 ft, together with a clock and six bells. There are several stone effigies in recessed arches.

Amongst the chief charities in 1939 were £5 for the improvement of the town and £5 for coal for the poor. The education charities amounted to £27 3s 10d, being interest from Consol shares left by John Andrews, Joseph Wriford and a few others, part of which went to the vicar for religious education and the balance for school prizes. A Mr Hill donated £7 per annum for nursing.

Modbury must have been fairly self-sufficient with Mr Bickford the miller at the lovely old water mill at Sheepham, a monumental mason called Mr Ash, Percy Ford the saddler, Mr Williams the blacksmith, Mr Burring the bootmaker, Mr May the tailor, farmers galore and dairymen like Mr Phillips and Percy May. Then there were bakers like Mr Brown who also made delicious ice cream using fresh cream, and later Arnold Fox who would let villagers pop pasties or chickens into his bake-ovens. Luckily his son Colin owns the baker's shop in Broad Street and still bakes behind the shop. There was a flourishing printers called Trinick, now the post office.

Several doctors, dentists and veterinary surgeons kept the people and animals in good health and of course there were the old inns – the Exeter Inn, full of character, the pretty Modbury Inn, the Red Devon Inn, which in recent times was taken down to widen the road, and also the old White Hart.

Today there are many attractive new estates with lovely gardens, and new generations of children filling the old school and creating traditions of their own.

In the 1950s there were still cobbles 'up along' Galpin Street but today there are good roads and all the old cottages are being renovated, most of them with imagination and using the best of materials to make lovely homes with the traditional look.

Molland 🐑

Molland is a small community on the southern slopes of Exmoor, with only about 284 people, mostly connected with sheep and cattle farming, remote from motorway traffic and a very peaceful place.

The approach to Molland from the South Molton road runs uphill through a tree-lined valley with the chance of a deer crossing the road unexpectedly, watched by the herons standing sentry in the trees opposite. On reaching Molland the road divides, one branch leading to one of the oldest houses in the village at West Molland Barton, a manor house of the Courtenay family, whose arms are still carved over the front door. In the mid 18th century it was leased by the Quartlys, a Huguenot refugee family said to have originally been called Cartelois. The most famous of the Quartly family was Francis Quartly, who with his brother farming at nearby Great Champson, started the Devon Herd Book with the famous Red Devon cattle. The family died out in 1910 when the last Quartly went to Canada.

Back in Molland village the right hand fork of the road leads up a short steep hill passing the London Inn, reputed to be 700 years old, with a warm and cosy bar and a pleasant garden outside – meeting place for local farmers and summer visitors. Beyond that is the church of St Mary Magdalene, parts of which date back to Norman times, particularly the massive font and the base of the tower. An aisle on the north side is called the Courtenay Aisle with many of their family memorials and a three-tiered pulpit. Most noticeable are the tall box pews.

Swallows find the porch a perfect nesting place and no wonder, the view from there is most lovely, over fields and hills and a glimpse of Dartmoor in the distance. Beware if it is too clear, rain is on the way! Follow the road still further up the lane, bordered with primroses and bluebells in spring, until you cross the cattle grid and come out on Exmoor, where it seems all Devon lies below you like a patchwork quilt. Only larks and cuckoos disturb the peace and if you are lucky you may see the Exmoor ponies and their dancing foals in the spring or red deer in the autumn.

But what do we do in Molland? Well – play darts, have men and women's skittles teams, a cricket club and a gardener's club which holds a flower and produce show every September, a garden fete in the summer and a Christmas bazaar. The WI hold an open meeting in August with films about Exmoor and the Red Deer for summer visitors to raise money for the local hospital, and a carol concert at Christmas with the Town Band from South Molton to help various childrens charities.

Monkokehampton 🦢

Monkokehampton is a small village situated some three miles from Hatherleigh. The name itself means 'an enclosed farm on the river Okement' and also relates to the village's former associations with a monastic community. An area about a quarter of a mile west of the parish church is known locally as Monk's Mill. Here is the ruined site of a former monastic grange associated with Tavistock Abbey.

Today the village is smaller than in former times. More recently there has been a slight increase but the parish still only has about 140 inhabitants. The real focus is now the post office and the blacksmith's forge, one of few survivals as a working village smithy in Devon. The post office has been in existence for over a century and throughout the whole of its history has been run by members of the Vanstone family. The village forge is still run today by Mr Herbert Vanstone, who has succeeded his father and grandfather in the occupation.

In former times the village supported another forge near the Old Swan Inn, the remains of which can still be identified, as well as a wheelwright's business operated by the Fairchild family.

Village recreation was catered for by the parish reading room, which is still an attractive thatched building in the centre. The village has one old packhorse inn, The Old Swan Inn, but in the 1820s it certainly had a New Swan Inn too!

The west end of the village is overlooked by the parish church of All Saints. The church has a particularly fine 15th century tower with impressively lofty pinnacles. Following a serious fire most of the rest of the church was rebuilt by F. Harper in 1855. Internally its most striking feature is the east window, which was shown at the Great Exhibition in 1851 and provided for the church by the Northcote family. Beside the lychgate at the edge of the churchyard the old National school building still stands and is also still used today for parish activities.

Monkokehampton has, throughout its history, been dominated by farming. The two most architecturally interesting former farmhouses to survive in the parish to the present day are the secluded 16th century Beer, and East Lake, an almost completely 17th century structure off the Winkleigh road. Today the centre of farming life in the village has shifted to the Hatherleigh road, in particular to The Mills and Church Stile farms, which themselves have been a major influence on the parish for over a century.

A 19th century three-storey mill is today situated in a beautiful setting on the river, just outside the village. It has two pitchback wheels each driving two pairs of stones and is still operational. Present inhabitants can also remember when the village had its own tucking mill.

A long lived custom is associated with the Colehouse and Clapp's charities. Still supervised by a group of village trustees, these date back to the early 18th and early 19th century respectively. They were founded to provide bread, fuel or cash for labouring men or widows in the parish who were not receiving any poor relief. In 1971 the charities were amalgamated and today the trustees distribute a small payment every few years to widows or persons living on their own in the parish.

The village is still very peaceful and unspoilt. There has been hardly any new housing built in recent years. Perhaps the essence of the village is still the occasional striking from the blacksmith's forge – a true echo from yesteryear!

Morchard Bishop 🦢

Morchard Bishop is a large pleasant village with a population of just under 1,000. The parish includes several hamlets and many farms, mainly dairy.

Its history can be traced back to Celtic times when there was a settlement in or near the 'Great Wood', the meaning of Morchet. Archaeological excavations have revealed an Iron Age settlement in the south-west of the parish, while the name Harestreet in the east testifies to its Saxon past. At the Conquest Morchard became Crown property but in 1166 it was purchased by the Bishop of Exeter, and from that time became known as Bishop's Morchard.

The church tower is a prominent landmark, standing as it does on the highest point in the village. The church was built in the middle of the 15th century, when the Bishop was offering indulgences to all who helped with the work of building. This was probably done to keep the villagers out of mischief, as a few years earlier he had been writing stern letters threatening excommunication for those who were caught poaching deer and other animals from his Park!

The present thriving village school was built in 1872, but an earlier one was founded in 1733 which was a 'Blue Coat' school.

Passing through the centre of the village is the Two Moors Way, and a stone near the school marks the midway point of the walk. On the southern side of the village are the remains of a pound, which records mention as early as 1682. This has now been restored and is cared for by the Gardening Club. Further down the hill are the local blacksmiths. The family of Webber have been blacksmiths for at least three generations but the family can be traced back to the 17th century.

One of the greatest events of the year for villagers used to be Morchard Great Fair, which took place on the Monday following the church Harvest Festival. Horse racing took place in the fields to the west of the village called 'The Parks', surely a remnant of the Bishop's park. Another red letter day was Whit Tuesday when the London Inn had their 'Club Walk'. On both of these occasions the village band took a prominent part, both in leading processions and giving concerts, still remembered by many of the older villagers.

There are several medieval farmhouses in the parish and many attractive cottages in the village. Most visitors are, however, enchanted by the continuous row of 13 pretty cottages in Fore Street. These were mainly built in the late 18th century, and are reputedly the longest row of thatched cottages in the county. Until 1830 Fore Street was on the main coaching route from Barnstaple to Exeter and ultimately to London, hence the name of 'London Inn' in the centre of the village. The opening of the road and railway in the valley in the first half of the 19th century, coupled with the decline of the woollen industry, led to a severe drop in both employment and population. The population was halved within 50 years.

Morchard's central position in the county has encouraged commuters to settle in the village and enabled many of its young local families to stay. Homes range from two small council estates to a private development of bungalows which were built in the late 1960s on the site of the old rectory and its garden. As the village is in a conservation area new building is carefully monitored, but several new houses have been built, while many of the older properties have been carefully modernised.

Fore Street, Morchard Bishop

167

Moretonhampstead ✑

Moretonhampstead lies on the B3212 road from Exeter, a road which used to be a main route into Cornwall years ago.

Fifty, even 40, years ago it was a shopping centre for farmers and workers from outlying hamlets and the shops sold the sort of goods they would need. There were four bakers, about a dozen grocers, a fish-monger, two butchers, a draper, a shoe shop, chemist, blacksmith and a large general store which sold everything from candles and bacon to buckets and nails. Nowadays there are still two butchers and a chemist but the general store has closed, the fishmonger went many years ago and until very recently there was no baker in the town.

It is now predominantly a tourist centre. On the outskirts of the town there is a large transport depot for container lorries. There is also a timber merchant, a travel agent, office accommodation for various organisations and several retirement homes. These provide work for some local people and the others commute to Exeter or to Newton Abbot.

The name Moretonhampstead was originally Mor Tun – a name dating back to its Saxon foundation in AD700. It appears in the Domesday Book as Mortona. The Hampstead part of the name crept in at a later date and is still largely ignored by the Moretonians today.

The church of St Andrew is in a commanding position on high ground at the end of Greenhill. The present building dates from the 15th century but replaces earlier churches dating back as far as Saxon times. During the Napoleonic Wars, when the prison at Princetown housed French prisoners, many of the officers on parole lived in Moreton and two of them died here. Their tombstones are now in the porch.

Near the church, in Cross Street, is a copper beech surrounded by a stone platform on which is the head of an old cross. This tree is a replacement of the old 'Dancing Tree'; an elm brought down in a gale in 1891. This was pollarded so that a platform could be supported in its branches and on this a fiddler and dancers could be accommodated. The stone cross is of 14th or 15th century origin.

There is nothing left today of the original Saxon settlement apart from the position of what is now Back Lane; this alley delineates what was the centre of the Saxon settlement. There has been a thoroughfare there for nearly 1,300 years but visitors will find no name plate – nor has there ever been one.

Many of the old houses were destroyed by four major fires which occurred between 1845 and 1892. There remain, however, some houses of antiquity – notably Mearsdon Manor. Parts of it date back to the 13th century and indeed one door is as early as 1150 although there is reason to suppose that this door may have been part of the first stone church. The Manor is now a restaurant and antiques shop but is still very much unspoiled.

Mortehoe 🌿

Mortehoe is an ancient parish nestling in the hills beyond Morte Point, a rocky headland jutting out into the Bristol Channel, with magnificent views towards Lundy Island and the Welsh coast.

The parish includes Woolacombe, a three-mile stretch of sands which today attracts a great deal of tourist trade, and the village of Woolacombe has grown from only a couple of farms at the beginning of this century to a thriving community which today tends to overshadow its more traditional neighbour. There are, however, several caravan sites around Mortehoe which blend into the landscape yet command extensive views of the rugged coastline and rolling hills. Whilst tourism is important, farming is one of the main occupations of the area.

There is evidence that the area was settled in Stone Age times, and the Domesday Book mentions Morthou as a small manor.

The church of St Mary in the centre of Mortehoe dates from 1109, though most of the church was built in the 13th century. It has Norman arches and a fine barrel roof.

Bull Point lighthouse, just north of Morte Point, was originally built in 1879, to the dismay of the many people of Mortehoe who relied on the frequent wrecks along this inhospitable coastline for extra income. In 1972, however, there was a landslide below the lighthouse, and cracks appeared in the building. A portable light from Crowe was used until the new lighthouse was completed in 1975, built higher up the cliffs, and incorporating many automatic devices. The light flashes three times every ten seconds. The fog horn blasts every minute in poor visibility.

Mortehoe consists of eleven farms namely Shaftsboro, Borough, Damage, Warcombe, Yarde, Easewell, North Morte, Town, Poole, Ossaborough and Willingcott. Ranging from an acreage of approximately 60 to 250, not one of these has a herd of dairy cows today. The main source of income on farms today is sheep, beef, tourism and barley in that order.

Tourism is nowadays the main source of employment in this area. Both in Mortehoe, and particularly in Woolacombe with its long sandy beach, catering for the holidaymaker during the few short weeks of the summer season is the chief concern of the majority of the local people.

In the main the impact of tourism has been well-controlled: the caravan sites are well-situated and are generally screened with trees; facilities which have been provided for holidaymakers on the camp sites, such as swimming pools, are not obtrusive; and the small number of shops and cafes catering to their needs are generally open all year round for the benefit of local people. On the whole, the rural atmosphere is being retained very effectively.

Musbury ✑

Musbury lies in the beautiful Axe valley with a population of about 500. This is still predominantly farming country, with a gentle landscape of green hills, the fields bounded by hedgebanks, and still blessed with many broadleafed trees. To be held up in the narrow lanes by a herd of cows plodding home for milking, or a flock of sheep being driven from one pasture to another, can be a blessing. This enforced slowdown gives the traveller time to observe more closely the variety of wild flowers and plants still surviving in this corner of East Devon but no longer seen in many other parts of the country. Through the spring and summer primrose and bluebell, periwinkle and foxglove, honeysuckle and dog rose, bloom in succession along the lanes.

There are farms right in the heart of Musbury, as well as all round it. They originally formed part of the manor. The traditional home of the local lords of the manor was the ancient house of Ashe. It was badly damaged by fire in 1644, and the present Ashe House, situated just out of the village was built some years later. Ashe House, home of the Drake family, was reputedly the birthplace of Sir John Churchill, Duke of Marlborough, hero of Blenheim and other battles.

The church of St Michael dates from the 13th century. It has been enlarged and restored over the years. It stands on a hill in a very attractive setting, with the small school beside it still, happily, serving the village's young children. Below it is a lovely thatched house with a stream running beside it, and gardens which are open to the public on certain days of the year. Church fetes and festivals held from time to time in the summer add life and colour to this tranquil spot.

Musbury Castle is the site of an Iron Age hill fort. Those who reach the grass-covered summit are rewarded with a magnificent view of the lower Axe valley.

Another vantage point is at the top of Mounthill Lane. A bench well placed for sitting to admire the spectacular view bears the inscription 'Mary Day Lewis 1902–1975'. Mary and her husband, the poet Cecil Day Lewis, lived in the pretty thatched cottage half way down the lane.

When the Romans occupied Britain, it is thought that Musbury was used as a camp, mainly by engineers who built roads, including the Fosse Way. Present day employment, in addition to farming, is found in neighbouring towns, with such companies as Racal Ltd at Seaton, Hoechst CeramTec at Colyton, and Axminster Carpets.

Musbury's shop and post office is a focal point of the village. There is a great deal of coming and going, with pauses on the corner to read the notice boards and exchange news, while tractors and Landrovers pass up and down 'The Street'. On a hot day, a young man on his way to the fields may stop his tractor and jump down to buy an ice cream, and the story is still told of the farmer who inadvertently drove through the village with his muck-spreader switched on!

Newton Poppleford with Harpford

Newton Poppleford and Harpford are separated by the river Otter, which runs under the bridge carrying the main A3052 road, to join the sea at nearby Budleigh Salterton.

The village of Newton Poppleford was founded as a new town in the 13th century by the lord of the manor of Aylesbeare, some three miles across the common. His original plan was for a market on the road from Exeter to Sidmouth, which soon became a permanent settlement. On the site of this market, in the middle of the village, stands St Luke's church. The village has a mixture of cob and thatch cottages, many bordering the main road. The long, narrow gardens still exist, originally plots termed burgages, given to the crofters to grow their own produce. Today, modern housing estates are springing up in the village.

St Luke's church was originally built in 1331 as a chapel of ease for Aylesbeare church. Only the tower and porch remain, the bulk of the present church was built in 1897. Harpford has its own church, St Gregory's. It was almost entirely rebuilt in 1884. The Rev A. M. Toplady, the author of *Rock of Ages* was vicar here in 1766. St Gregory's has a peal of bells, rung every Sunday.

Both villages use the village store and post office, where it seems possible to buy almost anything, and meet friends.

At the Exeter end of the village, at the Exeter/Exmouth crossroad, is the toll house, the oldest in Devon, built in 1753, a pretty 'listed' thatched building, occasionally used as an antiques/gift shop.

The original King Alfred daffodil was bred in Newton Poppleford. Sadly, its birth-place is now developed into a modern estate, but its name is forever preserved. The road through the estate is King Alfred's Way.

Communal life in the village is very active, and caters for all ages, from the village school and the Rainbow playgroup to the Over 60s who meet weekly in the village hall. The Playing Field Foundation maintain the extensive playing field, where, as well as a children's play area, there are pitches for the local football and cricket teams.

North Bovey

North Bovey is a picturesque and unspoilt Devon village, beloved of artists and foreign visitors. Its thatched cottages cluster round the green, which is shaded by a grove of ancient oaks, and marked with many granite memorials commemorating past Royal Jubilees and coronations, and the end of the First World War.

A prominent feature is the ancient granite cross which faces the church. This is not, however, the original village cross, which was broken during the Civil War, and which in 1943 was found to have been built into the wall of the parlour of the cottage opposite (at one time the village store and post office). The present one was found in 1829, lying in the Bovey brook being used as a stepping stone, and the Rev John Pike-Jones had it hauled to the green and set upon the old base.

The church of St John the Baptist dates from the 13th and 15th centuries. The church is light and airy and well looked after. The carved bench ends, with Tudor roses, are 16th century.

A brass tablet near the altar records the service of some 50 years of the Rev W. H. Thornton. He was a parson of private means and out of his own pocket was able to provide £600 to restore the church. The rectory is now the Glebe Hotel. He owned two pairs of greys for hunting and for his carriage. He wrote a diary, published in two books, one of which refers to North Bovey. He arrived here from Dunsford in February 1866 and recorded:

'My new parishioners were very turbulent people . . . the women were awful . . . the whole village was much addicted to scandalous gossip of the worst description . . . They tore each other's hair out by handfuls and they flung crockery and stones at one another, and one actually leaned out of a window, pistol in hand, and threatened the life of a policeman.'

But later on he adds – 'They were as generous as they were fierce.'

At one time the village was much larger, when there were more farm labourers. There was a post office, which the Sampson family ran for 75 years, a grocery shop, a blacksmith, a carpenter/undertaker, a thatcher, a coachman for the rector, a shepherd, and many more. Mr Hill was the miller, and corn was ground in the mill down at Blackaller until 1929.

The village shows much evidence of the generosity of Lord Hambledon. He extensively restored the church from 1916 to 1918. He built the thatched parish hall (formerly stables), constructed roads, and replaced a row of derelict cottages (one of which is reputed to have been an inn – The Court) with the New Buildings, for his staff at the manor.

The Ring Of Bells is very old. The late Mr J. H. Brackenbury, landlord, held a National Hunt permit to train steeplechase horses. Their stables were attached to the inn. Mrs Brackenbury was the last woman to ride a postal round on the moor six days a week in all weathers, on a twelve mile circuit.

Northleigh & Farway

The two adjoining villages of Farway and Northleigh have a population of between 400 and 500. They are situated in a rural area of outstanding natural beauty with a wealth of flora and fauna. It is mainly a farming community – many families and their ancestors have farmed in the area for generations, but there are a number of residents who have retired to these lovely, peaceful surroundings from busy towns and cities.

Apart from Dartmoor, Farway Common has the largest amount of Bronze Age barrows in the county. 'Boycombe' was the original manor house, which is still occupied and has been since it was built in the 16th century. In the churchyard of the medieval church of St Michael are two magnificent yew trees, several hundred years old.

Netherton Hall is now a school for deprived children, and adjoining the Hall is Netherton Barton, said to be haunted by the ghosts of children on a rocking horse. Several occupants of the house were insistent that from time to time they heard rocking noises, and a few years ago the house was exorcised by the vicar, the Rev F. Gilbert.

Northleigh village church of St Giles is well worth a visit – on entering the church through a Norman arch will be seen the Norman font, and the beautiful old carved woodwork on the chancel screen and the pew ends is quite exceptional, being some 500 years old. It also possesses a rare set of four medieval bells which are still rung. There is an old Charity Board in the porch worthy of note, and the charity is still administered.

The burning of the Ashen Faggot took place on 24th December each year – made up of branches of ash some 5 ft in length, bound together with strips of hazel and weighing as much as a hundredweight, it was placed in the huge fireplace of the local inn and set alight. Each time a strip of the binding was burned through, the landlord would serve drinks and refreshments to all the customers. This custom was last carried out at the New Inn, Northleigh on 24th December, 1952. Sadly the inn has now closed and is occupied as a private house.

Many farms and cottages go back to the 16th century and John Buchan, the well known author of spy stories, lived at such a farm – 'Summerdown'. Another author, Mr Coxhead, who wrote many books about rural Devon, lived at nearby 'Hawkswood' in a clearing in the woods. On his death, a few years ago, he willed the area, which is massed with azaleas, rhododendrons and many other colourful shrubs intermingled with a great variety of wild flowers, to the Devon Conservation Trust.

North Molton 🦡

The village stretches for more than a mile from west to east, rising from the lovely wooded valley running between North and South Molton to a peak where stands the parish church of All Saints overlooking the Square, an area of conservation. The road then winds steeply downhill to the river Mole.

There is evidence of a Neolithic settlement in this area and North Molton appears in the Domesday Book. Other records are scant but it is known that by 1314 there was a fulling mill by the Mole and a plentiful supply of local wool for the village to develop a woollen industry.

Mineral wealth in the area has been intermittently exploited since Saxon times. Iron, copper and silver mines in and around Heasley Mill were worked until about 1851. Many of the miners lived in North Molton. Even today some houses and cottages are still named after the miners who lived in them.

Farmland and small areas of woodland surround North Molton making it a truly rural village. It is chiefly sheep country with some cattle and a few crops. Two of the farmhouses are still situated in the village and not so long ago Joe, who was old and bent, could be seen herding cows to Lower Pool Farm for milking. Horses and riders are part of the daily scene and during the hunting season the huntsmen, hounds and followers often pass by.

With a population of just under 1,000 you may wonder what all the people do who are not working on the land or in the village. South Molton, a market town which also has several small factories, is just three and a half miles away and provides employment for some.

North Molton is well provided for with a very good primary school, three shops, a post office, two pubs and bus services to South Molton and Barnstaple. Twice a week a doctor's surgery is held in the village hall.

The parish church and the Methodist church each have well loved pastors who help to foster the really good community spirit in the village. Voluntary help ensures that all age groups are cared for. Just a few years ago a splendid Sports Club was built by voluntary labour under the keen eye of one of the builders. Football and cricket have for ages been the main sports. The club boasts two football teams and a good cricket team.

Most of the traditional village craftsmen and women are still to be found including a thatcher. Annual events like the village hall fete held in the grounds of the Poltimore estate, are part of village life and promote goodwill and fellowship.

North Tawton 🌿

North Tawton is in the centre of Devon and has a population of some 1,500. It can be traced back to Roman times at least; ancient maps show a roman road passing through at North Tawton.

In 1086 it was recorded in the Domesday Book as Tawland or Tawetona with a population of 200. by 1158 it was known as Tawton and then in 1199 as Cheping Tawton. A market charter was granted in 1374, from which various fair days evolved. Most of these have now

175

lapsed but during the present century cattle have been penned and sold in the Square.

The reputation for trading has been kept up. The wool factory and bark stripping business situated at the bottom of the town provided employment up until the Industrial Revolution. Devonshire House, purpose-built as a school in the 1860s and now the doctor's surgery, was the home of the North Devon Water Board from 1895 to the 1930s. The Devon Serge warehouse had an extensive tailoring trade sending high class clothing and clerical suits to many parts of the world.

In the late 1800s ginger beer was manufactured. It is said that the owner of the factory was the inventor of the ginger beer bottle with the glass marble in its neck. This method of sealing the bottles using the pressure of the gas in the ginger beer was quite ingenious.

Today employment is provided by the Express Dairies cheese factory (the largest in Europe), and by the local firm of Gregory's who provide warehousing and run a fleet of container trucks.

Part of North Tawton was destroyed in two major fires, the old Gostwyck Hotel being one sad loss. Nevertheless many old buildings remain, St Peter's church with its 13th century shingled tower, and Broadhall being among the oldest. Broadhall, situated in the Square and now the home of the chairman of the Town Council and Avery's the ironmonger's, is a pre-Reformation building, parts of it dating from 1467. There is considered to be an underground passage from Broadhall to the church. Some of the houses still inhabited in North Street (originally known as Lakeway) date back to the early 1700s.

North Tawton has housed many famous personalities. Today the present Poet Laureate, Ted Hughes lives at Court Green, an ancient manor house. William Budd, born at Melhuishes in 1811, is perhaps its most famous son. He made the vital discovery that typhoid fever could be spread by bad drinking water or milk. Subsequently he was able to contain future outbreaks at both Bristol and North Tawton.

There are no ghosts but there is a curious legend concerning De-Bathe Pool. It is said that this overflows (even in dry weather) immediately prior to some national disaster or bereavement. Strangely enough this happened just before the deaths of Nelson, Pitt, Wellington and King Edward VII, and when the First World War broke out. This somewhat strange phenomenon was spoken of by Thomas Westcote in 1630!

176

Oakford 🦢

Oakford lies in a very attractive part of the Exe valley. It is bounded by the Exe on the east and south-east, Somerset on the north, parts of Rackenford and Stoodleigh on the west and the 'Iron Mill Stream' on the south.

The main activity of the area is farming and as this is carried out chiefly by the farmers and their families together with an odd helper, many of the other inhabitants commute to Tiverton or Exeter to earn their livelihood.

The earliest known man-made structure in the parish used to be a tumulus at the extreme south-west corner, now unfortunately lost under the plough. At Domesday (1086) Oakford consisted of seven manors which are still recognisable though the names have changed somewhat; and their constituent holdings still largely retain the same boundaries.

The parish church of St Peter, established well before 1260 and rebuilt more than once – the last time in 1838 – retains a 15th century tower which houses a peal of eight bells presented in 1827 by the rector of the day, the Rev James Parkin jnr. These are said to be among the best-sounding bells in the county. A monument now on the north wall of the church (originally on the west wall) records the death in 1693 of a Margaret Spurway, an ancestor of the present owner of the manor house, whose family has held land and manorial rights in Oakford for more than 800 years.

The older houses in the village itself have, of course, undergone considerable alterations and several of the exteriors have been stripped to show the original stonework. Quite a number have the old bread ovens as have several of the farms in the further reaches of the parish. Prior to 1872 the rectory was at what is now Parsonage Farm and the old tithe barn which served it is still in use there.

Oakford has a village shop-cum-post office, a new and well-used village hall with extensive parking space, and a pub – The Red Lion. This was an old coaching inn and today is a free house offering accommodation as well as meals and snacks. There is a large trout fishery on the Exe. There are also one or two listed buildings, the most interesting of which is an old flour mill, now a private house. There has been a mill on the same site since before Domesday and flour only ceased to be ground there in about 1965.

Oakford is a very pleasant friendly village whose residents are always ready to help one another in times of difficulty.

Otterton ❧

Otterton, tucked into the fold of the hills to the east of the river Otter, derives its name from that river. From early times the area further to the east, on Mutters Moor, had been the home of prehistoric man and by Saxon times a settlement had developed on the river, which was then a large estuary with direct access to the sea, two miles to the south. Otterton became a small port.

After 1066, William the Conqueror granted this settlement to monks from Mont St Michel in Normandy, who built their priory on the high ground where the church stands today and erected a mill on the river below.

From these beginnings the village grew and eventually at the Reformation in the 16th century came into the possession of the Duke family. By this time a shingle bar had developed at the river's mouth and the estuary silted up. Ships were no longer able to reach Otterton.

By developing the agricultural potential of the district, however, the Dukes and their successors in later centuries, the Rolles and Clintons established a considerable number of farms. The village became the centre, with many farmsteads in the village street. Virtually the whole village was owned by these landlords until very recent times and it has therefore managed to retain its old world charm. Many cob and thatch cottages and the typical Devon cross-passage farmhouses stand in the main street, interspersed with 20th century cottages of various styles, built for estate workers. These blend with the older properties to create the atmosphere so loved by holidaymakers.

Today a fair proportion of inhabitants are either retired or active estate workers or workers who commute to neighbouring towns, villages or farms. In comparatively recent years the landowners (Clinton Devon Estates) have sold off much of the village for private ownership. This mix of population has produced a lively, friendly community who organise a number of interesting events during the year – some traditional. Besides concerts, pantomimes and flower shows, on Boxing Day there is the raft race on the river, followed in April by the Duck Race, where model ducks are dropped over Otterton bridge to float downstream. At Easter the schoolchildren have a parade through the village and in August a chariot race is held in the village street and a Donkey Derby on the playing field.

Below Mutters Moor lies the Ladram Bay holiday complex and a considerable number of people from throughout the British Isles spend their summer holidays here.

Ottery St Mary 🌿

The famous poet Samuel Taylor Coleridge was born here in 1772. He was the son of the vicar of the large and beautiful collegiate church of St Mary.

During the Civil War, the Roundhead Generals Cromwell and Fairfax with their soldiers stayed in Ottery throughout the winter of 1645, during which bubonic plague broke out. There were many deaths and it is said that the casualties were buried in what is now known as Long Dogs Lane.

Every 5th November Ottery has a carnival night when young men carry flaming tar barrels through the main street and teams vie with each other.

There is also the tale of the pixies who attempt to abduct the bell-ringers from the church in order to stop the bells proclaiming their joyous sound and calling people to worship. But, when someone is heard to say 'Bless my Soul', they all disappear and the ringers live to ring the bells again.

To the south is a cave high up on the bank of the river Otter known as the Pixies Parlour. It was here that the young Coleridge hid when he ran away in sorrow after his father died.

In 1866 on a very hot day in summer a fire broke out in Yonder Street and swept along all the thatched cottages from one end of the town to the other. The result was devastation, even recorded in the *London Illustrated News*.

There used to be a whistling cock weathervane on the church, which did indeed whistle when a storm was brewing. When it was taken down in 1977 after nearly 600 years it was repaired but the modern technicians were not able to replace the whistle. The one they put in screeched like a banshee at a slight breeze, and the townspeople had to ask that it be stopped.

Henry VIII founded 'Kynges Newe Grammer Scole of Saint Marie Oterey' and this school still operates today.

There was a famous serge mill here which exported its goods to Europe. It became a lace mill in the 18th century. Now it is an engineering mill, which together with Otter Nurseries provides much employment.

Payhembury 🍃

Payhembury is roughly equidistant from the towns of Cullompton, Ottery St Mary and Honiton. It has never been a single manor with an overseeing lord or squire but belonged, in parts, to some several manors – including Forde Abbey. This was responsible for its development into a village with a character very different from others around.

The village has always had a reputation for being independent and self-supporting. Indeed, in the last century, as well as farmers, it supported a wheelwright, carriage maker, baker, brickmaker, smith and harness maker. Evidence of this thriving community can be seen as one walks through the village, but, sad to say, the builders have left for larger premises elsewhere and the agricultural contractor has retired. Until very recently a mill produced animal feed, and was involved in furniture making, and motor and farming repairs, but now, alas, it has closed. Harness repairs can be done locally – but only as a hobby. Within recent times, villagers have themselves built a road to the playing field, fenced the latter and the village green and decorated the parish hall – they still have a reputation for sturdy independence!

The land is fertile, with local springs and wells abounding. Indeed, the local 'Shute', near the hall, has never been polluted, run dry nor frozen – a boon in times of drought or when domestic pipes burst. The water it offers is still preferred by some people to that supplied by the water authority.

The church of St Mary contains some of the earliest known stained glass windows in Devon, a fine medieval screen and Jacobean pew ends – even though it was extensively renovated, at the incumbent's own expense, in the late 19th century. The church is still a centre for many activities, having a peal of six bells and a thriving Sunday school.

Cromwell and Fairfax are both purported to have stayed here – in The Lower House, a thatched house which has an Elizabethan window. 'Bittery' Cross, just outside the village and aptly named, commemorates the six Payhembury men hanged for participating in the Monmouth Rebellion – perhaps sentenced personally by Judge Jeffreys, reputed to have slept at Colestocks House.

Like most villages, Payhembury had a traditional fair which later became known as Club Day, organised by its own Friendly Society, and celebrated on Whit Monday on the green. In the 1970s this fair was revived to raise money for the new playing field.

The stream which bisects the village, alas no longer supports eels, nor

Payhembury village

is the wild watercress recommended to be edible. But as it meanders through pastureland it keeps the village centre rural. The land of four big farms, which used to dominate the village in past times, has now been sold off for housing or incorporated into one large farm. However, two other dairy farms on the outskirts of the village centre counterbalance this.

Four hamlets – Colestocks, Tale, Upton and Cheriton, are farming communities, each with its own character, and from each, inhabitants play an important part in corporate life. These include preparing the monthly free parish paper, bell-ringing, running a cricket club – and supplying a Father Christmas!

There is a thriving primary and infants school, two garages, a village stores, a pub, and a post office. Twice a week, a bus takes shoppers and others to Honiton.

Peters Marland 🍃

This parish is fairly rural, being five and a half miles from the nearest town of Torrington. The population has dropped in the last 200 years – from 289 in 1801 to about 200 today. The majority of the land is farmed by about twelve farmers. The main road from Torrington to Plymouth used to run through the parish in the days of coaches and horses.

The parish consists of three hamlets, apart from Peters Marland itself. They are Yard, Winswell and Woolaton.

The village of Peters Marland contains the church of St Peter (rebuilt in the 1860s), the rectory (now a boys school), the old school and school house. Apart from one other old house the remainder of the dwellings (six) are modern.

Apart from the parish church, the other place of worship is the Methodist chapel, originally the Bible Christian chapel built in 1870 and about one and a half miles outside the village. A smithy was once attached to this chapel.

There used to be two inns in the parish, one, the New Inn, burned down and the second, the Sheepwash Inn, was on the old main road to Plymouth but is now a cottage.

On the church lands there used to be four cottages for occupancy by paupers. They were given £5 per year and received bread at Christmas.

Twigbear (now the post office), Week (now a farm), Winscott and Winswell were all pre-Norman Conquest estates. Stone was also once a small manor.

The clay works (owned by North Devon Clay Company) have been in existence for over 300 years and they are the only industry in the parish, apart from agriculture. Following much capital investment, the operation has changed from being very labour-intensive mining to highly mechanised open-cast and only 45 people are now employed. The ball clay goes to make a wide variety of products, eg face powder, toothpaste, drain pipes, toilets, bone china.

The hamlet of Yard largely consists of a row of cottages which originally belonged to the clay works and which housed some of the workers who used to travel by train to work. The train stopped at Yard station on the Torrington to Halwill line, now sadly pulled up, and was known as the North Devon Joint Light Railway.

Winswell mainly consists of a small group of cottages which belonged to the Winscott estate and the Moore-Stevens family. Various tradesmen on the estate lived there, eg the blacksmith, carpenter, etc. A house had stood at Winscott for many centuries but was replaced in 1865 by a new one. After the death of Col Moore-Stevens in 1932 Winscott was sold and it gradually fell into decay and was eventually demolished in the late 1930s. All that remains are the lodge and entrance gates.

Woolaton has some very attractive thatched cottages, one of which used to be a smithy. Other tradesmen also lived in this hamlet, eg cobbler, cooper, rough carpenter, bag maker and butcher.

It seems now that, in common with many rural parishes, apart from the farming community most people travel outside to work. It is sad that the village school closed in 1949, and the two inns have gone. The school, which was built by Col Moore-Stevens in 1872, is now used as the village hall.

Pilton 🐝

Pilton is an ancient parish on the edge of Barnstaple. It is a charming village which still retains its character, with its main street lined with shops, houses and cottages spanning many eras. Atop the main street is a glimpse of the church behind the very old and picturesque almshouses. Pilton came into existence long before Barnstaple, which has now developed into a sizable town.

On the edge of Pilton village is the main hospital and community college and a few new housing estates, but in no way do these detract from the charm of the village.

The earliest evidence of man living in Pilton was in the Iron Age as there is a defensive earthwork hill fort on the edge of the village. In Saxon times a settlement was made below the hill fort and the name Pilton is Saxon for 'farm by the creek'. The village is surrounded by the river Yeo and Bradiford Water, and a causeway eventually joined Pilton to Barnstaple. Because of all this water there were many mills along the rivers and leats and Pilton was a thriving cloth-making community for some years. The 1394 Wool Tax showed that the Pilton area was producing more wool than Exeter.

The parish church stands on the site of a Benedictine priory which was dedicated to St Mary the Virgin and was mentioned in the Domesday Book. The lower part of the tower and north aisle still remain. A legend exists that it was founded by the Saxon King Athelstan and the ancient seal of the priory is in the Athenaeum. It shows King Athelstan and his arms on one side with the Virgin and Child between two angels on the other side.

Outside the church in the churchyard is an area called Ladywell where there is an ancient stone bowl – Our Lady's holy well, where one can still dip into the water with its restorative powers.

At the bottom of the village street is the site of the former leper hospital called St Margaret's, and the St Margaret's Hospital Charity is still in existence today, surviving from the 12th century. The names of two males and one female are taken from the electoral role to receive a regular pension. Today the feoffees, 18 men and women, administer through the United Pilton Charities the many almshouses in the village.

Plympton 🐑

'Plymouth was a fuzzy down when Plympton was a borough town.' This old rhyme is often quoted by the older folk who can remember how an outing to Plymouth used to be a special occasion. The city's modern development has crept eastwards along the marshy estuary of the river Plym, engulfing Plympton and including it within its boundary in 1967. However, Plympton people are proud to think that the former old borough retains its own identity – captured in the names of its districts: Plympton St Maurice, Plympton St Mary, Ridgeway, Underwood and Colebrook are all names of ancient settlements that have grown together to form a modern suburb of Plymouth.

Plympton, in medieval times, was a port on the Plym estuary. It became a borough in 1194 and returned two members to Parliament for over 500 years. Today two of the borough's maces can be seen in the ancient Guildhall while the third is carried in procession at the Lord Mayor's choosing ceremony in the city. Plympton has some justification in considering itself to be the 'mother' of Plymouth as the tiny settlement of Sutton, from which Plymouth was to grow, belonged to the priory of Plympton until 1439. The wealthy priors owned land from the moors to the coast and west into Cornwall. After Henry VIII ordered the destruction of the priory local people used the stones in the building of their houses. While very little of the priory remains, carved and ornamented stones can be seen in the walls of many of the older buildings in the district.

In the church of Plympton St Mary, the church built by the priors for the parishioners, the tomb of Sir Richard Strode can be seen. He was a local Member of Parliament in the 16th century and lived at Old Newnham, one of the many manor houses in the Plympton area which date back to Domesday times. Plympton had been designated, in 1328, a

184

stannary town like Tavistock, Ashburton and Chagford. Tinners were required to bring their metal to be checked at weekly tin courts in these towns. Sir Richard, in 1512, introduced a bill into Parliament to curb the mining on Dartmoor as he claimed that the process of streaming, where the metal was washed out of the gravel, was causing rapid silting of the Plym and its tributaries. He was tried at the stannary courts, convicted of acting against the interest of the tinners and imprisoned in Lydford gaol. After his release and return to Parliament a statute was passed granting him, and other Members from then on, immunity from legal action. Thus it was a Plympton man who established the basic right of Parliamentary privilege.

The ruins of a Norman castle stand high above the streets of St Maurice. It was twice besieged in the wars of King Stephen's reign, and was a Royalist headquarters during the siege of Plymouth in the Civil War. Musket shot and cannon balls are still dug up in local gardens! From the top of the castle motte there is a fine view over the roofs of the old houses to the medieval boundaries of the borough. Old records show that the bailey has always been used for festivities and celebrations and nowadays a Lamb Feast is held every June.

Although modern development has obscured much of Plympton's past, many old buildings remain. A weekly cattle market reminds us of the close links of Plympton with the South Hams and Dartmoor. While most Plymptonians work in the city they seek their leisure in the woodlands of the Plym valley and the countryside of south-west Devon.

Ringmore ✤

Ringmore is a very attractive village situated on the south Devon coast, west of Kingsbridge. It has some interesting 16th to 18th century buildings.

The church of All Saints was built around 1300, although parts of it are Norman, dating from an earlier church on the same site. Before the First World War the rectory was well and truly occupied, with a big family, eight servants and two gardeners, plus a handyman. Today the rectory is part of the farm and used for storage. Who would believe that garden parties were held on the rectory lawn, where well-to-do people met and enjoyed themselves? Fetes were also held there, when the highlight of the afternoon would be the folk dancing.

The Journey's End pub was nearly always full (it was known as the New Inn then). The local shop was there too. Before that the local pub had been at the top of the village in a house now known as Challaborough Cottage. Over the years about five different cottages have housed the post office.

Mains water came to the village at the end of the 1930s and with it came changes. Council houses were built at the top of the village and a few new bungalows, as well as a new rectory. The farms have changed hands. The school has been closed for some time, and is now a very attractive cottage.

Salcombe

Salcombe was once called Saltcombehaven – salt being panned from the sea here.

In the 19th century it was famous for its waterfront boat yards where they built the famous fruit schooners which brought back oranges and pineapples from the Azores. It is said that cottages were built so close to the boat yards that they had to remove their windows to make room for the bowsprits when the boats were moved! Fishing has always played a large part in the life of the town, and Salcombe crab fisheries were (and still are) among the largest in the UK.

As a harbour and local centre for farming, Salcombe once had five butcher's shops, with an abattoir behind the one surviving butcher's shop. Livestock was brought in for slaughter on the ferry from East Portlemouth, and driven in on the hoof from Kingsbridge market to be held in a field at the top of Bonfire Hill awaiting slaughter.

At that time there were also eight bakers, all of whom baked and sold their products on the premises. On Sunday mornings the villagers took their joints and potatoes in their roasting tins to the bakers to be cooked for Sunday dinner. Today only one baker's shop remains, but it still cooks bread and cakes on the premises and is a firm favourite with visitors.

As recently as the 1930s Salcombe was a self-supporting working community. There was no need to go out of the town for supplies. There was even a milliner who made hats to order. At that time almost every house was occupied by local families, every one knew his neighbours, and mutual hospitality was the order of the day. Boat building and fishing continue on a smaller scale, and there is a small construction and service trade.

The ferry boat between Salcombe and East Portlemouth was originally owned and run by the Great Western Railway and the fare was one halfpenny in each direction. A larger ferry plying between South Sands and Salcombe jetty originally cost 4d.

Placed where it is, it was natural that Salcombe should become a lifeboat station. There was a major lifeboat disaster in 1916 when the *William and Emma* got into difficulties. The lifeboat from South Sands, a rowing boat, put out but could save only two of the crewmen. Coming back over the bar it capsized and sank. A brand new lifeboat was handed over to the Salcombe lifeboatmen in June 1989. It is called the *Baltic Exchange II* after its donors.

The Second World War was an exciting if traumatic time for the small and previously quiet community of Salcombe. One thousand of the children evacuated for safety from the bomb-ravaged East End of London were billeted in Salcombe. This large number was bound to cause some problems.

By far the most important contribution to the war effort, however, was that a large part of the secret build-up of American forces that were to take part in Operation Overlord (the Normandy D-Day landings) assembled at Salcombe. The military arrived and requisitioned virtually the whole of the town. Large houses were taken over and troops billeted, and nearly all movement was prohibited. Many of the American troops settled in the area, while some local girls married and went to America. This has left the town with a flavour of the New World which exists to this day.

Today Salcombe is a holiday resort that has benefited from the increase in second/holiday homes, and a boom in sailing. The estuary is a natural harbour and a place of great natural beauty.

Sampford Courtenay 🌿

'From Bloodshed to Blossoms' – Sampford Courtenay has strayed on many occasions from the popular conception of a typical sleepy Devon village.

Henry VIII placed his mark on the area when in 1538 he had Henry Courtenay, the Marquis of Exeter executed. After confiscating his lands and possessions, the area passed, in due course, to King's College, Cambridge, who became lords of the manor in 1570.

After some years of tranquillity his son, Edward VI, decreed that Church services should henceforth be conducted in English and not, as previously, in Latin. The use of the new English Prayer Book on Whit Sunday 1549 marked the beginning of the Prayer Book Rebellion.

Parishioners, after heated exchanges, killed one William Hellyons on the steps of the church house. Having burned their boats, men of Sampford Courtenay joined like-minded men of Cornwall and all marched on Exeter gathering thousands of supporters en route. Exeter was besieged for six weeks before superior Royal troops defeated the poorly equipped rebels. The final battle was fought in the village street on 17th August 1549 with hundreds of deaths ensuing.

After some centuries of comparative calm, the farms and cottages were offered for sale to the occupying tenants in 1929. Most properties then passed into private ownership – King's College only retaining tiny token areas of land to fulfil the original covenant between Henry VIII and themselves.

The London and S.W. Railway brought the line to the village in 1867. This was closed to passenger traffic following the Beeching rationalisation of the network in the 1960s.

During the past 20 years, Sampford Courtenay has become well known as the Britain in Bloom village of the West Country, and has seen hundreds of visitors yearly walking the village street, admiring some 600 floral displays in gardens, tubs and window boxes. In 1985 great excitement was felt when a telephone call from Switzerland revealed that the European Trophy (for small villages under 500 population) had been won in competition with eleven other European countries.

Sadly, but inevitably changes in village community life have been brought about by the transfer of many cottages to holiday homes.

Sampford Spiney 🌿

Sampford Spiney is a small and very old parish bordering on Dartmoor. Mentioned in the Domesday Book, it has never been a village in the true sense of the word, having no centre of population, and consisting of scattered farms, houses and cottages, though after the Second World War, a row of eight council houses was built more or less in the centre of the parish to house farm workers. These, owing to mechanisation and the consequent reduction of employed labour, are now housing people from quite a wide area.

There are six farms in the parish – mostly sheep or cattle rearing, and very little arable or dairying. They are all family farms and employ casual labour only at the busy times of lambing and sheep shearing.

There is no shop, post office or pub, the nearest being either at Horrabridge or Walkhampton, each over a mile away. There used to be a pub near the boundary with Walkhampton, but it is now a private house. Until the boundary change this century there were two or three shops at one end of the parish, but these are now in Horrabridge.

The lovely little church stands at the moorland end of the parish and dates from the 14th century, if not earlier. It is very small as befits such a small population – 115 according to the latest electoral roll. It consists of a nave and a south aisle. It has no choir stalls, and there is room for only six people to kneel at the altar rail.

There are two hatchments to the Hall Parlby family who were the last 'true' lords of the manor, owning most of the land in the parish. The last was the Rev John Hall Parlby, who died during the First World War, when most of the land was sold except for some acreage round the old Hall Farm or Manor Farm as it is now called. This building and 'Eastontown' are two of the oldest houses and date back to the 16th century. At one time the manor was owned by Sir Francis Drake, and continued in Drake ownership through Drake's brother Thomas.

Sampford Spiney is a beautiful little parish, most of it standing from 400 to 700 ft above sea level. Owing to its remoteness and lack of public transport, only three houses have been added during the last 50 years. Most of the inhabitants feel this is a good thing, as the narrow lanes bordered by high hedges are not suitable for increasing traffic and they feel they are fortunate to live in such a small and friendly place.

Sandford 🦢

To the passing motorist Sandford would probably appear to be a fairly typical Devon village with a church and chapel, post office and general store, school and parish hall, some attractive thatched cottages, a varied collection of other architectural styles and some modern council houses. There is also the Lamb Inn in the village square and the Rose and Crown as you enter from Crediton. It is somewhat surprising to discover that there has been a settlement at Sandford since well before Domesday.

The church at Sandford, dedicated to St Swithin, is thought to date from the 12th century and was then a chapel of ease for the parishioners because the road to the Mother Church in Crediton was 'so foundrous and unsafe'. The earliest story about the church dates from around 1125 when during matins, two men had a 'very great dispute in so much that one murdered the other'. They are thought to have been two rabbit catchers in dispute about their territories.

As a result of the murder, the church was closed for several years. To commemorate this event, a small stone sculpture was erected on one of the church pillars some time in the late 15th century.

About a mile north of the village is Dowrich House, a large grey stone house with an interesting gatehouse. The Dowrich family settled here before Domesday and occupied the land until 1717. The last of the line, Lewes, was cursed by an old woman who had told him he would die by drowning, afterwards returning to the house by 'Cock's Steps'. This meant he would go up the hill towards the house at the rate of a cock's stride in every moon, ie about six inches a month. It was calculated that he would take 256 years to get from the bridge where he fell to his death to the house, a distance of about 525 yards. Because of this tale, successive owners of Dowrich have kept the bottom step at the gatehouse entrance, at least 18 inches high.

The distance calculated meant that Lewes's ghost would reach home in 1973, provided he carried straight on and did not have to retrace his steps. Incredibly, one summer afternoon in 1973, a gardener, cutting the lawns, did actually see a man, sitting on a black horse, in the garden! At that time, a new drive was being constructed and a hole had been made in the wall for a cattle grid. In the short time that the way was clear, Lewes must have seen his chance and came home without having to negotiate the steep step!

Would you expect to find a Greek temple in a Devon village? This is the design of the primary school, built by the local squire, Sir Humphrey Phineas Davie of Creedy Park, in 1825. So keen was he that the local craftsmen would get it right, that he had a model of his design made so that the builders could see what they were expected to produce. Few Devon masons and carpenters would have actually seen a Greek temple in 1895. This model is still kept in the school. Originally designed for 250 pupils, today, with an additional classroom, it is not really large enough for 100. Apart from its classical design and the model, the school is unique in another way as it is built mainly of cob, thought to be the highest cob walls in Devon.

For many years there was an annual market held in the Square, and a fair on St Swithin's Day. Another market began in the 19th century at the end of March. The St Swithin's fair eventually became the Sandford Revel when the market ceased – about the end of the 1930s. Traditional Revel Biscuits known as Pig's Ears are still baked and sold.

Seaton ✒

Seaton's old name was Seton, a port at the mouth of the river Axe. In early days the Phoenicians landed here bringing tin. It was thought to be the site of a Roman station – Moridunum. A house called Honey Ditches was built on the site of a Roman villa, and, for a time, the late St John Ervine, publisher and playwright, lived there.

It is rich in historical and legendary lore. Wednesday used to be market day, and the annual fair was held on St Gregory's Day.

For forty years from 1723 Abraham Sydenham was the Salt Officer. Salt pans then existed on the marshes nearby, but they are not used now.

In 1817, there was a shipwreck off Seaton, *The Queen Charlotte* foundered, and eight seamen perished. There used to be a Coastguard station near the golf course.

Nowadays the local inhabitants either go to Exeter to work, or to the carpet factory at Axminster seven miles away, or to Racal's or Peco's factories in Seaton. Many people take in seaside visitors, while some of the men go fishing. There are two holiday camps, and these people add considerably to Seaton's summer population. One of these camps was an internment camp during the Second World War. The railway ran from Axminster to Seaton and brought visitors close to the beach. It closed down under the Beeching plan in the 1960s and its loss is still lamented by older residents.

The parish church, St Gregory's, dates back to the 1100s, and there are several quite old houses nearby.

Before 1939, Seaton had nine large hotels, it now has only one. Several of them are now used as elderly people's homes. There are now several shops down a steep narrow street, where formerly there were only two shops in Seaton. A steamer used to call at Seaton taking passengers to Torquay, but smaller boats now come from Beer to collect any passenger traffic.

There was a 'Bath House' run by a Mrs Walsh. People now bathe from beach huts along the front. The sea wall running right along the East Front was built a few years ago, following violent storms which flooded houses on the front, causing much devastation.

Seaton has the oldest concrete bridge in Britain, across part of the Axe valley. It also has a new hospital, built in 1988 after a great deal of voluntary fund-raising.

The population of Seaton in 1891 was about 1,350. It now numbers over 5,000.

Sheepstor ✍

The Tor itself is the fabled haunt of pixies and said to be rich in precious minerals stored there by these tiny folk. Bronze Age people lived on the lower slopes and practised their rites at the Yellowmead stone circles. During the Civil War, Sir John Elford of Longstone Manor concealed himself successfully from Cromwell's troopers in the Pixies' House, a cave on the side of Sheepstor. He was fed by his faithful tenants from Sheepstor village and passed his time by painting pictures on the cave walls. These were still discernible in 1800.

The village is now centred on the church and its holy well in the churchyard wall. Mainly a 15th century building, St Leonard's was much restored in the late 19th century. Its rood screen includes panels from the original and there is a curious sundial over the porch door, depicting wheat growing out of a skull. The lychgate is well preserved, with its central coffin rest. Amongst the many who have passed this way were the white Rajahs of Sarawak.

Sir James Brooke, the first Rajah, bought Burrator House in 1858 for his retirement. He and his successors are commemorated by large granite tombstones in the churchyard, the largest, surprisingly, not of local stone. Elizabeth (Didi) Brooke, one of the daughters of the third and last Rajah, married Harry Roy, the ebullient dance band leader of the 1930s. He wrote the popular song *Sarawaki* for her.

Next to the church is the old vicarage. There is now no resident vicar, but the date, 1658, on the wall above the arched front door shows the antiquity of parts of the building.

A stone stile and steep steps opposite the south porch of the church lead to the small St Leonard's Hall and to the Bull Ring. In 1929 L. A. G. Strong wrote in *Dewer Rides*: 'The bull-ring, still preserved, is solid evidence of the purposes the churchyard served upon profane occasions. White witches practised their charms under the tower, and to this day children are brought to St Leonard's Well to be cured of small diseases.'

Sheepstor was once a thriving village, centre of extensive tin mining activity, with numerous farms and much warrening, and with its own school and inn. All that changed. Tin mining declined and ceased altogether many years ago. Burrator Reservoir was opened in 1898 and the dam raised in 1926, to supply water to the fast growing population of Plymouth. Several farms and Longstone Manor were drowned. Other farms in the catchment area were all bought up by 1916 and evacuated to avoid contamination of the clean upland surface water, which did not receive full chemical treatment until 1959. The inn was closed because it was on the wrong side of the watershed and the school was transferred to Meavy in 1926.

Despite the loss of its pub and school and having no post office or shop, Sheepstor retains a very strong community spirit. Almost all of its 45 adult population are on the electoral roll of the church. Many of the residents are elderly and there is no local employment apart from a little farming. There are few commuters and the road through the village leads only to the open moor.

Considering the extent to which Burrator Reservoir was responsible for its decline, it is ironic that there are still four properties served by a leat system off the moor and it was not until 1956 that most of the village received piped water from the mains. Prior to that the Sheepstor Brook was kept clean by locals and acted as a natural leat. Tim Powell used this pure, untreated water to help make his high quality, hand-made paper, much in demand by private presses – appropriately enough one of his watermarks is a sheep.

Sheepwash ✒

It all happened rather quickly – relatively speaking. Since the 18th century, Sheepwash had been just a rather obscure little village. Then it was designated a conservation area and, almost overnight it seemed, it became a tourist attraction. Now it's probably known to more people outside Devon than to Devonians themselves!

To the tourist, the village is four picturesque streets converging in a central square that must be every city dweller's dream of peace. A pink chestnut, two cherries and a village pump; the church to the back, the inn to one side, thatched and colour-washed cob cottages all around. Rush hour is two tractors meeting or a brewer's lorry arriving at the same time as the mobile library.

In this small, lively community of all ages, they work hard. Farming is in the blood – those who don't own their own, work on someone else's. They play hard – skittles, darts, table tennis, pool, snooker, bingo. There are fetes, drawing in people from neighbouring villages, clay pigeon shoots; there's a visiting hunt, bowling, shooting. The headquarters of the Dartmoor Dog Training Club is here, running dog agility classes.

One of the highlights of the year is the air show. Yes, Sheepwash has its own Flying Association! It meets regularly and circulates its own magazine to some 50 members and annually, small planes, delicate as butter-flies, arrive from all over the country to put on displays.

Many of the villagers have never lived anywhere else. Their roots go back several generations – the post office for instance has been in the same family for a hundred years. Newcomers are soon absorbed, adding their own enthusiasm to all that goes on.

Looking round now, it's difficult to believe that this small village, with a population of around 260, was once regarded as a very important centre in North Devon. Fire put an end to that claim, when, in 1743, most of it was destroyed and it lost its weekly market to a neighbouring town. A smaller market returned during the 19th century and again in the 1920s. The latter lasted some 30 years.

Traces of its antiquity are everywhere. Its name, for instance, is of Anglo-Saxon origin, Schepewast.

Over the door of the old rectory is one of a pair of the original plaques from the ancient market pillars and the surviving pillar stands in the entrance to the rear of the inn.

Downstream of the bridge are 'the Sheepwash Strips', known locally as 'South Commons'. These are a set of long, narrow fields, thought by some authorities to be the most perfect remaining specimens in England, retaining the original outlines laid down in the days when an open field system of agriculture prevailed.

Even the bridge has its story. It owes its existence to a fatality in the 17th century when stepping stones provided a crossing place. When his only son was drowned in a sudden spate, John Tosbury was so devastated that he dedicated money to build a bridge. By 1695, trustees had been appointed and as the income from his farms and lands was more than enough to maintain the bridge, he gave instructions that the surplus should be used for the benefit of the people of Sheepwash. So the Bridgeland Trust was born and to this day, the income provides money for deserving cases of hardship, the upkeep of the church and chapel, outings for children and pensioners and a Christmas box for the elderly.

The delightful little church of St Lawrence is the third to be built on the site since the original in the 14th century. The one that stands today was rebuilt in 1880.

By the 19th century, the village was a busy, working place with an average population of 430, three pubs and all the usual trades needed to support itself. A cottage industry was introduced in the 1850s, in the form of silk glove making. Later they were made under one roof in the Foresters' Hall, now the village hall.

By the 20th century, the village was run down and neglected by the landlord who owned most of it. Many of those who didn't work on his estate were farmers in their own right, whose fields were dotted about in such an inconvenient way that several herds of cows criss-crossed the square four times a day for milking, leaving roads ankle deep in muck. Added to that was the market, bringing its own peculiar brand of chaos until the 1950s.

About the same time as the closure of the market, many of the cottages came up for sale, and for the first time people moved into property ownership. Almost overnight, Sheepwash became a prettier, cleaner place. Even so, houses were lying derelict as recently as 1968 and it wasn't until the importance of an entire village that contained some of the finest examples of thatched and cob-walled houses in Devon was realised that the committee for Torridge Council's Development and Trading Services stepped in and designated it a conservation area.

Today it has its niche in tourist brochures; its inn, famous among the fishing fraternity, draws hundreds of people a year from all parts of the world to try and tempt salmon and trout from the peaty brown waters of the Torridge.

Shirwell

Shirwell is a tiny scattered parish situated some four miles from Barnstaple on the Lynton road. The village is divided into distinct areas, the cluster of houses around the church – the main part of the old village – being called Shirwell 'Town'. The name of this historic village, mentioned in the Domesday Book, means 'clear water' and even today the area abounds in natural springs which bubble out of the ground.

Today the adult population of Shirwell is about 230 souls. There is an ancient parish church, a Methodist chapel built in 1902 on ground given by Admiral Sir Edward Chichester, a historic house of some note, a very old village school, a most unusual skittle alley, a village hall and a general stores with post office and petrol station. In days gone by the village boasted two public houses, but alas both have closed leaving the nearest pub some three miles from the centre of Shirwell.

The historic house – Youlston Park – which is not open to the public, and is now in private hands, was the ancestral home of the Chichester family. The house is famous for many features including highly decorated plaster ceilings, a magnificent staircase and a room which is decorated in hand-painted Chinese wallpaper dating from 1760. Sir Francis Chichester, the famous 'round the world' yachtsman was born in the village at the old rectory where his father was, for many years, the rector. Both father and son lie buried in the churchyard; one to each side of the south porch, and even today many come to visit his grave and perhaps combine it with a visit to nearby Arlington Court, also a former home of the Chichester family, and now owned by the National Trust.

The ancient parish church of St Peter also lays claim to a saint who was martyred for his faith in the 16th century, being hung, drawn, and quartered. He was born in Shirwell, the son of a tenant farmer and was baptised in the Norman font which is still used for baptisms today. The school also has a Chichester connection, for it was founded in 1830 by the Chichester family and it has been in continual use ever since.

The skittle alley is also steeped in history. It is a railway carriage that once belonged to the Royal train of Queen Victoria and is a Grade II listed building. It is full of nostalgia of days gone by and is still lit with gas lamps. It is in frequent use by the very active skittles team.

Today, as in the past, Shirwell is mostly a farming community, although the influence of easier travel and the motor car has brought an influx of 'vurriners' into the village, some of whom work in nearby Barnstaple, and some further afield. There is still a core of families who have lived in the village for generations and many of the houses are mentioned in records of hundreds of years ago. New building has been kept to a minimum. Though the village is not stagnant, but growth is slow, probably because there is no mains drainage in the parish. Many houses, even today, still have their own well water and not everyone in the parish is connected to the mains electricity supply.

Sidford ❦

Sidford, East Devon, is a village within the parish of Sidbury. It is situated in the beautiful valley of the river Sid, lying two miles to the north of Sidmouth, a popular seaside resort, and one mile south of Sidbury village. It is overlooked by Sidbury Castle, an Iron Age hill fort. Here the Roman road from Dorchester to Exeter crossed the river; Sidford Bridge was built around 1100 and the northern parapet is that of the old packhorse bridge, which was widened in 1930 to allow for modern traffic. The Roman road is now the A3052, a busy route, especially in summer when used by holidaymakers on their way to the south of Devon and Cornwall.

The centre of the village is known as 'The Cross' and here the Sidmouth to Honiton road crossed the A3052. This is the original part of the village and some lovely cottages can be seen adjoining the roads. About 50 years ago, three farms were occupied in the village, but these have all been modernised, one now being a cafe, one a guest house and the third was turned into flats. Farm buildings were pulled down to make way for a car park, shops and houses. In School Street on the Honiton Road, three of the cottages have beautiful stonework chimneys dating from 1636. The small school which was situated in one of the cottages was closed in 1922, the children since going to either Sidbury or Sidmouth.

The Blue Ball Inn is a delightful hostelry, complete with thatched roof and huge fireplaces dating back to 1369.

St Peter's church was built in 1873 and is a typical Victorian brick structure with some beautiful stained glass windows. In 1930 a Methodist church was built near the centre of the village, replacing a cob chapel which had served the village for many years.

The recreation field lies a short distance from the main road, and soccer and rugby football are played here during the winter. Adjoining the soccer pitch is a very flourishing tennis club with three floodlit hard courts, enabling members to play all year round. Opposite the recreation field is the village hall dated 1907: the younger members of the village formed a new committee and after much hard work and fund raising, it is a hall of which to be very proud.

There are numerous lovely walks in the surrounding hills, but the most popular is a level walk to Sidmouth known as 'The Byes'. Meandering through fields and eventually along by the river Sid, the lower meadows were given to the National Trust in 1937 and these are well maintained by the local council.

In August, the Sidbury, Sidford and Salcombe Regis Horticultural Society holds its very popular show on the Sidford recreation ground. The society was formed in 1922. Also on the recreation field on Spring Bank Holiday Monday, weather permitting, the Sid Vale athletic meet takes place. This is also a very popular event, started in 1956.

Until the 1930s the village had changed very little, but development started about 1933 on the hill towards Exeter, known as High Street, and also towards Sidmouth. Building recommenced in the late 1940s with new council-built homes. After that, many private estates were developed, so that Sidford is now virtually joined to Sidmouth, except one field which has been ear-marked for a bypass, now talked about for 60 years!

Although it may appear to be a suburb of Sidmouth, this is still very much a busy, happy village community, served with good shops of all descriptions, three doctors' surgeries and a veterinary clinic.

Silverton

This is a large attractive village equidistant from Exeter and Tiverton and standing above the valley of the Exe. It was bypassed in 1819, thus saving it from 20th century traffic.

The name Silverton is Saxon, but the only lasting reminder is the Saxon name for the open space in front of the church – the Bury or Berry (a place of safety for women, children and stock in times of peril).

It is a very pleasing village, containing many cob and thatch buildings ranging from the 16th to the 19th centuries.

In the 1300s Silverton was a borough with a weekly market and fair but by the end of the 18th century it had lost its market, and was down to two cattle fairs a year by the late 1800s.

Like other Devon villages, Silverton was built with just one main street, called Fore Street, in which everyone of importance used to live. But the Devon proverb runs 'Us can't all live in Vore Street', so there was a back lane for the rest.

There were two serious fires in 1837 and 1878 and many village houses were destroyed. The Silverton fire engine (which is now at Buckland Abbey) must have been very busy helping those who displayed a fire insurance plaque. You will see a copy of one of these from the Phoenix Insurance Company of about the year 1780 above the front

The Square at Silverton

198

door of Old Church House. This house was used in medieval times for the sale of church ale. It dates from 1480 and is described as a Devon longhouse.

The post office was previously a butcher's shop, and as recently as the 1970s cattle and sheep were still being slaughtered in the rear buildings.

One of Silverton's oldest and most interesting houses is Ivy Cottage. When some beams were being exposed just after the Second World War, a book was found in a niche cut into a beam, dated 1584. Unfortunately woodworm prevented all of its being read, but the British Museum interleaved every page and made an airtight box for it.

All of the fittings and tools of Silverton's blacksmith, Archie Tremlett, were taken over by Tiverton Museum when he died and there is a wonderful mock-up of the forge in the museum today. Opposite the Church House Gallery is Archie's cottage.

What was once a boys school endowed in 1724 by John Richards, a city of London wool merchant, is now the British Legion Club. John Richards is still remembered today in the Richards Trust which gives grants to Silverton school leavers for further study. It supports both the primary school and various youth organisations.

The present parish church of St Mary the Virgin dates from about 1450, although the list of the past rectors goes back to 1273. In company with so many other churches, it has suffered at the hands of two sets of 'improvers' but the west gallery is one of its best features. Outside in the churchyard there is a massive old yew tree, said to date from around 1100 and to have been a useful source for bows in the days of archery.

Slapton 🪶

Slapton is a peaceful, picturesque village nestling in a hollow of the hills of the South Hams. It is noted for early production of garden produce, evident at the annual Horticultural Show.

The De Brien family, from Pembrokeshire, owned Slapton by 1250. Sir Guy de Brien was King Edward III's Standard Bearer. In 1373 he founded a chantry, of which the ruined tower in the centre of the village, in close proximity to the Tower Inn, is the only trace left. The church of St James the Great dates from the 14th century.

Poole farmhouse is on the site of the former manor house. Here in 1600 lived Admiral Sir Richard Hawkins (kinsman of John of Armada fame) and his wife Judith. It is thought Judith was a haughty lady as she is reputed to have had a red carpet laid down from Poole to walk the three quarters of a mile to church!

In 1690, John Kellond left £100 to be invested for the education of poor children of the parish. His son gave £50 to apprentice a poor child annually. These legacies were not paid until 1746 when they were recovered with £205 interest. Charity Commissioners stated that the funds should be applied wholly for a Sunday school and books are still purchased for the Sunday school from this fund.

By 1850, Slapton had 726 inhabitants, compared with 450 in 1988. There were five carpenters, eight masons, two blacksmiths, three corn millers, two tailors, four shopkeepers, three shoemakers, two bakers, two publicans and 24 farmers! In 1989 there was one shop/post office, two fruit and vegetable shops and two inns!

In 1914, HMS *Porpoise* ran aground off Slapton Sands in fog. Tugs from Devonport tried unsuccessfully to pull it free, but hawsers snapped and sand had to be dug away after chains, cables etc had been offloaded. Shortly afterwards a Belgian vessel laden with galvanised iron started sinking near the shore. Much of the cargo was retrieved by enterprising locals who loaded it into a carrier's flat-bottomed wagon and sold it to a Kingsbridge scrap metal dealer!

Before the Second World War, the inhabitants were mostly farm workers and fishermen. During the winter the fishermen sought work on farms and cut reeds from the Ley. These were placed in pyramidal stacks at the edge of the Ley where they remained until early summer when they were bought by farmers for thatching ricks or by property owners for thatching roofs. There were two resident thatchers at that time.

In 1825, a hotel was built on the beach and named Slapton Cellars – later called Royal Sands Hotel (King Edward VII stayed there as a boy). In 1940, a land mine damaged the luxurious hotel and after further damage during the evacuation of 1944 the ruins were flattened after the war. The large car park now covers this site.

At the end of 1943, the villagers, with those from surrounding villages, were evacuated as the area was used by the US forces preparing for the Normandy invasion.

Flora and fauna abound in the countryside around Slapton, much of which is under the management of the Slapton Ley Field Centre. The reserve is leased from the Herbert Whitley Trust and is designated a Site of Special Scientific Interest. A steady flow of students from all over the UK attend courses there regularly. The centre is the largest employer in the village, with 30 employees. Horticulture and farming are the other occupations giving employment and there are several guest houses.

Sourton 🏵️

The village of Sourton lies north-west of Dartmoor, rising at Sourton Tor to a height of 1,447 ft. Sourton is a large parish acreage-wise, but inhabitants only number approximately 500.

The church of St Thomas a Becket stands at the base of the moor. The tithe map of 1844 shows the 'High Road', known also as 'King's Way', running beyond the church along the moor edge, probably where the railway was later built.

The men working on the railroad bought their tankards of ale from the alehouse at Sourton Cross a few yards from the listed old farmhouse, which is now a public house named The Prewley Moor Arms. The old alehouse has long been demolished.

St Thomas a Becket's church is 14th to 16th century. It was built mainly of moor stone with three bells; now there are five.

In about 1870 spring water was tapped and left to freeze in stone tanks. These slabs of ice were transported to Plymouth by waggonette to be used in the fish trade. This business collapsed because the distance was too far, and the ice melted in transit! Ruins of the old freezing store are still on Dartmoor.

Peat works also existed on Dartmoor and a tin streaming business, and there was tin mining at Rattlebrook. A tin mine still stands today.

Sourton schoolchildren, years ago, walked through Sourton quarry bridleway to school. Farmers used it, and it was also a favourite walk between Sourton and Bridestowe. However, in later years the gates were locked and it took a ten year struggle by the Sourton Parish Council before the bridleway was reinstated on the definitive map. The Sourton quarry with its wildlife and flowers is still a protected area. Guided tours can be arranged.

The recently re-sited Sourton Cross was moved, because of road developments, for the third time. The cross dates from about the 6th century. Letters on the stone denote a late Roman or sub-Roman military leader, probably a very important person in the locality. The arms on the cross may have been added later.

Every seven years the age-old ceremony of the Beating of the Bounds takes place. It is always organised by the Sourton and Bridestowe Commoners. It commences at 10 am when all walkers and helpers gather at 'Iron Catch Gates' on the moor. They are given pasties, sandwiches and ale then, after a short service, all move off, some on horseback, passing boundary stones marked 'S' which they strike or walk around.

The New Inn, a plain white building, now known as 'The

Highwayman Inn', was a meeting place for locals. It is now a tourist attraction.

Village events were held in the church room up to 1963, (it is now a cottage known as 'Cobweb Hall'), but with money raising efforts a parish hall was built on ground kindly donated by Lt Col Calmady Hamlyn.

South Brent ✧

Travelling along the new A38 very few people notice the village of South Brent nestling between prominent Dartmoor hills and surrounded by green fields and woodlands. The new dual carriageway now bypasses some half mile south of the village, but before the 1970s the heavy traffic on the old road cut the village in two.

If you should be tempted to turn off the dual carriageway at Marley Head the road signs will lead you along the old road and up to the crossroads by the police station, where new estates are increasing the population to over 3,000. They bring new life and surround the older houses and a village centre which dates back to the 16th century.

As you walk into the main street, you pass the Anchor Inn which has stood on this spot since 1546 when Henry VIII granted the village to Sir William Petre of Torbryan. A couple of doors on is the Old Toll House with its board of tolls (restored by WI efforts in 1960), payable by farmers who brought their sheep and cows to market when Brent's markets and fairs were among the most important in the county and when four major fairs were held annually between 1850 and 1950. The weekly pannier market was so successful that it rivalled that of Totnes and the annual pony fair brought buyers from all over Britain. Still, today, the village has houses and shops, butchers and bakers carrying on trade as they have for many years past.

St Petroc's church has an interesting history going back to the 6th century. The present church was enlarged and rededicated in its present form in about 1436.

In 1436 an incident happened at the end of Corpus Christi vespers. For some unknown reason a certain Thomas Wake (or Weke) dragged the vicar, Master John Hay, dressed in full vestments from the altar and through a small doorway and with the help of some accomplices beat him to death. It is thought that Brent is the only place in England where such a murder has taken place, apart from Canterbury Cathedral. The blocked-in remains of the doorway can still be seen.

St Petroc's church, South Brent

From the reign of Mary in 1556 South Brent held a charter as a properly constituted borough. By the end of the last century, South Brent was a place to be reckoned with. There were five mills working along the Avon river which runs down the valley from Shipley Bridge (where you can still see the remains of Ryder's Ring, a completely enclosed settlement inside which are a number of hut circles).

In 1848 the South Devon Railway Company opened the mainline from Exeter and in 1893 Brent was proposed as an important railway junction and an extra line was added to take a branchline from Kingsbridge. This was once a lovely country station with sub-tropical gardens. Demolition of the station buildings was started in April 1965 shortly after the final closure in 1964, although the signal box remains on what is left of the island platform. The railway track has now long since gone from the South Hams and nature has reclaimed the track bed. It is becoming progressively more difficult to trace the course of this once lovely branch line, known as the 'Primrose Line'.

South Milton ❧

In early records South Milton was called Middleton. On either side of the village are the hamlets Upton (Upperton) and Sutton (Southton). It is a small village of thatched whitewashed cottages, farm buildings, farmhouses, and stone barns all surrounding the church, which was originally a chapel in 1269.

During the last 100 years a very large family called Steer lived in the village, and nearly everyone was related. Among the inhabitants there was a parson, policeman, stonemason, builder, beekeeper, rabbit catcher, shoe and boot maker, blacksmith, fisherman, coffinmaker, nurse who laid out the dead and attended all the births, and numerous farmers. There was a carrier who plied between South Milton and Kingsbridge. This was the last horse-drawn carrier in the South Hams and the business ceased with the death of Jim Johns in 1977.

The big house, Horswell, now flats, was occupied by Major General Alexander who was a great benefactor to the village. He employed many local people as maids, grooms and gardeners. There are now only 18 parishioners living in the village who were born here and they are mostly all related.

The Thurlestone Rock is in the parish of South Milton, and has witnessed many shipwrecks in the bay, the sea being only a mile from the centre of the village. Some of the shipwrecks have had sad consequences, such as the *Chantiloupe* in 1772. A lady, on the foundering vessel, realising the danger of the ship sinking, put on all her fine jewellery, and she was eventually washed onto the beach. The local wreckers found her, saw her rings and cut off her fingers, and then realised that she was still alive. The last wreck was the Belgian ship *Louis Sheid* which ran aground after saving passengers from a torpedoed ship. Parts of this ship can still be seen at low water.

Limestone 'draying' was a particular type of work done by local men. At high tide the barges from Plymouth would anchor in the bay, and unload limestone into 'Goosey Pool' and 'New Way Gut' at South Milton Sands. At low tide the horses would drag the carts into the sea where they would be filled with stone, and then the cart would be 'lugged' across the beach, helped by a 'lug' horse. The load would then be deposited into heaps along the road where men would sit and split them into small pieces for road mending.

Life was gentle and slow, people walked the primrose-covered lanes, hares and rabbits were abundant, in every dairy there were large bowls of thick cream to be eaten with every meal, and a 'crab lady' came to the door selling live crabs at 6d each. In the month of August the farmers would all help each other with the harvest, and after a full day's work they would sit with the workers around the ricks with their cold tea, cider and drinkings (small fruit buns) whilst the thresher rattled on, driven by a steam engine.

There have been many changes since those days. Now there are more new houses, the roads are busier, caravans nestle against hedges in many fields, the cows have changed from Red Devon to Friesians, and new-comers both old and young have integrated into the village, which is still a picturesque place to live.

South Molton 🐝

Known as the 'Gateway to Exmoor' is the community of South Molton, a small market town which in the summer months throngs with visitors.

There is plenty for them to see – the Honey Farm, for instance, where they can see swarms of bees actually making the honey, two potteries, a shop specialising in antique lace, an art gallery etc. There are plenty of tea shops and pubs to cater for all tastes, a park, outdoor swimming pool, tennis and bowls.

For those who like to get off the beaten track, there are back alleys to wander down, where houses and shops are as they were built 200 or more years ago. Even a glance around the Square will reveal many interesting old buildings. The post office, for instance, was the old Corn Exchange. A 'Town Trail', available from the library, points out many interesting features.

There has been a settlement on the site since Norman times, when Sud Moltona was mentioned in the Domesday Book. The first charter of South Molton may date to the 11th century, the so-called Turbeville Charter. Then in 1590 the town was granted a more comprehensive charter by Queen Elizabeth I. This was renewed after the Restoration by Charles II. Both these charters are in the town museum, which won an award in 1987 as the best small museum in the country.

The church of St Mary Magdalene dates from 1864 in its present form and is well worth a visit. There is no doubt, however, from the records that the original site was built on long before the 12th century, and there have been numerous alterations in the last 800 years.

The people of 17th century South Molton were fortunate to have a benefactor, one Hugh Squier, who went to London to make his fortune, then came back and spent most of it on the town in various ways. He is commemorated with a bust on the façade of the Town Hall, and more recently a street has been named after him.

South Molton flourished with the wool trade and the town seal depicts this with a fleece, a bishop's mitre (which represents the fact that the town was granted a bishopric but never actually took it up), and a crown to show the town's allegiance to the King.

There is still a regular livestock market every Thursday but these days there are more cattle than sheep. Times have changed! Now we rely on the tourists and antiques dealers.

South Zeal

On the northern part of Dartmoor South Zeal lies in a hollow below Cosdon Hill, in the parish of South Tawton. South Zeal was known as Zeal Tony when the De Tonys, of nearby Blackhall, were lords of the manor.

During its history many important industries are recorded including corn milling, tin streaming, and lime quarrying, the latter having been worked for over 300 years.

The woollen industry flourished in South Zeal until the introduction of steam machinery in mills at North Tawton. Remains of a copper mine at Ramsley can still be seen and many of the village cottages were built to house the Irishmen who came to mine the copper. The chimney of the old mine stands sentinel over the village to this very day.

The long street of the village was once the main coach road to London and the mantle which once held the sign of the London Inn remains upon the building now converted into cottages. In the middle of the street stands St Mary's church which is thought to have originally been a guild chapel, founded by the burghers, and is referred to in the late pre-Reformation churchwarden's accounts.

Near the church, past where cottages which housed the 'penny school' once stood, stands the market cross, dating from about the 14th century, but probably replacing an earlier cross.

Further up the hill the thatched hostelry The Kings Arms stands guard on the road to Okehampton. Was this once the toll house for the road?

At the opposite end of the village stands a building in which John Wesley once preached the gospel. The building has had a chequered career, as a chapel where the organ was played, a scout meeting hall, and as a cinema, all within the memory of villagers today.

The author Eden Philpotts based his novel *The Beacon* upon the village, Charles Dickens stayed at the Oxenham Arms while writing *The Pickwick Papers*, and Charles Kingsley in his book *Westward Ho* wrote of the Oxenham family's legendary white-breasted bird which, to this day, is reputed locally to be seen before a death.

South Zeal is the setting for the annual Dartmoor Folk Festival, renowned for its preservation of traditional dance and music.

The ancient custom of Beating the Bounds, maintained every seven years, involves the majority of villagers, with those unable to walk the boundary being taken by hay cart to the ram roast and picnic celebrating the completion of the rite.

South Zeal remains a working village, its lands are farmed, the old cinema houses a woodwork company, artists, tradesmen and writers live and work here while others return to the close knit community after commuting to Okehampton or Exeter.

Gaze down upon the village from near the sentinel chimney of Ramsley mine and South Zeal's unique medieval 'Borough Acres' lie behind the cottages and houses in the valley. These strips of land remain as distinct a landmark today as when Devonian rebels laid siege to Exeter in 1549.

Sparkwell 🦢

Sparkwell is less than two miles from the main A38 Ivybridge to Plymouth road. Just across the main railway line – 1/42 incline, the longest in England! – the old signal box and siding can be seen. The disused Hemerdon siding is next to Moor Farm (now Parkside). Trains always stopped 'on request' for members of the Colborne family to travel from the siding in 'the good old days'.

The annual Sparkwell Fair is held in the meadows, through the Beechwood entrance gates, by the lodge, on the first Saturday in August each year, at the kind invitation of the Colborne Mackrell family, still of Beechwood.

To the left, at Beechwood Cross, is Hemerdon House, thought to have been built in about 1765, but on a much earlier foundation. This is the home of the Woollcombe family, who replanted the plantations around that area, and also Hemerdon Ball plantation up on the hill – which can be seen for many miles, especially by ships at sea. During the Civil War, Hemerdon Ball was the site of a battle between the Cavaliers and the Roundheads – a cannonball was found in about 1890 on the Smallhanger china clay works, which lies to the north.

The church was built in 1859 on land given by the 2nd Lord Seaton. The organ is of particular interest, as the ebony and ivory notes are reversed from the normal, with naturals being of ebony! The gates were made in about 1956, by the local carpenter and wheelwright, from wood supplied from the Hemerdon House estate.

Blacklands was built in 1847 by Isambard Kingdom Brunel, the engineering genius of the Great Western Railway, who designed the railway bridge over the river Tamar. He also built the lodge and the two cottages opposite the Treby Arms. The site of the house, Blacklands, is believed to be that of Welbeck Manor. It is now owned by the Hamlyn family, who have opened it as a restaurant.

Fursdon (originally Fursdown) is believed to have been on a very old site, but over the years it has been almost completely rebuilt. At present the Crowley family own the property.

A little further along the same road, is Baccamore, thought to be the oldest property in the village – 'Bachemora' is in the Domesday survey of 1086, and was at one time part of the Saltram estate.

Today probably the most famous property is Goodamoor, better known as the Sparkwell Wild Life Park. The house used to be owned by the Treby family, then the Martins, who owned the clay works at Lee Moor. Goodamoor is thought to have been erected late in the 18th century for the Treby family – one member of that family, a keen huntsman, once entertained Prince Albert, the Prince-Consort there for a few nights!

Starcross

Starcross is an estuary village on the west bank of the Exe. Its facilities for sailing are a great attraction – there is a club as well as private moorings. At one time the oyster beds were a real source of income for the village and now a shell industry is once more established.

The ferry, plying between Exmouth and Starcross, is a delight to many. In the 12th century, its rights were the property of the abbey of Sherborne. The city of Exeter seized the rights after the Dissolution of the Monasteries for they had always been jealous of the abbey, whom they alleged to have deprived the city of income by luring traffic away from its toll system. The ferry became the property of the South Devon Railway in 1848 and remained an excellent link, but its importance ceased when the Exeter/Exmouth line was constructed in 1861. At this stage, Lympstone ceased to send its mussels to Starcross for transport to

London. The Devon Dock and Steamship Company ran the ferry until the pier and ferry were sold in 1981 into private hands.

The ferry has undoubtedly been a real influence on the settlement and on its name too. It is said that the name, Starcross, originated from the cross which at one time surmounted the flight of steps at the landing – Staircross to Starcross.

The railway now provides the embankment and replaces the Courtenay Embankment, built in 1750. The rails, laid since 1972, provide for the Inter-City 125, a far cry from the Atmospheric Railway which Brunel first constructed for the line from Exeter, opened in 1847. Today, the Brunel Tower, one of the original and only surviving engine towers, houses a working model to illustrate the principle upon which the Atmospheric Railway was powered.

Along the land side of the embankment, a footpath runs north to what was the site of a dock, now a picnic site and car park. To the south is the Courtenay Arms; it was originally built in 1710, when at high tide it would be an island surrounded by floodwater. In the 19th century, it was the scene of festivities at regatta time – breakfasts and balls. Earlier in 1772, some gentlemen including the Earl of Devon were snowbound and they established a Gentlemen's Club, limited to 20/30 members. The other inns are the Galleon, there since 1490 and the Atmospheric Railway which houses much 'Brunelia'.

In 1864 the asylum was established. This was to be a dominant feature of the village until its closure in 1986 in line with national policy on mental health. The buildings were demolished and the site sold to developers. This site provided the last big development of the village, although the sports field became the property of the Parish Council.

Today, there are some shops, but not the variety which served the village at the turn of the century. Behind The Strand is the church, built in 1828 and the school built in 1839. Nearby are the almshouses which were established under the will of Henry Drew in 1901. Light industry contributes to the economy of the village, but it is essentially a residential community with the river the key to its attraction.

Staverton & Landscove 🦜

The name Staverton is believed to have come from 'the village by a stony ford', and there was a ford by the old Staverton mill, but now it is more often called Staverton on the Dart – a peaceful village famous for its bridge built in 1413 to replace the original which was destroyed in a flood.

The screen in the lovely Norman church dedicated to St Paul de Leon, is 57 ft wide and stretches the whole width of the church. It was restored in 1889 with the addition of a loft and rood, which was destroyed in Elizabethan times.

The village is also well known for its local pub the Sea Trout Inn, once known as the 'Church House Inn'. It is believed that once there were three or even four pubs in the village. One other for certain was called the Ring O Bells, but it has long since disappeared.

In the summer time on the first Saturday in August there is a Garden Show, where the pick of the local produce wins prizes and later on August Bank Holiday Monday the Elizabethan Fayre takes place. Both these events are held on the well kept and well used recreation ground.

The most famous industry is perhaps Staverton Joinery. Staverton station is one of the pick-up points along the Dart Valley Railway, once an extremely busy station all year round. The trip by steam train alongside the river Dart is a most attractive journey and highly popular.

The civil parish of Staverton is split into two parochial parishes, Staverton itself and Landscove. Miss Champernowne built a church, vicarage and school alongside the hamlet known as Woolston Green, in a field known as Landscove, and so this area has become the parish of Landscove. The church was consecrated in 1851. In those days a quarry was being worked and once over 100 men were employed there and many lived in the Woolston Green area. Nowadays it is really like a small village with its own shop, but the two parishes do combine in their activities and of course have only one Parish Council.

Sticklepath 🦢

In 1918 Lt Col Pearse, aide de camp to the Governor of Assam, was on a mission to the Nizam of Hyderabad. When Col Pearse was introduced the Nizam said 'Pearse? I know that name', and among some old documents, found bills for scarlet cloth bought from Pearse of Sticklepath. This cloth had been made into uniforms for the palace guards and at that time, 100 years later, they were still in use. The bales of cloth had been carried by packhorse up the old highway to Plymouth, for shipment to India.

Sticklepath lies on the banks of the river Taw, three and a half miles east of Okehampton. From earliest times the road has been the main

Exeter to Cornwall highway and from this the village derives its name, for its old route lay up a 'stickle' or 'steep' path which climbed the hill at the western end of the village.

At the beginning of the 19th century it was a busy centre of industry, having two woollen mills and a flour mill. The Cleave Mill was acquired by the Pearse family in the early 1800s. To work the machinery, the waters of the river Taw were utilised by means of a canal known locally as 'the leat'. This also provided the power for the industrial site of Finch's Foundry, a complex which operated three water wheels and two trip hammers. Until 1960, tools for agriculture and for the mining and china clay industries of Devon and Cornwall were made by hand. In 1966, a trust was formed to preserve the foundry as a Museum of Industrial History.

Before the building of the village school in 1870, local children received a smattering of knowledge from various dame schools. Mary Brookland taught a few of these children in one of the thatched cottages behind which the leat runs, and into which she slipped one day and was drowned. She was not missed until the foundry wheel refused to turn because of the obstruction in the leat above.

John Wesley preached in the village in 1743 and as a result of this and subsequent visits, a strong Wesleyan movement developed and the present chapel was later built. Several Sticklepath Quakers sailed with William Penn to help found the New World colony of Friends in Pennsylvania.

Although there are 24 buildings listed as being of historical interest, including two 17th century thatched inns, the village has grown so rapidly during the last few years, that there are now as many new houses as older ones.

The great Sticklepath oak, which stands proudly at the entrance to the new Oak Tree estate, had a preservation order put on it after the WI, worried about its future, petitioned for its protection.

Agricultural workers, copper and tin miners, stonemasons, blacksmiths, shoemakers, candlemakers and many others have all disappeared from the rural scene. Now most of the working population travel out of the village daily. To compensate, there is a road haulage business, a residential home and a nursery garden specialising in hostas.

Sticklepath had long been part of the parish of Sampford Courtenay, but after the Boundary Commission Review, it became an independent parish.

Stockland 🎕

Stockland is situated in the Yarty valley, amongst the Blackdown Hills. It is a parish of scattered farms, bounded on the east by the Yarty and on the west by the Umborne brook. In AD 939 King Athelstan gave ten hides of land to Milton Abbey in Dorset to provide food and clothing for the monks, and this was the first mention of Stockland. The village remained in the county of Dorset, an island surrounded by Devon, until 1842 when it became part of Devon.

There is evidence of much earlier settlement in the area. Stone Age man has left behind an abundance of tools and hand axes. There are also two Iron Age camps in the parish, the larger one unfortunately cut in half when 'Inclosure' roads were made on Stockland Hill. Parts of the ditch and banks are clearly visible on both sites.

The exceptionally large church was built in the 14th and 15th centuries upon earlier foundations. In the chancel, on a pillar, is carved the head of a monk, possibly a mason's mark.

There remain in Stockland an unusually large number of houses which date back to the 15th and 16th centuries, and early documents contain forms of surnames which are with us today. In 1394 we hear of Cubbel, now Kibby, and later Strobridge which became Strawbridge, Soutere – Salter, Toukere – Tucker. In 1288 Laurence de Crandon may have lived at the present Crandons Farm, and Gervas Borde probably lived at Boordais, now Broadhayes.

Although Stockland is some twelve miles from the sea, at one period smuggling was rife here. One family had to leave for New Zealand in some haste! Later they sponsored 23 other members of the family, who departed on the first emigrant ship, the *Dallam Castle*.

An interesting story appeared in *Dalwood Magazine* in 1885. It relates that 'A sexton was digging in Stockland churchyard when he came upon a skull, on the removal of which he discovered some old coins, 35 in number. They proved to be silver pennies from the reign of Henry III. The coins are claimed by the Crown, but application has been made by the vicar to the Lords of the Treasury that some of them could be sold for the church restoration fund'. Unfortunately the coins disappear from local records at this point so it is not clear who benefited from the discovery.

There is in Stockland a wealth of information gathered from ancient documents which gives fascinating glimpses of the lives of those who lived here in times past. In 1759 a certain Sarah Callard made her will.

She desired that 'My funeral may be performed early in the morning in the most private and frugal manner, and that my corpse be carried to my grave on men's shoulders, and that twelve poor men, usually employed at Ford House may be my bearers, and have one shilling apiece and a pair of gloves'.

Stoodleigh ॐ

Stoodleigh is a small village six miles north of Tiverton. It offers a pleasing variety of landscapes combining wooded valleys fed by streams, rising to nearly 1,000 ft at Stoodleigh Beacon, reputed to be one of the Armada warning beacons. The approach road to Stoodleigh is commonly called the Drive, as indeed it was once a private drive leading to Stoodleigh Court.

St Margaret's, the parish church of Stoodleigh, lies in the centre of the village, and although enlarged and restored at the end of the 19th century by Squire Daniel, still has much of its 15th century origin intact, which includes the tower. The font is reputed to be Norman and during renovations Roman tiles were discovered. The yew tree in the churchyard is over 500 years old, and was probably planted when the original church was built.

Stoodleigh Court was built around 1880 on the site of the old manor house by Squire Daniel of Stuckeridge. The Squire's wife, however did not take to it and they returned to Stuckeridge. In 1926 the estate was broken up, and Stoodleigh Court itself was bought by Ravenswood Preparatory School from Paignton, who have occupied it ever since.

The occupations of the people of Stoodleigh are wide and varied. Most of the dairy and sheep farms are family owned, Ravenswood School employs both teaching and domestic staff, whilst quite a few people commute. Many retired people have settled in the village, and the craftsmen working locally include a builder, carpenter, furniture maker, glass blower, potter, jeweller, artist and dressmaker. On the outskirts of the village there is a trout fishery.

Despite occupying a rather isolated position and being a long drawn out village, the community spirit is very strong. There are no shops, post office, pub and alas now no school, so folk without cars are dependent on the goodwill of others, and on the twice weekly market bus which is run by volunteers and serves Stoodleigh and the neighbouring villages.

Stoodleigh has some interesting tales – Gibbett Moor was the site of the gibbet, where many a sheep stealer was hanged, and in fact a local resident tells how her great-grandmother recalled going to Gibbett Moor to see one of the last men hanged there. Hangmans Hill has its memories too, and was so named because an old sailor returning from serving his time in the press gang had reached the vicinity of Hangmans Hill, when he saw an old crone who lived nearby walking towards him with a crow perched on her shoulder. This terrified him so much he went off and hanged himself. Whilst Quoit-at-Cross was not where quoits were once played, but the site of an old burial ground.

Stoke Gabriel ৯৶৹

The village of Stoke Gabriel lies in a fold of the hills by the river Dart, six miles upstream from Dartmouth and the same distance winding downstream from Totnes. The church stands sentinel above the creek and this and other buildings are mentioned in the Domesday Book.

Fishing and farming were always the main occupations and it was known as the 'Village of Orchards'. Most are now built over but some remain, including the Church Orchard leading to the millpond, bought by the Parish Council as a public open space.

For centuries Stoke Gabriel has been the centre of the Dart salmon fishing industry. Though no longer a full time occupation the netting rights are carefully guarded by those who own them and many visitors have watched with interest the working boats and enjoyed the delicious fresh salmon.

The quay is now a popular beauty spot with a cafe where once the ancient tidal mill stood by the dam. In the creek floats a pontoon for rowing boats, small sailing dinghies lie in a sheltered corner and there are many moorings for larger craft in the main river. In days gone by the river Dart was a busy trading route between Dartmouth and Totnes. The old paddle steamer called at Duncannon Point and the ferryman rowed passengers and goods ashore. The loads were then hauled up the steep path in trolleys known as 'three wheeled kits', which were often ridden scooter-fashion down again.

The village is now a mixture of old and new housing but the essential character remains with the cobbled walk to the church with its old cottages, the original schoolroom (now the parish room), the ancient yew tree and the much loved church of St Mary and St Gabriel. The verger's cottage has recently been restored for the new verger who has happily taken on these duties when the unbroken line of the Narracot family, who held this office for 500 years, finally ended.

A new vicarage was built in 1960 on the hill above the primary school. The old vicarage once housed the fiery 'Parson Neville' 1881–1916, who as a tall handsome bachelor inspired the love of a maiden living at Sharpham House across the river. She had a window specially constructed to look towards the vicarage, but as her love went unrequited it was later boarded up.

When the footpath to Duncannon was barred by the occupant of Duncannon House, Parson Neville went with a band of fishermen and smashed the gate down with his own hand. A tale retold with relish by older residents! The path remains a right-of-way today to the little river beach.

At Sandridge on the edge of the parish was born John Davis, sailor and explorer friend of Raleigh and the Gilberts. He was christened (the font remains unchanged) and married in Stoke Gabriel church. He discovered and named the Davis Strait between Greenland and Baffin Island. In 1592 he discovered the Falkland Islands, on his last voyage in 1605 he was killed by Malayan pirates. Later a house designed by Nash was built on the site of his birthplace.

In 1881 Stoke Gabriel was almost self-sufficient with 642 inhabitants. In addition to fishermen and millers there were twelve farmers

Stoke Gabriel from the river Dart

215

(five working farms remain today), a thatcher, two boot and shoemakers, a carpenter and undertaker. At the turn of the century there was also a resident policeman, a district nurse and a post office (fortunately still with us), also two general stores, a butcher, paper shop, hotel (once the home of the Churchward family), three pubs, two cafes, two nurseries, two holiday camps, a garage, Baptist chapel, village hall and until recently a pottery.

Stokenham ✤

At the southernmost tip of Devon, where the land juts into the sea, Stokenham has been the home of farmers and fishermen for a thousand years. The Saxons settled it first, around AD800. Then the Normans came, and made it the centre of a richly fertile manor, with good productive fishing from the sheltered sandy beaches.

Who was that unknown romantic who provided a lady's ring, lately found on the manor house site? It is a plain gold band, and the inscription is *inside* it, where only the lady wearer would know of it, but would know of it constantly. In large medieval letters it says, simply and enchantingly: MY HART YOU HAVE.

The closeness of the sea at all points provides a benign local maritime climate, protected from the extremes of heat in summer and of cold in winter. Spring comes early, and the banks at the sides of the deep-set lanes are, by April, vivid and fragrant with flowers. Even in mid-winter, if you know where to look, you can always find a small bunch of wild violets.

The centre of the village breathes a tranquil settled antiquity, especially when it is drowsing in the summer sun. The scattered houses, under their brown thatch, have their white cob walls clothed in colourful long-established wisterias or roses, and the gardens are similarly aglow. The two pubs, centuries old, have the same simple appealing character, and the square-towered dominant church of St Michael and All Angels, set on a slight mound, is a focus for everything.

Many modern houses have developed around the original core of the village, for people today, just as in the past, have found this a pleasant place to live. But all strive to keep it a gentle and beautiful place. The fact that the large church is so scrupulously well-kept is a symbol of that.

The community feeling of the village was specially expressed at the time of the Jubilee in 1977. All the families, old and new, joined in creating a time capsule into which they packed hundreds of small domestic articles. Then the capsule was buried at the centre of the village to tell the people of future centuries, with pride, what the village's present life is like.

Strete ❧

Strete stands 300 ft up on the cliffs overlooking Start Bay. This is the wide, half-circle of sea, the scene of many shipwrecks, which extends from the Mew Stone to the lighthouse at Start Point. It is five miles south-west of Dartmouth and the nearest beaches are Blackpool Sands to the east and Strete Gate to the west.

Strete may have got its name from the Romans as some old maps show that a Roman camp was formed near Slapton Ley. The spelling changed to Strete in 1870 to avoid postal confusion with Street in Somerset.

In the early 1700s there was an undercliff village. Here the fishermen built their cottages in the rocks but the village was swept into the sea during a storm.

Strete had its share of smuggling as did all the villages around the coast. Beneath an old coach house a cellar was found with steps leading down into the rocks, into what was most likely a smuggler's storeroom. Other stories are known of possible tunnels and secret passages from the beach to the village.

Before the Second World War, Strete was a very busy village. It had three farms, three building firms, a butcher, two bakeries, a post office, a shoe repairer, a resident doctor, a blacksmith, church, chapel, the reading room, a boys club and the National school.

The school was built in 1839, had two classrooms and educated children from five surrounding hamlets. Sadly it closed in July 1965. The building is now used as a restaurant.

The church was built in 1836 with donations amounting to £978. It was dedicated to St Michael and All Angels. It is built of stone in the Gothic style and consists of a chancel, nave, aisles, a south porch and western tower. Long before this there was a small chapel in the grounds of the Old Manor Farm.

There are just two shops in the village today. A general store/post office and general store/off licence. The Kings Arms pub has successful dart and quiz teams. The nearest doctors are now in Dartmouth.

In July 1943 all the people in the village were given six weeks notice of evacuation, when the whole area was used for training in preparation for the D-Day Normandy landings. Most people were away from their homes for well over a year. Many buildings were bombed during the practices. The reading room and the boys club were destroyed. With the compensation and other monies the village hall was built.

On the first Saturday in August the highlight of the year is Village Day. All the organisations in the village run stalls and side shows and the monies raised are split between charities and funds for the village hall. A marathon run which is recognised by the AAA is also held on Village Day.

The population is now 530 and quite a number of the residents are retired. Strete is a happy, sociable village and retains much of its old charm.

Talaton

Did they hang the rebels at Bittery Cross? It is said that men building Escot House ran away to join Monmouth and that those who were caught were condemned by Judge Jeffreys to die at Talaton. The route for the Rebellion did pass close by on its way to Honiton. The Roman bath in the field called Bath House is too overgrown to be authenticated and perhaps that is as it should be. Village folklore would be the poorer if all stories had to be 'cut and dried'. The Talaton hoard of six Bronze Age swords, three of which are in the British Museum and the others in Exeter are indisputable connections with local settlements such as Hembury Fort.

There have been dwellings in and around Talaton for hundreds of years. The Old Manor is a fascinating house which has an inner core of cob walls with outer ones of brick. There are also some simple flower paintings on the plank panelling which are dated as 16th century. The adjacent Harris Farm is an early example of brick and timber construction. Other old houses have walls of cob or of stone with brick additions. It seems extraordinary that the Manor in Deep Lane and St James' church are in a hollow, not in commanding strategic positions.

What excitement there must have been when the railway came to East Devon in around 1860. Lashbrook Farmhouse was in the way so it was demolished and a new house was built a little way off. One of the windows bears the scratch mark 'C. Chick glazier. December 23rd 1863'. The new home was ready in time for Christmas. The local halt, Sidmouth Junction, has long since gone and the connection to Ottery abandoned. The Waterloo train and small commuter two-coachers travel the line but the stations to use now are either Feniton or Whimple.

218

Various trades flourished here in the earlier part of the century. There was a butcher, baker, blacksmith, wheelwright, tailor, thatcher, carpenter, agricultural contractor, even a seamstress who, in spite of working all hours, always seemed to be very poor. There were a number of farmers and also a husband and wife who were doctors living and practising here with their surgery and dispensary in a shed adjoining one of the cottages.

Lack of rural transport is nothing new. In the 1920s and 1930s it meant that the tradespeople came to their customers. There were pedlars, patent pill merchants, fishmongers (one called 'Slippery Apple'), a tea specialist and the gypsies' wares. The village shop sold all the usual conglomeration of goods from flour and rice to paraffin and candles. A Mrs Robinson came from Manchester and opened the Oak Tree Stores to sell small articles of clothing while her husband mended bicycles. There is still a village shop with the post office but most of the visiting trades are no longer to be found.

The Talaton Friendly Society was founded in 1855. Whit Tuesday was Club Day. There was a parade through the village which collected the Rector en route and went to the church for a service. After this the parson was escorted home to change and the parade finished at the pub for a dinner. Following the normal Friendly society objectives it provided a

Harris Farm, Talaton

form of sick pay for its members. One of its articles of association states 'No member shall be entitled to any pay whose sickness shall be caused by fighting, wrestling or any misfortune of their own seeking or whom whilst receiving pay shall frequent any public house or any improper place for a sick person to resort to'.

Farming still remains the way in which the land is used although it is no longer a major source of employment. In recent years some small local industries have been started on the old saw mill sites on the edge of the village going out towards Feniton.

Tedburn St Mary

Tedburn St Mary lies in beautiful countryside which is full of colour at any time of the year. It was with the building of the parish church around the 13th century, that the village acquired the 'St Mary' part of its name. Hence a map of 1575 records it as St Marytetborne.

In 1683 a Mr William Hay was paid four shillings for pulling ivy from the walls of the parish church. Elizabeth Hay, most probably his wife, received four shillings for sweeping the church for the whole year!

Between the years 1793 and 1806 the population numbered 500, and were said to be mostly employed in agriculture and spinning. In 1988 the population was around 1,400, including the nearby Pathfinder Village and two estates that have been built since 1970. A great number of Tedburn people commute daily to Exeter and around. With the coming of the motor car and public transport this is made possible, but one wonders what our forefathers would have made of it – those members of a self-sufficient community, which in 1857 included 31 farmers, two blacksmiths, three boot and shoe makers and a builder-postmaster, among others.

In Victorian times, there are known to have been at least nine dame schools in the village, and even though the state school had opened in 1877, 'Mrs Holman's Private School' at North Park Lodge continued to operate until 1881. The first headmaster of the state school only lasted a year, when his certificate to teach was withdrawn by the Education Department. This decision was then shown to be quite justified when he proceeded to take, not only his leave of the school, but also the school fees and the stationery money that he had collected. A bad start for the School Board, but no doubt it added some spice to much of the conversation around the village!

In spite of the rapid growth of the village, in Tedburn the old community spirit lives on. There was, during the last century, a cattle fair on the Monday before Michaelmas each year, and the annual fair and flower show still attracts crowds each September. The village pantomime is still performed with gusto, and the WI is still going strong. It would seem that the more recently formed organisations, of which there are many, have captured the enthusiasm of the long established ones. As in times past, Tedburn can still provide its own amusement!

Tetcott ꙮ

Tetcott, referred to in the Domesday Book as Tetecote, is a small parish of approximately 300 inhabitants. It is situated near the confluence of the rivers Tamar and Claw, five miles south of Holsworthy. It has an adjoining hamlet called Luffincott, with aproximately 50 inhabitants.

Luffincott has its own church (adjoining Luffincott Barton) which is now closed and maintained by the Historic Church Trust.

Farmland in the parish is owned by the Molesworth St Aubyns and many farms are being farmed by the third or fourth generation.

The approach to Tetcott's 13th century church of the Holy Cross and the manor house is through parkland, known locally as 'The Wilderness'. The beautifully kept church has a tower and one bell.

The ancient manor is the home of the Molesworth St Aubyn family, but it is not open to the public. The Barton joins the manor house and an interesting early brick-built granary on brick piers stands nearby.

Social activities include an active WI (linked with Clawton), skittles teams and a horticultural show. Tetcott has a Methodist church which serves the area. It is also the home of the South Tetcott Hunt.

Thorverton ꙮ

Thorverton is a large and ancient village with a flourishing flour mill on the river Exe not far from the site of the old mills on the leat near the old railway station. It is surrounded by beautiful hill scenery. Crops, such as wheat, barley, apples and at one time locally famous apricots, flourish here. There are several old farms. Raddon Court takes its name from the range of hills nearby on which a clump of trees, Raddon Top, can still be seen. Red Hill was a Saxon estate. Other old farms are Upcott, Bidwell and Lynch. Traymill, to the north of the parish on the Exe, was built about 1400 and has traceried windows, arched doorways and still retains the original hall roof.

Thorverton bridge is the most recent of several bridges built to span the Exe. The first was built in 1307 probably made from timbers. Both old Thorverton and Traymill were Domesday watermills serving the manor of Silverton.

The main streets are followed by a channel stream as in several South Devon villages. There are also smaller channels running in the streets. This was the brain child of the daughter of a Victorian Rector, after a rather serious outbreak of cholera.

Two great fairs were held every year, one the last Monday in February chiefly for fat sheep, the other on the Monday after the 18th of July for lambs at which 4000 were frequently sold at one fair. A hundred years ago there were four bakers, three blacksmiths, one of which was a part time dentist, four grocers, two saddlers, four tailors, two shoemakers, two plumbers, two wheelwrights and a chandler. Also there was a parson and curate, surgeon, solicitor, an accountant auctioneer, veterinary surgeon, builder, corn miller, apple nurseryman and a maltster. Today the village can only boast one shop, a post office and three pubs.

The church, dedicated to St Thomas a' Becket, was built in the late 15th early 16th centuries and restored about 1834 when the nave was rebuilt. In recent times a portion of the east end of the church has been converted into a Lady Chapel and as if to balance this, a vicars chapel occupies the space beside the organ. The north transept was also enclosed and is now used for meetings and other occasions. There are also slate floor slabs to the Tuckfields of East Raddon, a hamlet one mile west of the village, where the abandoned workings of a stone quarry are still visible.

Thorverton stone was used to build many houses and churches in the neighbourhood of which Newton St Cyres is one. Charities of £60 was left by John Bury to be lent to poor tradesmen. In 1673 Thomas Adams left £100 part for bread and part for education and other smaller gifts were left for bread. In 1710 Margaret Tuckfeet arranged for bibles and coats to be distributed amongst the poor children. These charities are now contained in one separate fund as the value of money and circumstances are completely different in this day and age.

There is an up-to-date Trust Fund known as The Leonard Trust, founded by a local resident Chip Leonard. It is run by trustees who are very generous in giving a helping hand to any worthwhile cause in the village.

Throwleigh 🌿

As you enter Throwleigh ('ow' pronounced as in 'cow') either from Okehampton, Exeter or Chagford, you must be impressed by its peaceful beauty. Stand at the village cross and gaze at what has been described by another writer as the 'gem' of the village. Here is an exceptional view of the church of St Mary the Virgin, the thatched lychgate and ancient thatched church house, with other pretty cottages around it.

The lychgate was erected in memory of the late Rev Gambier Lowe who, in the early part of this century, renovated the old tithe barn (now a dwelling house) and built several houses in Shilstone Lane. This lane goes, uphill all the way, to Shilstone Tor, on the moor, at a height of nearly 2,000 ft and passes some 30 houses, all set back in pretty gardens. The steepest part is known as Golden Hill and this lane was once known as 'Petticoat Lane' because most of the homes were occupied by widows or spinster ladies, with as many as 22 domestic servants 'living in'. Times have changed – many of those houses are now occupied by retired people while those of working age, newcomers and local residents, commute to Exeter on the new A30.

Many of the old local families have nearly died out. The Endacotts of the 15th century Clannaborough farmstead, the Aggetts, highly skilled thatchers, and the Hills once formed the largest share of the population of about 300. In 1930 one third of the school children were Hill descendants. During the early part of this century the elder children were excused school to help plant potatoes in the fields and to harvest the corn. Practically all farming today is centred around stock breeding (bullocks and sheep) and the delightful summer scent of haymaking has changed to the winter smell of silage.

The Barton Farm 'longhouse' is now a delightful residence, the barn, stables and calves' house converted into cottages, all with the original granite walls. Two cottages stand on the old saw-pit and in the orchard; the bull's house and cart-shed have become modern garages. The forge has gone, after being in the Hill family for four generations, but the Forge Stores and post office are there to remind us of their original position at the beginning of the century.

There is much to see in the hamlets of Wonson and Providence. The Northmore Arms, once called the New Inn when it replaced the Royal Oak in Throwleigh, has taken its name from Wonson manor. This Norman fortified manor re-styled in the 17th century, once belonged to the Northmore family. The village hall, a cleverly converted Nissen hut, stands near the top of the hill where there are three things of interest – the beautiful high curved granite wall of Wadman's Garage (once a wheelwright's shop), a Victorian letter box and a horse chestnut tree, planted by a local tree-lover to commemorate Queen Victoria's Diamond Jubilee. The wheelwright's stone for binding his cart and wagon wheels with iron bands is there now and also one at the forge which the blacksmith used when executing repairs.

Providence is the home of the Methodist chapel, which has celebrated its 150th anniversary, and the local school, now closed and used as a Field Centre. Nearby is 'Bloody Meadow' where fighting took place during the Chagford battle between Royalists and Parliamentarians in the 17th century.

Thurlestone ✍🏼

The parish is in the South Hams of Devon, about four miles from Kingsbridge, and consists of the village of Thurlestone, and the hamlets of East and West Buckland and Bantham.

The village of Thurlestone is attractive, with its old thatched cottages lining the main street which dips towards the sea and the ancient parish church, a view which has changed little for many years.

The well-preserved 13th century church of All Saints has a Norman font, some ancient memorial plaques, and decorative bosses in the chancel. At the time of the Armada a fire-pan kept in the church tower was ignited as a warning beacon.

In the 16th century a church house was built on land acquired from the rector, and in consideration of this a pair of gloves and a copy of the deed was placed annually, from 1536, on the high altar on All Saints' day. The custom has not been followed since 1922 but it is hoped to re-start the practice. With the coming of the Puritans, however, the church house was converted into dwellings, then into a poor house. It is now cottages and these are protected as being of historic interest.

Smuggling became almost an industry at one time, and spirits were shipped in great quantities from France. It is said that the kegs were stored at what is now 'Whiddons' at Bantham and on top of the church porch at Thurlestone, with a keg being left handy for the parson in return for this convenience. This went on until a new rector arrived in 1839 who 'indignantly refused it'!

Buckland has some attractive thatched cottages clustered on the steep sides of a sheltered valley inland between Bantham and Thurlestone. Its former Wesleyan chapel is now converted to a house, and what was once an old mill, complete with leat, became a butcher's shop and is now a house.

Bantham, at the mouth of the Avon estuary, is well-known for its 'ham' – the dunes adjoining the large sandy beach. Its unspoilt beauty is largely due to the Evans family (Evans Estates) who own most of the land and who have not allowed building on the river banks or coastline. They rent the river bed and part of the foreshore from the Duchy of Cornwall. A little inland from the 'ham', a small number of cottages and houses make the village, with its ancient Sloop Inn and a small shop/post office. From May until October the river is full of holidaymakers' boats but after that it reverts more to what it must have been like at the beginning of the century.

Boat trips from Plymouth continued to visit Bantham up to the First World War. There was also commercial traffic with boats from Brixham bringing limestone to be processed in the lime-kilns that are features of the estuary, and boats were guided up-river by a Harbour Master until 1928. At Bantham Quay the old boathouse was rebuilt in 1937. Just above the quay are the old pilchard cellars, a reminder of the days when fishing was an important local occupation. There is also a Surf Life-Saving Club and a Sailing Club at Bantham.

Thurlestone's pub, The Village Inn, contains some old oak timbers reputed to have come from a Spanish Armada ship wrecked at nearby Hope Cove.

The sea around Thurlestone is often very blue but at times, when the south-westerlies are blowing, there can be spectacular storms and rough seas. Even today ships will lose their deck cargoes and then what bounty on the beaches! Onions, oranges, soap and timber are some of the things that have been salvaged . . . but you have to be quick before the Customs men arrive!

Topsham ✑

Topsham is on the Exe estuary, five miles downstream from Exeter. It was once a thriving port, delivering goods to all parts of the Continent, most of the cargo being the thick, smooth, heavy serge made in and around Exeter. After the Napoleonic Wars, trade to Europe declined, so the merchants of Topsham transferred their business to the Americas. In time all the trade went to larger, more efficient, ports.

Today Topsham has a small boat building yard, some salmon fishing and a very large fleet of private boats sailing on the estuary.

Topsham (pronounced Tops-ham, not Top-sham!) derived its name from a Saxon landowner named Toppa. It is a town in its own right, being given a charter by Henry III who permitted a three-day fair, each July on St Margaret of Antioch's feast day. In those days if you were large enough to run a three-day event, you were large enough to call yourself a town!

Topsham has one main street, Fore Street, with small lanes and courtyards running down to the Passage Way (where at one time all the work was done) alongside the estuary. Many of the buildings that remain in Fore Street were built between the 14th and the 17th centuries. Many have been modernised of course, but the original outlines can still be seen.

The parish church, St Margaret's, was rebuilt in 1876–8, except for its medieval red sandstone tower.

It is an elegant little town which has not 'rusticated' with the passage of time, with plenty to do and enjoy. There are still nine public houses (there were once 36!), many dating back to the 13th century, and four restaurants. There is also a local museum housed on The Strand (area of ships and sails) in one of the original houses built with bricks brought from Holland as ballast. This building was bequeathed to Topsham in the early 1980s.

Uffculme

Uffculme is one of a number of compact villages found all over Devon, but more frequently east of the river Exe.

The village has a population in excess of 2,000 and is the largest settlement in the upper Culm valley. It is situated mid-way between Taunton and Exeter, about a mile from Junction 27 on the M5. It was once an important centre of the woollen trade and a market town and is in a large parish of some 6,000 acres.

The former wealth of the village is reflected in the size of the parish church of St Mary, which has a medieval west tower and a nave and chancel rebuilt and refitted in 1843. The most striking feature of the church is an early 15th century rood screen which is, at 67 ft, thought to be the longest in Devon.

Another feature of the village is the shambles, a wooden construction like a lychgate, which is a relic of the markets once held in the village

226

square. The latter is a wedge-shaped sloping area pleasantly surrounded by early 19th century frontages and opening onto the grounds of Ayshford House, a former grammar school, now used for housing.

Uffculme possesses a wealth of other buildings of architectural or historical interest including Bradfield House, once the home of the Walrond family (now a residential school), Coldharbour Mill, a wool spinning factory (now a working wool museum), part of a former steam brewery (now a day centre), The Old Parsonage, Gaddon House and Craddock House.

Agriculture has always played an important part in the life of the village and, despite changing techniques, still contributes to its delightful setting. It is also at least partly responsible for the many miles of footpaths with which the parish is blessed. Some of these lead to the areas of common land which have also survived in quantity despite the pressures of industry in the shape of sand extraction and block making.

Like so many Devon villages, Uffculme is changing and growing. Some of the changes and the rate of expansion are not entirely appreciated by the indigenous population. Nevertheless, for country lovers it remains a delightful place to live and an excellent base from which to explore this part of the West Country.

Umberleigh ✇

Umberleigh lies in a beautiful valley in the north of the county. It is bisected by the river Taw which divides the village between the two parishes of Atherington and Chittlehampton. At its centre is a public house, village shop, cafe and guesthouse, the post office, an agricultural engineering business, village hall, church, chapel and railway station, but very few houses. These are scattered amidst the surrounding countryside in small clusters, often grouped around an old farm.

Even today the village is mostly agriculturally based and covers an overall area of about 1,200 acres, mainly livestock farming with some arable. In the past, many acres of fruit prevailed, cherries in particular, and old field names like 'Mazzard Close' record evidence of these old cherry orchards. However, a lovely hanging wood, now preserved as a nature reserve, hides an old coal mine within its depths, indicative of a previous, more industrialised community – a complete contrast to its present tranquillity!

A further important asset in Umberleigh is about three miles of trout and salmon fishing on the river Taw. It was the setting for Henry

Williamson's story of *Salar the Salmon* and it is still possible to observe salmon fighting their way upstream, along with sightings of kingfishers and herons. Some people have even been fortunate enough to see an otter. The bar of the Rising Sun pub displays many pictures of proud fishermen with their catches, including one of the late Eric Morecambe with a 3 ft salmon. This looks very impressive until you realise that he is holding the wooden fish sign which normally hangs over the pub door!

Heavy rain on Dartmoor results in a considerable rise in the river level here about twelve hours later. In the past it has burst its banks and in 1968 dwellings by the bridge were flooded to a height of about 5 ft. Each August the river hosts a raft race, organised by the Round Table, and usually attracts about 100 entries.

Umberleigh's origins can be traced back to Umberleigh Barton itself where, in AD936 King Athelstan built a palace. Later a chapel was built, dedicated to the Holy Trinity, but only a bricked-up archway now remains and much of its fine church furniture was transferred to Atherington church. The estate, however, continued to prosper and has frequently been associated with female inheritors known as 'The Ladies of Umberleigh'. It passed through various families until 1460 when it came to the Bassett family with whom it remained for nearly 500 years. When part of the manor was being rebuilt a stone was found, inscribed thus:

> I, John of Gaunt, do hereby give to thee and thine,
> from me and mine,
> the barton fee of Umberlee.
> And so the world may know its truth
> I hereby seal it with my tooth.

This was inscribed with the impression of a tooth!

The present village of Umberleigh prospered with the coming of the Exeter to Barnstaple railway line on 1st November 1873. An annual garden show and carnival meant the London to Barnstaple express had to make a special stop here that day, and passengers also came once a month to the popular livestock market until that ceased in 1961. A small church, made of wood, is built on leased railway land and one of the conditions of the agreement is that it has to be painted brown and cream – the old GWR colours.

Today the school and church still thrive, the garden show is still an annual event, and current reports indicate a possible return to the golden age of steam along the railway track, wending its way through this delightful valley.

Uplyme 🦥

Uplyme lies on the south-east border of Devon, close to the counties of Somerset and Dorset. The main road runs through a valley between wooded hills. Visitors dash through the village to reach Lyme Regis, a mile away, little realising the history and beauty of this large Devon village.

The river Lym rises above the village and flows through to the sea at Lyme Regis. Around it the settlement grew and became the source of life and industry. Sheep grazed on the hills and estates thrived. Mills were built along its length from the 14th century to the 18th century. The Waterside cloth factory provided a market for all wool produced in the parish, progressing from undyed coarse cloth to dyeing, weaving and napping cloth of a fine quality. It is said that the scarlet serge for Queen Elizabeth I's soldiers was made at the mill and the red dye for the footmen's uniforms of Queen Victoria was supplied from here. Near the mill is the old thatched Uplyme corn mill, still standing beside the water.

Two other industries provided work for the people of the village, the Yawl Mineral Spring Factory started in 1896 and the stone quarry also at Yawl. The farms are still working today and many families have been living here through generations. The large houses at Harcombe and Rhode Hill on the eastern boundary are now boarding school accommodation for the comprehensive school 'Woodroffe' on the Uplyme border. The Uplyme primary school, Mrs Ethelston's School, was built in 1854, in memory of the rector's wife, and is beside the church.

All around lies the history of Uplyme. The western boundary follows an ancient British ridgeway passing several tumuli. Beacons were lit around here to warn of invasions. The site of a Roman villa, excavated in 1850, rises on a hill above Cannington Farm. This was found to be built over an Iron Age settlement. Dominating the whole valley is the Cannington Viaduct, built to take the railway through Uplyme to Lyme Regis. The banks of the railway are now covered with trees, shrubs, grasses and wild flowers.

On the southern boundary is the wonderful nature reserve at Ware Cliff, part of the famous landslip overlooking Lyme Bay.

On the hill above the river, in the heart of the village, is the church of St Peter and St Paul. It stands on an ancient site beside the Old Manor Court Farm and the church is said to have been founded about 100 years before the death of King Alfred. Over the centuries the church has been restored, but the beautiful Perpendicular tower, built in the 13th century, is the oldest part and still stands above the village with its bells ringing on holy days and for other celebrations.

The land below has always been the meeting place of villagers through the ages. It is still a thriving community and the three village shops keep it alive and busy. The recreation ground has taken the place of the village green and, with the village hall, is a centre for all the various clubs and institutions. The local people have formed the Uplyme and Lym Valley Society to help to preserve and protect this village of outstanding beauty.

Upottery

The village is tiny, and has been known since Saxon times as Up-Ottery, as it is the first village the stripling river Otter passes as it comes out of the hills. In the Domesday Book, Alric the Priest was the chief inhabitant; his little wooden Saxon church, however, was soon to be replaced with a Norman stone one, of which you can still see traces in the present largely 13th/14th century building.

As the village grew more prosperous with the wealth from wool in the late Middle Ages, the villagers built themselves a fine church tower with a peal of bells. The latter lasted for 300 years, and their six successors still peal for services and can be heard for miles around on New Year's Eve, ringing out the Old Year and ringing in the New.

The village is the nucleus of a sprawling parish of scattered farms, set in a bowl of the hills, protected from the east and north winds. From this quiet valley, great lorries can be seen crawling towards London on the skyline, as the A30 climbs up to meet the A303 and cross the plateau towards the Somerset-Dorset border.

A son of the manor, Henry Addington, became Prime Minister in 1801 and was created Viscount Sidmouth. The pub proudly displays a letter to him from Nelson, and there is a detailed account of the huge festivities in the village when Napoleon was defeated.

The Sidmouth family did a lot for Upottery, restoring and rebuilding much of the centre of the village in a 19th century 'picturesque' style. It blends well with the thatched homes of an earlier age, one of which used to be the forge, while another held the old hand-operated fire engine. The resultant cluster of buildings round the old church is highly photogenic, and we are also indebted to the Sidmouths for the magnificent trees which are a feature of the village. It is only in the last quarter-century that the Sidmouth connection with the village has come to an end, and the great mansion, whose gates still open on to the centre of the village, has been pulled down. The influence of the family who ruled the village for so long as much-loved despots can still be felt, and incomers must bow to a traditional way of doing things, because 'that was how old Lady Sidmouth liked it'.

Villagers are proud of the fact that this is still a living village, with a working dairy farm in its midst (look at the road surface in summer for proof!), a lively inn, a beloved church and a well-attended school.

Weare Giffard ❧

Travellers on the main road between Bideford and Torrington have a good view of Weare Giffard, strung out for about three miles along the east bank of the river Torridge, between the flood plains and the steep wooded slopes of the valley.

In the Domesday Book it was called Were. The Giffard addition to the name came later, after the powerful Norman family who owned the manor in the 13th century. The tombstone effigies of Sir Walter Giffard, dressed as a Crusader, and of his wife, can be seen in the church.

There was probably a building on the site of Weare Giffard Hall in Saxon times, but the present building was erected in 1450 by Martin Fortescue, son of the Chief Justice to Henry VI, who had come into the Giffard inheritance by marriage. The manor remained in Fortescue ownership until recent times.

As one of the few medieval manors licensed to be fortified, it was defended by the Royalists during the Civil War, but was taken by General Fairfax who ordered it to be razed to the ground. However, it was reprieved, and only the defensive walls levelled, leaving the gate-house tower standing isolated from the house as it is today.

Little Weare Cottage, well out of the village on the road to Gammaton, is probably the oldest existing house in the village, as it has been dated back to the 13th century. A crest with the date 1616 is preserved in a bedroom. Tradition has it that the house was originally a medieval 'meeting hall'.

Weare Giffard was a more 'industrial' village in times past than it is now. There were at least two mills. The large flour mill which can be seen in the middle of fields near the present post office, was modernised in the 1890s and then became one of the first to be driven by a turbine and lit by electricity. Its grinding equipment, the most modern and efficient available, was specially obtained from Manchester. There was also a tucking mill, now a builder's yard, where skins were prepared for the glove industry in Torrington, for which many of those living in Weare Giffard were outworkers. Boat building was carried on in Weare Giffard until the 19th century, and the remains of the dock can be seen by the old 'Dock Cottages'.

Until the 19th century there was no bridge over the Torridge between Bideford and Torrington. Halfpenny bridge was then built to allow farmers access to the lime-kiln on the far side of the river, and the halfpenny toll charged gives it its name.

But until very recently, Weare Giffard was best known as a strawberry-growing village. Large crops were harvested from the south-facing slopes and sent by railway to markets up-country. Now only one or two growers are left, but many older folk can remember summer trips up the river to Weare Giffard for strawberry teas.

West Alvington 🍂

West Alvington, or Alvantona in the Domesday Book, is situated on the crest of the hill from Kingsbridge to Salcombe, in the South Hams. Houses, shops and inns were built on either side of the main road, with a few cottages on the lower side of the road.

In the 18th century an order to widen the roads in the village so that a coach might use them (they are not much wider in places now!) put the parish to great expense as the stone for the work had to come by sea, the local variety not being suitable.

In its heyday, the village had two bakers, a butcher, grocer and haberdasher, post office, newsagents and stationers, as well as builders, thatchers, a rope walk, blacksmith, ship's chandler, maltsters, two dairies and a cider brewer. Today there is only a post office and a builder, the last remaining shop having closed.

All Saints' church, Perpendicular in style except for the tower which is Early English, stands on the site of earlier churches. The porch was used as a school at one time. There are six bells in the tower, and West Alvington bell ringers are well known all around for the number of competitions they win – the walls of the ringing chamber being 'papered' with certificates.

Since the Second World War much new building has taken place, including 53 council houses and flats, many of which are now privately owned. For many years Gerston was the principal manor in the parish. With its mild climate its one-time owners (the Bastard family) were able to grow oranges outside all year round and supposedly once gave them to

George II. It is now a farmhouse. Bowringsleigh, originally built in 1303 but much altered since, is the only manor house left.

When gas came to nearby Kingsbridge, the gasworks was built at the lower end of West Alvington parish and a supply was laid on at the same time. At the end of the 1800s, however, most of the outlying parts of the parish (the gas works included) were ceded to neighbouring parishes, very much reducing West Alvington's size.

In West Alvington graveyard there is an unusual headstone with the following inscription:

"Here lyeth the body of David Jeffrey the
son of Michael Jeffrey and Joan his wife
He was buried ye 2 days of Sept, 1746 in the 18th
year of his age. This youth
when in sickness did lay did for the
minister send that he would come and with
him pray but he would not attend. But
when this young man buried was the minister
did him admit. He should be carried into
Church that he might money get. By this
you will see what man will duo to geet money if
he can. Who did refuse to come and bury
by the for said young man."

This inscription alludes to the custom of a fee paid to the minister when a corpse is carried into the church. Actually the youth died of smallpox, very suddenly, and in spite of the scandalous falsehood the minister, the Rev M. Pyle, allowed the epitaph to stand as a specimen of village poetry.

West Hill 🦋

Although much changed in character in recent years the village of West Hill, on the western side of the beautiful Otter valley, remains what it always has been, a small rural community, surrounded by farmland and meadows and set, wherever the plough could not reach, amongst tall trees.

In the distant Bronze Age our ancestors built a 'ditch and bank' earthwork into the hillside above the larger settlement in the valley bottom a mile or so below – a place that in Norman times took the name of Ottery St Mary. For man and beast alike West Hill's earthwork was a place of refuge when raiders came from the sea and crossed the high moorland to the east of the village. Today that reminder of the distant past is all but cloaked with trees and carpeted with bluebells every spring.

Many of the big houses of the village have now gone, yet the old vicarage remains (built on land given to the church in the bounty of Queen Anne) and is still connected to the church of St Michael (1846) by the tree-lined 'Vicar's Walk'. The church with its beautiful stained glass windows is worthy of a visit.

Before the church came into being West Hill had a thatched chapel. It also had a post office, almost from the time that postal services began, although it was no more than a small room in a private house (still standing) which has now become a private house again. So too has the sweet shop where children were served humbugs and home-made fudge in twists of paper through an open window, its sill serving as a counter – and took them to suck as they watched the smith shoe a horse. The sweet shop and the post office are now contained in a smart new mini-market a little further along the road beyond the war memorial. There was also a mill built in 1815 worked by water which took the farmer's corn to grind for animal feeding stuffs or flour, but this has now been converted into three private houses.

West Hill nowadays has become a smart place in which to live and many of the new generation of villagers work in middle and senior management positions in companies in Exeter.

One of the area's most celebrated sons (excluding Samuel Taylor Coleridge of course who was properly an Ottery boy) was John Billiat, who is buried in the little churchyard. He was one of the explorers who crossed the uncharted Australian interior in the mid 1800s, in the Stuart expedition, surveying the route for the continent's first overland telegraph between Adelaide and Darwin.

Westward Ho!

In the middle of the 19th century the name of Westward Ho! was non-existent. The area was just a rural part of Northam, and is still part of that parish today. It was only after Charles Kingsley wrote his popular novel *Westward Ho!* about the seafaring folk of Bideford, Northam and district that the name was adopted from his title to cover the district now known as Westward Ho!

It was at this time that Westward Ho! began to develop, possibly due to the arrival of the railways and improved system of horse-drawn passenger transport. The excellent surroundings, the beach, the Burrows and even the golf links (then one of the few in the country) were soon appreciated and became a big attraction to visitors and to locals alike.

Westward Ho! depends for its survival on the Pebbleridge; without it the sea would eventually return to its one time shoreline along Atlantic Way.

Behind Westward Ho! looms Kipling Tors — beloved of Rudyard Kipling, who went to school at the old United Services College. It was while he was receiving his education at this college that Kipling began his journalistic writings. His *Stalky and Co* tells the story of his school life and his adventures on Kipling Tors. The actual college is now a series of flats and the old gymnasium has been converted to the Westward Ho! community hall, known as the Kingsley Hall.

A lively challenge to all golfers is presented at the Royal North Devon Golf Course, the 'Royal' being bestowed by the late King Edward VII who played on these links when he was Prince of Wales. Commoner's or 'Potwalloper's' rights allow sheep and horses free grazing on these links, sheltered by the Pebbleridge.

The origin of the term Potwalloper was as a voting qualification and applied to all people who had a separate hearth on which to boil a pot. The Reform Act of 1832 removed this as a voting right but the term Potwalloper lived on. Nowadays Potwalloping involves a community effort in manually throwing back into place the pebbles washed from the ridge by the spring tides.

At the western end of the seafront is the 'Lido' (Patio), a house and swimming pool, at one time the home of a Duchess of Manchester. It was in this pool that Captain Webb did part of his training for his English Channel swim. At the other end of the sea front is Bath House, so called because it incorporated baths for 'Ladies only'. This is now an amusement arcade.

An attempt was made to build a pier at 'Seafield' but the heavy Atlantic breakers soon destroyed these plans. The uprights are still visible at low tide.

Whitchurch ♈

Whitchurch village lies on the western edge of Dartmoor, one and a half miles south of Tavistock and the parish covers roughly five square miles of farmland and several hamlets. The name Whitchurch is derived from the white elvan stone found on Roborough Down which was used to build the parish church of St Andrew, which is of Saxon origin.

The present church dates from the 13th century, partly built in the Perpendicular style, with a tower containing an octagonal staircase and a fine peal of six bells.

The village pub stands in the grounds of the church. Owned by the church, it was originally a resting place for monks journeying between Tavistock Abbey and Buckfast Abbey, the way marked by granite crosses on the moor between these two places.

Mining in the 19th century produced tin, copper, arsenic, lead, silver, zinc, iron, wolfram and uranium. Tin is known to have been mined in medieval times and again in Elizabethan and Victorian times. The quarry at Merrivale has produced granite for the building of London Bridge, New Scotland Yard, and a memorial stone was made here for the victims of the Falklands War.

On the moor above Merrivale are the remains of an ancient standing row, believed to have been a burial ground.

Walreddon Manor was built of granite and local hurdwick stone. The coat of arms of Queen Elizabeth I adorns a parlour wall.

Church of St Andrew, Whitchurch

At the beginning of this century John Edward Eyre lived here. He was noted for his interest and protection of the Aborigines on his arrival in Australia. He was a great explorer and Lake Eyre in Australia is named after him. He held administrative posts in New Zealand, Antigua and St Vincent, before becoming Governor of Jamaica in 1864. He was recalled and suspended for the great severity with which he suppressed a negro insurrection. He is buried in Whitchurch churchyard. Also in the same churchyard is the grave of Mary Metters, mother of five children, who was murdered by her servant with a bill hook. Her assailant was subsequently tried at Exeter assizes, found guilty and was hanged there.

The Priory was built in the 19th century with a 14th century square tower which was part of a chantry for four priests. There is a spring at the Priory which has never been known to dry up.

Honour Oak has for several hundred years marked the boundary between Whitchurch and Tavistock. In the 19th century the oak tree marked the boundary for French prisoners of war, imprisoned at Princetown, on parole in Tavistock. In a great hollow in the tree money was deposited in exchange for food during a cholera epidemic in 1830 when the town was virtually cut off to all outsiders.

Whitestone

Whitestone is a large and hilly parish approximately three miles west of Exeter, with a very scattered population of 650. The parish is like a hand with three fingers extended eastwards, the highest ground being 809 ft above sea level, from where there are extensive views of Dartmoor, north towards Exmoor, eastwards over Exeter and the hills beyond, and south-east down the Exe estuary. Between the three ridges are deep valleys through which run the Nadder and Alphin brooks.

The name Whitestone is derived from the ancient saltway which ran from the salt pans in the Teign estuary northwards to Crediton.

The beautiful little 13th century church of St Catherine of Alexandria, stands high on one of the ridges overlooking the village with wonderful views towards Exmouth. In the old days it was a mark for sailors entering the estuary and to this day the church has the right to fly the White Ensign.

The main part of the village on the old coach road from Exeter to Okehampton, is not old, but there are many beautiful old houses and farms in the parish. The visitor should take time to explore the side lanes and high ridges where every gateway reveals a different view or a hidden valley.

The famous A. J. Coles, who created the wonderful Devonian character 'Jan Stewer', once owned a farm here and finally ended his days in one of the first caravan homes in Pathfinder Village.

Widecombe in the Moor

When in ancient times men dwelt on the moor, leaving the remains of their homes as the stone hut circles we see today, they must have looked down with wonder on the deep combe filled with withy trees. Later, monks who travelled across the moor between their abbeys, leaving stone crosses as guides to a safe route, ventured into the valley and erected granite crosses where they had preached and perhaps had drunk from the well which now is covered with an impressive granite canopy in the centre of the village.

The tinners who toiled so hard on the moor, scarring the hillsides with large gullies, must have appreciated the shelter of the valley in the wild winter days. They loved it so much that in the early 16th century they helped to build the present church, dedicated to St Pancras and known as the cathedral of the moor. On one of the roof bosses they left the tinners' symbol of three rabbits, each with one ear joined at the top to form a triangle. The majestic 135 ft tower was almost its downfall when in 1638 it was struck by lightning during a service, injuring many folk. Many a story followed of how the Devil had galloped through the sky on his steed followed by his whisht hounds, and it has become a legend.

Within the parish there is so much evidence of past activity – prehistoric sites, the remains of medieval granite posts incised with crosses to mark church paths, large boulders marked with crosses where coffins were rested when being carried to the church for a funeral by neighbours from distant farms. Another boulder with a hollow in its top where manorial dues were paid, gateways with granite posts wider apart at the top to let packhorses through when they were the only means of transport. Mould stones left by tinners, granite troughs and quern wheels, also a wayside stone marked '1 MOIL' as a boundary from the days of the Napoleonic War prisoners, denoting the limits of their parole. Clapper bridges and so many more items of interest. An old church house which once was an alehouse, later the village school, but is now the village hall.

So deeply rooted in the past, the village remained almost unknown until in 1850 the vicar decided to hold an annual fair and another well known Devon vicar, Sabine Baring-Gould, popularised an old folk tune which made Widecombe world famous. Each year thousands come to see where Uncle Tom Cobley and his friends visited the fair and their poor old grey mare died.

Willand &

The earliest name recorded (in 1086) for the village was Willeland. Until the Reformation it formed part of the lands of Taunton Priory.

For many centuries it was small and quiet. In the 1920s a section of the A38 was built which bypassed the old village so that Willand was passed through almost unnoticed by the thousands of travellers who used the A38 as the gateway to the South West. Before the opening of the M5, this road effectively divided the old village on the east side from the newer part on the west, and traffic was so heavy that a long wait to cross it was always expected.

In the old village is St Mary's church and a cluster of attractive old cottages, one of which houses the post office, some being built of Devon cob with thatched roofs. There is also the old National school, which was in use from 1844 to 1872, and the old board school, both of which are now private houses.

The church of St Mary the Virgin dates from the 14th or 15th century and has a very beautiful carved rood screen, still showing some of its original colour and gilding.

In the western part of Willand most of the houses were built in this century. Here also is the fine village hall, which was built and is maintained by the people themselves and opened in 1957, the youth club, tennis courts, the Methodist church and the modern primary school, opened in 1948.

At the edge of the village is the Lloyd Maunder abattoir and processing plant, which is the largest local employer. It came here in 1913 and produces meat and poultry products which are sent to all parts of the country and to Europe.

There is also a tannery and several smaller businesses on a recently-designated industrial estate. The older businesses were originally developed round Tiverton Junction station, which was on the main Exeter–Paddington line, but in 1987 this station was closed and replaced by Tiverton Parkway, some three miles away. Near the old station a cattle market was begun in the early years of this century, and continues to operate weekly, an unusual feature in a village of this size.

Another unusual thing is that there is no pub in the centre of the village – the White Horse Inn in the old village closed and became a private house before 1890, and the Railway Tavern was demolished to make way for the M5, but the Halfway House, an old coaching inn, still stands almost on the boundary of the village.

The greatest change has been brought about by the building of two very large housing estates, which has doubled the population. Many newcomers have chosen to live at Willand because of its position which gives easy access to the M5 at Junction 27, and main-line rail travel from Tiverton Parkway. They have also found a lively, welcoming community with organisations catering for many different interests.

Withleigh 🦢

Withleigh is a small village on the A373 from Tiverton to Witheridge. It is one of the largest parishes in Devon. The parish church of St Catherine was erected in 1846 on the site of an ancient chapel. The surrounding countryside is hilly with many sheltered valleys and some woodland.

The farming land was mainly owned and worked, for much of the 19th century, by the large Carpenter family. It was their generosity which made the building of the church possible; the churchyard bears witness to their numbers.

The church was declared unsafe in the early 1960s and was closed for a time, services being held in the unoccupied vicarage and later in the village hall. Extensive alterations and refurbishment took place to the interior, many of the local people helping with scrubbing of pews and other safe but dirty jobs. On completion in 1966, a service of dedication was held attended by all those connected with the restoration.

In 1846, George Crook was the first churchwarden and sexton. He was also the local carpenter, coffin-maker and gravedigger and he was followed by his son John, and his son Percy who was churchwarden and sexton for 35 years. His sister, Hilda, ran the post office and delivered the letters to outlying farms, walking miles each day across the country in all weathers. Other members of the family farmed in the area, but now like the Carpenters the name has died out here except in memory and in the churchyard.

The first Luxton arrived here in about 1900, his family having farmed in Rackenford. Today, while still owning and working much of the land in and around the village, his descendants hold occupations as diverse as carpentry, road haulage and training racehorses. The methods of farming have changed too and we no longer hear the cows being called twice a day for milking nor the milk churns being clanged about in the early morning. Now alongside cows, pigs and sheep are goats, riding horses and poultry, and the cart horse has been replaced by the tractor.

The Congregational chapel closed in the 1950s. This, like the school, is now a private house. Close by was the mill where farmers took corn to be ground. The water-wheel was still in use until about 1930, when it was replaced by an engine. The mill and adjoining cottage have been thoughtfully restored and it is hoped the wheel will be repaired in the future. Mr 'Jimmy' Norrish, the last miller, was born at Mill Farm, one of several Devon longhouses in the parish. He did not remember the farm as an inn but before 1860 it is thought to have been one.

Although there are still a number of original dwellings in the village, there has been quite a lot of new development, mainly bungalows built in the last 20 years. The Luxtons and the Brittons between them have built 15 new homes since 1935. The good community spirit is noticeable at the annual events, ie dog show, gymkhana and harvest thanksgiving.

Ours is not a picture post-card village. We have no pub or village green or school and to the ordinary passer-by, we seem to be just a row of houses on the A373. But it is a thriving community, and a great deal goes on here thanks to the many people who contribute to village life.

Withycombe Raleigh 🐚

The village of Withycombe was mentioned in the Domesday Book of 1086. Up to some 60 or 70 years ago the village was just one long road, and a couple of lanes leading off, with the Withy brook meandering through. It was surrounded by farms with green fields. There was a flour and corn mill with its water-wheel dating back centuries, which came under attack during the bread riots of 1867 and was stoned by a mob. A sluice gate in Farm Lane controlled the mill leat, but during the severe flood of 1960 the mill was destroyed. The wheel has now been resited within the town of Exmouth.

There were many thatched cottages past which the drovers would herd their animals to market. There was a forge with a blacksmith shoeing horses for the milk carts – deliveries twice daily, laundry vans from the two hand laundries, two bakeries where you could take your dinner and have it cooked for a penny, a saddler, and a wheelwright who was also the undertaker. Private traps and dogcarts added to the bustle of a busy village. There were two pubs where they made their own beer and cider; the children used to pick up the apples in the orchard for a penny an hour.

There were several large houses in the village. Motor cycle racing was held in Phear Park, the winding and hilly paths being the track; the pond was sandbagged but many went in with the ducks! The Rugby Club added to village social life holding whist drives, socials and concerts. The year they won the Devon Junior Cup most of the villagers went with the team to cheer.

What is the village like now? The main roads and lanes have been widened and are now through roads with almost continuous traffic. There are no working farms, the green fields where the larks sang are covered with semi-detached houses and bungalows. The large houses are now no longer private, some have been flattened, some are schools or nursing homes. The school at the bottom of the village is one of the largest community colleges in the country.

The mill and the forge are no more, the pubs have been up-dated, but there are still a few thatched cottages. The brook is still there and the Park is more or less the same, but now with tennis courts, bowling greens and a golf course.

Woodbury

The earliest spelling of the name of the village is Wudbirig (c1072), closely followed by Wodeberia (1086), both clearly indicating woodland plus ancient earthworks.

Woodbury Common is a beautiful area, with woods, gorse and heather. The Beacon, an earth mound crowned with pine trees, is the highest part of the common. Originally a Bronze Age burial mound, it was known as Fire Beacon c1200 and served as an Armada beacon in 1558.

In the old days everyone knew everyone else in the village. Those were the days when maids went into service – and anyone wanting a servant had only to go to the village school to find out who was leaving at the end of term. Boys worked on one or other of the many local farms, nearly all of which belonged to the Clinton estates of Lord Rolle; or at the quarry on the common, for local builders. Many young men, too, were employed at Woodbury Mills and at Ware and Sons, leather merchants, in Gilbrook.

In 1960 and again in 1968 the many open brooks flowing through the village were turned into raging torrents after heavy rains and the village was badly flooded on each occasion. A flood prevention scheme was finally brought into operation in 1972.

Nicholas Stone was a famous person born in Woodbury in 1587. The son of a stonemason, he was given an official position as 'Master Mason' under James I and was responsible for architectural work at Holyrood Palace, St James' Palace, Somerset House and Greenwich. He sculpted several tombs in Westminster Abbey, worked with Inigo Jones on buildings in Whitehall and on the old St Paul's Cathedral, and as an architect at Windsor Castle.

Another famous man who came to live in Woodbury in his later years was the Rev W. Keble Martin, author of *The Concise British Flora in Colour*. He died, much loved and respected, in Woodbury on 29th November 1969 at the age of 92. Embroidered kneelers at St Swithun's church, depicting wild flowers illustrated in his book, are a lasting memorial to him.

The church lychgate, Woodbury

The village has some interesting old buildings. Nutwell Court is Woodbury's biggest and most historic house and was occupied by members of the Drake family from 1685 to 1941. The parish church of St Swithun is full of interest, the south side, which dates from the 13th century, being the oldest part. The fine tower was added to the existing building early in the 15th century and consecrated by Bishop Stafford of Exeter on 23rd September 1409.

Many changes have taken place over the years and now the majority of the working population commute from the village to their place of employment. New housing estates have been built, along with specially-designed and warden-supported dwellings for the elderly and disabled. There is a community centre, a splendid new surgery and health centre for the two resident doctors, and an enlarged village hall.

Woodbury Salterton

Woodbury Salterton must be one of the youngest parishes in Devon, having only achieved that status in 1845. Earlier this scattered collection of small farms had simply been a part of the neighbouring parish of Woodbury.

Among the cob and thatched cottages, three stone buildings stand out, namely the church, the school and the vicarage. These edifices, together with a conduit which provided the villagers with water for over a century, were the gift of Miss Marianne Pidsley of Greendale.

The church, in Victorian Gothic, was constructed of stone from an old tithe barn at Woodbury and as this was insufficient, further supplies were quarried on the beach at Exmouth. The people of the small village contributed to the church furnishings. Caroline Anne Pearce, later the wife of the first headmaster, embroidered the back of the chancel chair, a stupendous undertaking as each square inch contained over 1,000 stitches. The stained glass windows were hand-painted by volunteers in the village and took ten months to complete. While the building was in progress a pair of robins nested in the chancel and reared their young. This was commemorated by carvings of the birds on the bosses on the chancel arch. The locks on two of the doors have key-holes on the outside only. This is because they were obtained from a prison in Exeter which was being demolished at this time.

By the time the third building, the vicarage, came to be constructed, perhaps money was running a little short, for although the front is of the same stone as the other buildings, the rear walls are of brick.

The village inn which had served the inhabitants with beer and cider for 500 years, was acquired by an Australian after the Second World War and the name changed to The Diggers Rest. The inn sign now portrays a swagman taking his ease, perhaps under a coolibah tree!

Lord William Brewer, the founder of Torre Abbey, gave the farm of Greendale Barton to the foundation in 1197. In the years that followed further lands and grazing rights were donated to the abbey. A mill was built and twice yearly the abbot travelled to Woodbury Salterton to hold a manorial court and to collect the income from the farm.

Among the few reminders of this time are the first few courses of blocks of red stone on which stood the monastic barn, the leat which supplied the mill and the name of Honey Lane. Bee-keeping was one of the occupations of the tenant of Greendale Barton, which supplied the only sweetener in the villagers' diet and the beeswax for the church candles.

Woolfardisworthy West 🐑

Woolfardisworthy West is commonly called 'Woolsery' by its inhabitants, so much so that highway signs need to display both names. It is quietly situated amid rolling fields and leafy lanes.

The village centre embraces the core of village life – the pealing of bells may well be your introduction to All Hallows' church, with its beautifully carved 15th century bench ends – the one of the Crucifixion, remaining unmutilated, is very rare. The fine knight's tomb (often referred to as 'Old King Cole', due to his name), still retaining glimpses of its original greens and gold, is just one example of the beauty and majesty to be found here.

Across the village green is the thriving village shop and post office, the Farmer's Arms – an 18th century thatched inn, a fine Wesleyan chapel and the village hall, a centre of activity for all. Recently remodelled, but retaining the original Victorian facade, the village school dominates the outlook from the main street.

Parish House was built in 1850 on the site of the garden of the old poor house (now Sunnyside). It is now a private home, retaining the original fireplace and large beams incorporating the iron pulley used to raise and lower the oil lamps.

On the last Monday of every July, the one day village show is held in Woolsery. Originally a horse fair, the show still retains its 'horsey flavour' with local pony clubs competing and the ever-popular display of the huntsmen in their vivid coats of red and the pack of hounds in the ring. It is a grand opportunity for the farmers to exhibit their sheep and cattle, for the gardeners to show their best produce, for flower arrangers to show their talents, fine examples of needlework to be examined, and for our famed West Country cooks to bake a saffron cake or Devon scones.

Yarcombe 🌿

The village, dominated by its tall 14th century church tower, huddles picturesquely astride one of the two major routes from Somerset to Honiton and the west. It commands unrivalled views down the chequered pattern of fields in the broadening Yarty valley, and lies at the foot of the notorious twisting uphill climb of the main road through woodland to Honiton.

If the church tower dominates the clustered homes of the village, its ancient inn is equally strategically sited in the centre. It began life in the 14th century as a guest house for the monks of Otterton Priory, when both church and manor were administered by them. Thereafter the building became the Angel Inn, and following extensions, allowing greater accommodation for stage-coach passengers interrupting journeys to and from Exeter, the hostelry became known as the Yarcombe Inn.

National history touched the parish when, during the reign of Elizabeth I, Sir Francis Drake acquired the manor of Yarcombe. For many years heirlooms of that great Devon seaman and adventurer were preserved in the manor house, Sheafhayne, romantically sited on a platform overlooking the Yarty valley, and partially hidden from the lane by high flint walls and overgrown rhododendron bushes. Glimpses of its mullioned windows, stone gables and slate roofs, together with its lozenge-faced clock, frozen in time, remind one forcefully of Dickens' graphic description of Miss Haversham's mansion in *Great Expectations*. To this day, the Yarcombe estate, consisting of the major part of the parish of Yarcombe, remains the property of the collateral descendants of Sir Francis.

The church itself, dedicated to St John the Baptist, treasures a copy of the 1560 'Breeches Bible', the name referring to the fig-leaf breeches it describes as being made and worn by Adam and Eve. However, the unique possession of the church is its 14th century stained glass light, high in the north transept north window, portraying a contemporary pedlar, complete with his knapsack of wares.

Almost a separate hamlet, at Four Elms or 'the Meeting', a small group of colour-washed dwellings clusters around the second place of worship in the parish. Though the elms have long since disappeared, happily in this heartland of Nonconformism the whitewashed, galleried little Baptist chapel of 1829 survives.

Former industry in the village is recorded in many of the names on the local map – Tilery, the Old Forge, Mill Green and Foundry Farm, where agricultural implements, farm carts and charcoal bread ovens were made in the late 19th century. The foundry employed some 40 people at its peak, many of them walking considerable distances to work from as far as Chard and Axminster, five and seven miles away respectively. But always the mainstay of local employment has been agriculture, and dairy farming in particular. Woodlands, including Forestry Commission plantations, afford employment for a small work force.

The village school, having survived as such for 93 years, closed in 1965, after conversion reopening as the Belfry Hotel. Finally closing its doors in 1988, the village shop and post office was duly returned to residential use, though happily, through the initiative of the Parish Council, a community post office and council office were opened in other premises. Until recently the name plate 'Coppers' on a village house betrayed the fact that it had once been the residence of the village policeman. However, much enlarged and improved in recent years, the Silver Jubilee Hall, so named because building commenced in that year of the reign of George V, still remains the centre of the social life of the village.

Outdoor activities once included ploughing matches, but more recently unusual sporting occasions such as barrel-rolling races, steel-ball throwing, terrier racing and the East Devon sheepdog trials have all featured, not to forget the ubiquitous inter-village skittles competitions.

Yarnscombe ✍️

The village is approximately nine miles south of Barnstaple and situated between the two main roads which lead to Exeter and Plymouth. It is just over two miles from Huntshaw Cross, the highest point above sea level in North Devon.

In the Domesday Book of 1086 the name is recorded as Hernescombe, derived from the 'valley of the eagles', probably buzzard hawks which

247

still frequent the area. The landscape and scenery here of open country-side is quite lovely. At Westcott Cross the views stretching towards Exmoor, Dartmoor, and the coast towards Hartland must be about a radius of 100 miles, with Lundy Island just visible on clear days. Much of the parish was once part of the large Rolle estate at Stevenstone in the parish of St Giles, and was sold off, mainly to the tenants, on 24th July 1914.

The 15th century tower of St Andrew's church is a well known landmark. There are six bells, the oldest dated 1440 and engraved with a medieval ship and the arms of the Cockworthy family. The vestry was added in 1846. Huge granite pillars of Dartmoor granite each weighing three quarters of a ton were brought here on sledges.

The Methodist church built by Mr Albert Darch was opened by his wife in 1908. It replaced an earlier wooden church situated on land at 'Ward'. The Darch family were local carpenters and builders, but later moved to Torrington. The village blacksmith lived at Sparkes, and together they made wheels for farmers' carts, shoed the horses and were kept fully occupied supplying the needs of the local farmers and landowners.

There are three parish charities, the main one being the Ashridge Trust. In 1593 a lady donated the rent of Ashridge Farm, two thirds to go to the church and one third to the schoolchildren to pay for books or boots as needed. Later they were given the money, about eight shillings per year each. It is now in the hands of the Charity Commissioners and the village receives £40 per year. The Bread Charity was donated by the owner of Westcott Farm, to buy twelve wheaten loaves for the poor of Yarnscombe. Sometimes the bread became dry before it could be collected, so now the money is given instead. In 1796 John Champney left £20, Mrs E Nicholls £5 and an unknown person £25, to be invested for the benefit of the aged and infirm. These two charities now allocate £1 per year to the recipients.

The upsurge of building recently has doubled the number of houses around the village, and whereas almost everyone once worked in conjunction with the land, very few now do so.

Yealmpton

Before the First World War Yealmpton was a real Devon village, although only seven miles east of Plymouth. The village itself, stretching along the A379, comprised two pubs, a small school which catered for all age groups, a 12th century church and, of course, Mother Hubbard's Cottage.

Built on the river Yealm, it boasts two bridges, one on the main road leading to a small community and the little hamlet of Dunstone, and one on the Newton Ferrers/Noss Mayo road leading to the area to the south called Torre.

Most employment was on local estates with their surrounding farms or in light industry such as saw mills. The railway line, the main link to the city of Plymouth, stopped at Yealmpton.

Yealmpton's main claims to fame were then the picturesque cob and stone cottage built, it is said, 400 years ago for the housekeeper at the Kitley manor house and around whom the famous rhyme *Old Mother Hubbard* was written, and the Kitley limestone caves where green marble was quarried, a unique colour for limestone; there is an arch of it in the British Museum.

After the First World War the village started to expand with the building of the first council house estate on land above the river on the outskirts of the village. No more building took place until the early 1950s when a second council estate was developed at the other end of the village. Thus were Yeo and Yealm Parks brought into being.

Then in the late 1950s and early 1960s Yealmpton was designated as a development area and the first of several housing estates, Stray Park, was built at the eastern end of the village. Since then at least seven more have sprung up, mostly south of the river in the Torre area.

During the Second World War folk from the village and as far afield as Plymouth took refuge in the Kitley caves. These caves have been developed and are now open to the public, proving a popular and interesting feature. The tiny hamlet of Dunstone now houses the National Shire Horse Centre, a flourishing place of interest and entertainment.

Zeal Monachorum

Much of the Devon landscape seems unchanging; the flowered lanes and banks feel ageless and we take for granted the permanence of cob and thatch. Even so, the yew tree which has been standing for 1,300 years in the churchyard, 400 ft above the sea, has seen many changes. The view across to Dartmoor, for example, 500 years ago was thickly wooded with oak, but now is bleak and bare. Much of that oak was turned into the beams which are such a feature of our older houses.

King Canute who gave the manor to Buckfast Abbey in the 11th century, hence the name which means 'cell of the monks', would be baffled by the tarmacadam lanes with their street lamps and traffic; to say nothing of the RAF training jets which scream overhead at what, at times, seems little more than treetop height.

It is interesting to reflect on the way the village must have been in the past. No cars or planes, of course, but over 700 people in 1831 compared with the current population of about 250. Then there were three pubs, whereas now there is only one; and that opened as recently as 1980. The village school, now the village hall, had an attendance of 94 in 1875.

Perhaps the most surprising thing is to discover the variety of trades once practised here. There were two forges; a watermill for the wool trade, now a ruin; a shoe and boot maker; a wheelwright; a tailor and an agricultural implement maker. The family of the Brealys, stonemasons in the last century, still live in the village as do the Quicks, Rounsleys and Vicarys, all farming families. What is now Partridge Cottage was once the bakery.

At the crossroads there stands a monument, the lettering of which is now virtually illegible, to Richard Davy of Burstone who, in 1887, 'Paid to have a reservoir constructed and pipes laid conveying a supply of water throughout the village.'

People can still remember when the post office was in Yew Tree Cottage. Now it is part of the village shop, which carries a range of goods which would have astonished our grandmothers and sometimes even surprises us. By way of a link with the past, the post office still franks parcels with the original Victorian stamp.

The parish church, St Peter's, has the distinction of being the birthplace of The Devon Bellringers Association. Sadly, its own bells now stand silent until extensive restoration work being carried out on the tower is completed.

251

Index

Abbotsham 9
Abbotskerswell 10
All Saints 11
Alphington 12
Appledore 14
Ashburton 16
Ashprington 18
Ashreigney 19
Atherington 20
Aveton Gifford 21
Axmouth 22

Bampton 23
Bantham (see Thurlestone) 224
Beaford 25
Beer 26
Bere Ferrers 27
Berrynarbor 29
Bickington (North Devon) 30
Bickington (South Devon) 31
Bigbury 32
Bishopsnympton 33
Bishops Tawton 33
Bishopsteignton 35
Bittadon (see Marwood) 156
Blackawton 36
Blackborough (see Kentisbeare) 130
Black Torrington (see Holsworthy) 120
Bovey Tracey 38
Bow 39
Bradninch 40
Bradstone (see Kelly) 129
Bradworthy 41
Bratton Clovelly 42
Braunton 43
Brentor 44

Bridestowe 45
Bridford 47
Brixham 48
Buckfastleigh 49
Buckland Brewer 50
Budleigh Salterton 50
Burrington 51

Calverleigh 52
Chagford 54
Charleton 55
Cheriton (see Payhembury) 180
Cheriton Bishop 56
Cheriton Cross (see Cheriton Bishop) 56
Cheriton Fitzpaine 57
Chillaton 59
Chipley (see Bickington, South Devon) 31
Chittlehampton 60
Chivenor (see Heanton Punchardon) 116
Christow 61
Chulmleigh 62
Churchstow 63
Clawton 64
Clayhanger 65
Clayhidon 66
Clearbrook 67
Clovelly 69
Clyst Honiton 70
Clyst St Mary 71
Cofton 72
Colaton Raleigh 73
Coldridge 74
Colestocks (see Payhembury) 180
Colscott (see East Putford) 101
Colyford 74

Colyton 75
Combeinteignhead 76
Combe Martin 77
Cornwood 79
Cornworthy 80
Cottwood (see Ashreigney) 19
Crediton 81
Croyde 82
Cruwys Morchard 83
Culmstock 85

Dalwood 86
Dartington 87
Dartmouth 89
Dawlish 90
Denbury 91
Diptford 92
Dittisham 93
Doccombe 94
Dolton 95
Dunchideock 96
Dunkeswell 97
Dunsford 98
Dunstone (see Yealmpton) 249

East Allington 99
East Buckland (see Thurlestone) 224
East Budleigh 100
Easton (see Bigbury) 32
East Putford 101
East Raddon (see Thorverton) 222
East Worlington 102
Exbourne 103
Exminster 104

Farway (see Northleigh) 173
Fleote (see Axmouth) 22
Folly Gate (see Inwardleigh) 125

Fremington (see Bickington, North Devon) 30
Frogmore 105
Frogwell (see Calverleigh) 52
Furley (see Membury) 160

Georgeham 106
Gittisham 107
Goodleigh 108
Great Torrington 109
Guineaford (see Marwood) 156

Halberton 110
Harbertonford 111
Harpford (see Newton Poppleford) 171
Harracott 113
Hawkchurch 114
Haytor Vale 115
Heanton Punchardon 116
Hennock 117
Higher Netherton (see Combeinteignhead) 76
Holcombe Rogus 118
Holne 119
Holsworthy 120
Hope Cove 121
Horndon (see Mary Tavy) 157
Horrabridge 122

Iddesleigh 123
Inner Hope (see Hope Cove) 121
Instow 124
Inwardleigh 125
Ipplepen 126
Ivybridge 128

Kelly 129
Kentisbeare 130
Kenton 131
Kilmington 132

Kingskerswell   133
Kingsteignton   134
Kingston   135
Kingswear   136

Lamerton   137
Landkey   138
Landscove (see Staverton)   209
Lapford   139
Lee   140
Littleham (North Devon)   142
Littleham (South Devon)   143
Little Torrington   144
Liverton   145
Loddiswell   146
Lower Loxhore (see Loxhore)
   147
Lower Lympstone (see
   Lympstone)   151
Lower Netherton (see
   Combeinteignhead)   76
Loxhore   147
Loxhore Cott (see Loxhore)   147
Loxhore Town (see Loxhore)   147
Luffincott (see Tetcott)   220
Lurley (see Calverleigh)   52
Lustleigh   149
Lutton (see Cornwood)   79
Lydford   150
Lympstone   151

Malborough   154
Manaton   155
Marwood   156
Mary Tavy   157
Meavy   159
Membury   160
Middle Marwood (see Marwood)
   156
Middlewood (see Cofton)   72
Milltown (see Marwood)   156

Milton Abbot   161
Modbury   162
Molland   163
Monkokehampton   164
Morchard Bishop   166
Moretonhampstead   168
Mortehoe   169
Muddiford (see Marwood)   156
Musbury   170

Newton Poppleford   171
Nomansland (see Cruwys
   Morchard)   83
North Bovey   172
Northleigh   173
North Molton   174
North Tawton   175
Nymet Tracey (see Bow)   39

Oakford   177
Otterton   178
Ottery St Mary   179
Outer Hope (see Hope Cove)   121

Palmershayes (see Calverleigh)   52
Payhembury   180
Pennymoor (see Cruwys
   Morchard)   83
Peters Marland   182
Peter Tavy (see Mary Tavy)   157
Pilton   183
Plympton   184
Prixford (see Marwood)   156
Providence (see Throwleigh)   223

Quither (see Chillaton)   59

Riddlecombe (see Ashreigney)   19
Ringmore   185
Roborough (see Beaford)   25

Salcombe 186
Sampford Courtenay 187
Sampford Spiney 188
Sandford 189
Seaton 191
Sessacott (see East Putford) 101
Sheepstor 192
Sheepwash 193
Sherford (see Frogmore) 105
Shirwell 195
Sidford 196
Silverton 198
Slapton 199
Smallridge (see All Saints) 11
Sourton 201
South Brent 202
South Knighton (see Bickington, South Devon) 31
South Milton 204
South Molton 205
South Zeal 206
Sparkwell 207
St Ann's Chapel (see Bigbury) 32
Starcross 208
Staverton 209
St Giles (see Beaford) 25
Sticklepath 210
Stockland 212
Stoodleigh 213
Stoke Gabriel 214
Stokenham 216
Strete 217
Sutton (see South Milton) 204

Taddiport (see Little Torrington) 144
Talaton 218
Tale (see Payhembury) 180
Tedburn St Mary 220
Tetcott 221
Thorverton 222

Thriverton (see East Putford) 101
Throwleigh 223
Thurlestone 224
Topsham 225
Tuckenhay (see Cornworthy) 80

Uffculme 226
Umberleigh 227
Uplyme 229
Upottery 230
Upper Lympstone (see Lympstone) 151
Upton (see Payhembury) 180

Waytown (see Inwardleigh) 125
Way Village (see Cruwys Morchard) 83
Weare Giffard 231
Wedfield (see East Putford) 101
West Alvington 232
West Buckland (see Thurlestone) 224
West Hill 233
West Putford (see East Putford) 101
Westward Ho! 234
Westwood (see Cofton) 72
West Worlington (see East Worlington) 102
Whitchurch 235
Whitestone 237
Widecombe in the Moor 238
Willand 239
Winswell (see Peters Marland) 182
Withleigh 240
Withycombe Raleigh 241
Wonson (see Throwleigh) 223
Wonwell (see Kingston) 135
Woodbury 242
Woodbury Salterton 244

Woolacombe (see Mortehoe) 169
Woolaton (see Peters Marland)
  182
Woolfardisworthy West 245
Woolsery (see Woolfardisworthy
  West) 245
Woolston Green (see Staverton)
  209

Yarcombe 246
Yard (see Peters Marland) 182
Yarnscombe 247
Yealmpton 249
Yelverton (see Clearbrook) 67

Zeal Monachorum 250